Mairs & Power at 90

George Alexander Mairs Jr.

Founded in 1931 by George A. Mairs Jr., Mairs & Power was led by the Three Georges until 2004. Today the firm is employee-owned and led. These oil portraits were painted by Merry DeCourcy, St. Paul, Minn., in 2011. Photos courtesy of Mairs & Power.

George Center Power Jr.

George Alexander Mairs III

Mairs & Power at 90

A RICH HISTORY,
A BRIGHT FUTURE

DAVE BEAL

RAMSEY COUNTY HISTORICAL SOCIETY

Ramsey County Historical Society
St. Paul, Minnesota

Published By

RAMSEY COUNTY HISTORICAL SOCIETY

Ramsey County Historical Society
Suite 323 Landmark Center
75 West Fourth Street
St. Paul, Minnesota 55102
USA
Telephone: (651) 222-0701
www.RCHS.com

Mairs & Power
W-1520 First National Bank Building
332 Minnesota Street
St. Paul, MN 55101
Telephone: (651) 222-8478
www.mairsandpower.com

Printed in Canada.

Editorial and Production Services by John M. Lindley, John M. Lindley & Associates.
Design & Typesetting Services by Wendy Holdman, Wendy Holman Design, Ltd.
Graphic Art by Patricia Isaacs, Patricia Isaacs Cartography and Graphic Design
Printed and Bound by Friesens, Altona, Manitoba, Canada

Library of Congress Cataloging-in-Publishing Data is available.
ISNB: 978-0-934294-00-3 (hardcover)

Contents

Foreword

The founder of Mairs & Power, George A. Mairs Jr., and my father, Philip Stringer, were close friends throughout their adult lives. As a result, I was a boyhood friend of George Mairs III, even though I was a few years younger. Geordie, as his family and close friends always called him, was a good friend and trusted advisor to me and Geordie's younger brother, Angus, throughout our respective life journeys. I am deeply honored to have been asked to write the foreword to this remarkable book.

Author Dave Beal, the now-retired Business Editor of the *St. Paul Pioneer Press*, whose journalism career focused on business and finance, largely in St. Paul and the Twin Cities, was a natural choice to write this important history. After all, the very first substantive local newspaper story about Mairs & Power was written by Dave back in 1995.

While I naturally had a better knowledge of the firm than most St. Paulites, it was during my stint as a Trustee of the Mairs & Power mutual funds (starting in 2002) that I became fully aware of the unusually high quality of the organization and its people, and that it truly was one of the best-kept secrets in the Twin Cities financial world and beyond. My friend Geordie was clearly the architect of what made the firm the investment powerhouse it was becoming by the time I retired from the Mutual Fund Board in 2010. It has been no surprise to me to have watched it grow to become a firm managing nearly $12 billion in assets today.

The thought of reading a book about the history of a local company may seem dry and unappealing, but I can assure you that this story is not that. As a history buff who once served as Board Chair of the Minnesota Historical Society, I promise you that you will find this story to be a fascinating tale, beginning with the ancestors of the remarkable Mairs and Power families and ending with the firm of Mairs & Power being poised for even greater things in its next 90 years. Geordie, a history buff as well, especially St. Paul history, would be as pleased with the book as I am. Enjoy!

Edward C. Stringer
September 2021

Preface

I spent many years working for daily newspapers, most of them as a business and financial journalist. Along the way, I was privileged to interview countless executives, employees, and assorted outside observers—many of them quite accomplished and fascinating—who populated this panorama. But typically, my stories or columns were due the following day, or a few days thereafter. Generally, if we spent too much time dwelling on yesterday's news, we would miss tomorrow's stories. So, when Jon Theobald called my landline—I almost missed the call—and asked if I knew of anyone who would be interested in writing a book about the history of Mairs & Power, I raised my hand. Here would be an opportunity to go deep, I thought, instead of skimming off the top of another iceberg and moving on. I knew just enough about this firm, and George Mairs III, to be dangerous. Early in 1995, I somehow became the first Twin Cities journalist to write about him and his enterprise in any substantive way.

"When George Mairs III calls his 64-year-old investment advisory firm a plain-vanilla operation, he isn't kidding," my story, spread across the front page of the *St. Paul Pioneer Press* Sunday business section, began. "Mairs & Power's quarters, tucked away at the end of a narrow corridor on the 20th floor of the First National Bank Building in downtown St. Paul, looks like a bank or a law firm out of a 1940s movie. There are no glitzy appointments. There's no expensive artwork. The place does have some views, way out to the east suburbs—at least those that aren't blocked by the big air conditioning units parked atop the roof of the extended floor below."

The leaders at the firm wanted this history to help mark their 90th anniversary as a free-standing, independent firm. I realized at the outset that one of the "known unknowns" would be how any firm in this ever-turbulent corner of our economy could come through nearly a century and not be rolled up into a rival, wither away, or just flat-out collapse. As a business journalist, I had watched or read about these situations for decades. Think the 1930s. Or the financial crisis of 2008-09. Or any of the constant gyrations in the securities markets that frequently jolted many of their players out of their orbits. So, curiosity about how Mairs & Power endured and wound-up prospering despite all this uncertainty drove me from the start to the finishing line.

Weeks after I agreed to take this on, along came the Covid-19 crisis, our first full-scale pandemic since 1918. Archives, libraries, and universities everywhere shut down. Another complication: it quickly became clear that while the firm's founder, George Mairs Jr., and his iconic son and successor at the firm, George III, had been deeply interested in history, they preserved very little about their firm.

This is not "my book." It was a team effort. I needed a few lucky breaks, and I got them. In one of their wisest moments insofar as this project has been concerned, the firm's leaders hired John Lindley as the editor and consultant to pull this book together. Everybody needs an editor, and John had been the editor at the excellent magazine published by the Ramsey County Historical Society (RCHS) for 13 years. He has a doctorate in history from Duke University, has written six books himself, and has managed the drill of shaping an idea into a full-blown book on ten occasions. He worked around the covid restrictions to vacuum the archives at the RCHS, the Minnesota Historical Society, and a few other grottos of history for this project. He also understood, as even I did, that we couldn't adequately tell the story about the history and changing culture of a long-standing institution by looking at its own timeline. We needed to match up the internal history with the broader narrative of what was happening beyond the institution. And if we just wrote about a firm that got started in the depths of the Great Depression without exploring the social and economic backdrop that existed in the 1930s, the picture would be incomplete. Similarly, we needed to consider the environment in St. Paul and Minnesota during the long run-up to 1931, when George Mairs Jr. founded the firm.

I was fortunate to gain the cooperation of Ron DeSellier, the only living soul who was at the firm throughout most of the 1970s and 1980s. Ron saved everything. Without his help, that stretch would have been too much of blank slate. Todd Driscoll helped considerably, by unearthing and making available records of the Driscoll family's accounts that George Jr. managed in the 1930s. Erik Moore, head of the University of Minnesota's archives, contributed significantly, by digging into its vaults on the banks of the Mississippi River in Minneapolis at the peak of the pandemic to call up and send to me George Jr.'s master's thesis. This project provided important insights into how he was thinking when he opened the doors at his firm.

I need to offer a heads-up about the streams of assets and other dollar amounts, sometimes over many decades, that are presented in various parts of this book. Almost always, they are not adjusted for inflation. If you want to get a sense for the importance of that factor over many decades—and this is often no small consideration—call up the inflation calculator on your screen whenever that seems appropriate.

I frequently cite data from the firm without footnoting sources. In those cases, the information usually comes from the annual reports of the firm's mutual funds. Mairs & Power provided me with a complete file of those reports, dating back to the inception of the Growth Fund in 1958.

Initially, the leaders at the firm envisioned this project as something more akin to a thick booklet, 75 pages or so. John and I persuaded them that this was something more. Mark Henneman, Mairs & Power's CEO, agreed. He and the other three members of the management committee that runs the firm—Andy Adams, lead manager of the Growth Fund and chair of the Investment Committee; Rob Mairs, president; and Andrea Stimmel, chief operating officer—opened important doors for me. Jon Theobald, now retired and Henneman's predecessor as CEO, was my principal contact throughout this project. He put up with endless questions from me about this or that detail about the firm and the growing number of arenas and networks it plays in. In the end, I hope we have stamped out all the errors that were in early drafts of the material for this book; any that remain are my responsibility.

Special thanks go to Dusty Mairs, who played a huge supporting role in George III's life as his spouse from 1982 until his death in 2010. She loaned me a thick scrapbook of news clippings, virtually all of them after 1994, when George suddenly became the most unlikely celebrity I have ever known (see Chapter 8). She also provided us with many family pictures to choose from and was always available for questions about George or his family. Teedie Frankenbach, the sole survivor of the blended family led by George Jr. and his wife, Louise, was helpful on the Mairs family history. Diane and George Power III were invaluable sources on the history of the Power family.

Special thanks, too, to our book designer, Wendy Holdman, our graphics expert, Patti Isaacs, and to Annette Lance, the firm's coordinator on various aspects of this project. Among the others whose help should also be acknowledged: Jim Alt, Richard Arpi, Tom Bengston, John Bergstrom, Philip Brunelle, Dr. Edward Cheng, Norb Conzemius, David Crosby, Mary Schmid Daugherty, Chuck Dietz, Colin Dunn, Chip Emery, Priscilla Farnham, Ann Mairs Farrah, Liz Fedor, George Ficocello, Matt Fink, Bill Frels, Joan Gabel, Nicole Garrison-Springer, Bob Garland, George Gephart Jr., Susanna Gibbons, Melissa Gilbertson, Don Hall, Peter Heegaard, Ellen Holt-Werle, Scott Howard, Jim Johnson, Louis Johnston, Roger Katzenmaier, Patrick Kennedy, Tom Kingston, Russel Kinnel, Peggy Klema, George Latimer, Michelle Lindenfelser, Don Mains, Bonnie Mairs, Helen Mairs, Todd Mairs, Malcolm McDonald, Brent Miller, Richard Nicholson, Dean Nelson, Doug Platt, Dan Ritchie, Peter Robb, Mark Salter, Carol Schleif, Al Sedgwick, Fred Speece, Ed Stringer, Bob Struyk, Lori Sturdevant, Tony Thomas, John Wareham, and Stephanie Wolf.

Also, thank you to all the people, past and present, at Mairs & Power. They kept the flag flying throughout all of the potentially disruptive events that came their way. Finally, thank you to my wife, Caroline, who over the years has put up with all the diversions that took me away from my family as I pursued my career in journalism, surely still one of our most addictive vocations—save possibly for investment and finance. This effort was enabled most of all by her.

Dave Beal
September 2021

Prologue

In 1936, *Fortune* magazine published a remarkably unfriendly portrait of the Twin Cities. Earlier, the magazine had undertaken similar expeditions to Philadelphia, Boston, Pittsburgh, and other large cities, but its portrayal of the Twin Cities was hands-down the worst—a horror-show of labor-management strife in Minneapolis and, in St. Paul, a hopelessly corrupt city controlled by a cabal of politicians in bed with gangsters. Presiding over it all was Floyd B. Olson, elected as governor of the most radical state in the union on a platform pledged to abolish capitalism.[1]

Beneath this grim landscape, the seeds of what would become a very different story were taking root. In 1931, one of the scariest years of the Great Depression, George Mairs Jr. founded an investment firm in an obscure office on the 10th floor of the Pioneer Building in downtown St. Paul. He marketed himself as "one of the few investment counselors in the West," ran his enterprise as a one-man band, and managed to emerge from the dark days of the 1930s basically unscathed.

Ninety years on, the firm he started, now Mairs & Power, manages nearly $12 billion in assets. Imagine that one of your ancestors had bought $1,000 worth of shares of the Mairs & Power Growth Fund at its inception in 1958 and that you and your offspring had left them untouched. Now your shares would be worth $991,058.[2]

Mairs & Power has survived to prosper as the oldest continuously independent investment management firm in Minnesota in a tumultuous industry littered with the remains of countless peers that collapsed or were rolled up into larger firms. It has done so largely by developing a laser-like focus on investing for the long term. This is the fundamental investing philosophy articulated by Benjamin Graham

An undated portrait of George A. Mairs Jr. that was probably made in the 1930s. Comence Art Studios photo. Photo courtesy of the Mairs family.

in his classic texts, *Security Analysis* (written with David Dodd) in 1934 and *The Intelligent Investor* in 1949. It is a creed that distinguishes Mairs & Power from numerous money managers and traders fixated on reaping profits for the next quarter, or sometimes the next few weeks, days, hours, minutes, even seconds.

THE THREE GEORGES

For more than 75 years, the firm was led by "The Three Georges"— George Mairs Jr., his son George III, and George C. Power Jr. George Power Jr. joined the firm in the mid-1940s. George Mairs Jr.'s son, George Mairs III, joined them in the early 1950s. George III led the firm from 1984 to 2007. His decision to sell his controlling stake in Mairs & Power back to the firm (which could then spread it more widely among existing employees) rather than fetch a significantly better price by selling to outsiders makes the firm's continuing in-dependence far more likely. "It was his greatest legacy," says current CEO Mark Henneman.[3]

In 2016, *Wall Street Journal* columnist Jason Zweig, one of the country's most prominent financial journalists, called George III "a model of how to run a decent mutual fund that differs from the market and makes its clients feel as if they are part of a distinctive community." Zweig then re-posted his December 1994 column about George III's low-key, intuitive approach to investing. "I think it has more than historical interest; it offers some guidelines for how the investment business could do better," he wrote. "At Mairs and Power, phones don't ring off the hook, nor do frenetic traders buy and sell with half-eaten pizzas littering their desks."[4]

George C. Power Jr. in the late 1930s following his graduation from Carleton College. Photo courtesy of Diane Power.

But the other two Georges also played critical roles—George Jr., in founding the company and seeing it through years of the Great De-pression, war, and an agonizingly slow recovery of the stock market, and George Power Jr., so highly regarded by his clients for his tailored investing and caring manner. As have their successors, the managers and professionals who reshaped the firm to compete well in today's constantly changing, increasingly complex, and always uncertain financial world.

The firm's flagship Growth Fund owned just 27 companies in 1994, nearly 80 percent of them launched within 20 miles of the firm's downtown office. "Mairs and Power Growth has a 4 percent turnover rate, meaning it holds onto its average stock for an astonishing quarter of a century," Jason Zweig wrote. He suggested that the firm, managed like a tortoise, runs like a hare.

On June 30, 2021, 59 percent of the assets managed by Mairs & Power were in three mutual funds: Growth, $5.52 billion in assets; Balanced, $985 million; and Small Cap, $420 million. The rest of the assets are in separately managed institutional and individual accounts and the new Minnesota Municipal Bond Fund. This is an exchange-traded fund launched by the firm in March 2021. Its focus is consistent with the firm's emphasis on Minnesota stocks in the sense that it invests entirely in the bonds issued by Minnesota governments: the state, its counties, cities, school districts, and other government agencies.

George Mairs III about 1955. Photo courtesy of the Mairs family.

Flash back again to 1936. St. Paul business leaders were outraged by *Fortune*'s harsh dismissal of their city. The magazine gave them their say in a follow-up story but stood its ground. Seven months later, the Mairs household was shaken to its core when George Jr.'s wife, Jean, fell ill with pneumonia and died. In 1928, Louise Power had also lost her spouse, Robert E. Power, at a time when the couple had one child just 15 months old and she was carrying their second child. In 1938, Louise and George Jr. were married. He adopted her two children; she adopted his four. Louise and George Jr. went on to raise all six children in a large, early modern Georgian revival home on Summit Avenue in St. Paul. One of Louise's children, Robert P. Mairs, was the father of Rob Mairs, today the president of Mairs & Power. One of George Jr.'s four children was George Mairs III. George C. Power Jr., the other George, was Robert E. Power's nephew. Miraculously, the marriage of Louise and George Jr., enabled by their earlier tragedies, turned out to be a remarkable success that foretold the business partnership that would become Mairs & Power.

By the mid-1950s, the Three Georges were settled in at the firm and it had taken on its present-day name of Mairs & Power. In 1954, the Dow Jones Industrial Average finally topped its 1929 peak. Then, the Georges concluded that stocks were headed for a bright new dawn. Dealing with smaller clients, defined as those with less than $100,000 of investable assets, was taking too much time; mutual funds offered a more efficient means of channeling their money into securities. The firm started with the Growth Fund. Three years later, it added a second fund to offer clients a broader mix of securities.

COMMON DESTINIES LINK FIRM, REGION

From 1966 to 1972, the Growth Fund went on a tear. Its assets shot up sixfold as the firm identified fresh investment opportunities in its backyard. During these years, the Fund discovered or added more to its existing holdings of a cluster of rising Twin Cities companies: Medtronic, H.B. Fuller, Deluxe, Ecolab, Toro, Graco, Tonka, and Jostens.

Fortune's sister publication, *Time*, spotted the rise of these companies and much more. In its August 13, 1973, issue, the magazine shot a cover portrait of Governor Wendell Anderson flashing a broad smile as he displayed his catch for the day, a snaky northern pike. The governor and his bounty were framed by a background of one of the state's storied lakes. Inside the magazine, *Time* ran a lengthy story describing Minnesota, driven by the Twin Cities, in glowing terms. The so-called "fish cover" became emblematic of the good life in Minnesota. The magazine found that the business landscape had been flipped on its head from the scene a generation earlier when Fortune had described the Twin Cities in such foreboding terms.[5]

All told, *Fortune* reported that in 1973, 27 of the country's 800 largest and mostly publicly held corporations were headquartered in Minnesota—3.4 percent of the nation's total, almost twice the state's 1.9 percent share of the nation's population. By then, many of these companies had landed in Mairs & Power portfolios: Control Data, Dayton Hudson, First Bank System, General Mills, Honeywell, Northwestern Bancorp, Northwestern National, St. Paul Companies, and 3M. The rise of these companies, from regional to national and in some cases international markets, became the engine that would fuel the ascent of Mairs & Power.

Jason Zweig asked George III why he so often ended up shopping for investments so close to home. "This is a tough state to do business in," he replied. "With high taxes, workers' compensation and health-care costs, companies have to be run extremely well." If you can make it in Minnesota, he explained, you can make it anywhere.

For Mairs & Power, making it in Minnesota has also meant living with the ups and downs of securities markets that can be notoriously

The celebrated cover of the August 13, 1973, issue of *Time* announcing "The Good Life in Minnesota."

unpredictable. Unlike many other firms, its investing strategy—looking for companies with a strong franchise and often based in Minnesota or nearby—means its performance can lag in growth markets but excel in down markets. The firm has always been prepared to deal with and wait out disquieting times: the 1973–1982 stretch when stocks struggled; the financial crisis of 2007–2009; and the stock market's frightening plunge, however brief, sparked by the pandemic in the spring of 2020.

The highest moments at the firm have been the best of the best. In 1994, its Growth Fund, still unavailable to most investors beyond Minnesota, ranked with the top national performers with a 5.6 percent return, more than four times the S&P 500's gain. In 2012, Morningstar Research named Growth Fund co-managers Bill Frels and Mark Henneman as domestic stock fund managers of the year.

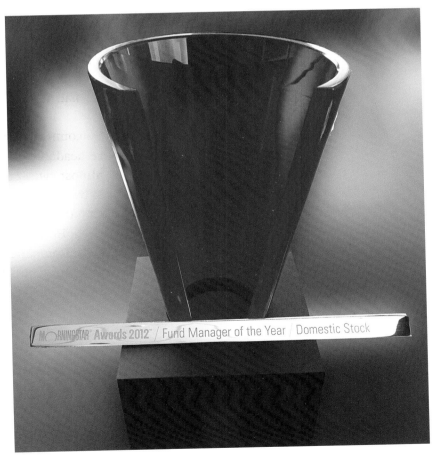

In 2012, Morningstar Research named Bill Frels and Mark Henneman, the co-managers of the Mairs & Power Growth Fund, the domestic stock fund managers of the year. Photo courtesy of Mairs & Power.

What else, beyond its investments in successful companies in Minnesota and nearby, has made Mairs & Power's journey so special? Its unchanging culture, which features judicious use of resources and an aversion to pricey and pretentious marketing practices. This helps keep client fees to a minimum. Also stamped into its culture: a preference for face-to-face relationships with clients; a capacity for seizing opportunities to build its staff; and despite its emphasis on regional stocks, a willingness to invest beyond the area as well. The firm stresses relationships, as opposed to the transactional dealings that have become commonplace in so much of the investment business. Women make up half of its staff now, including several in top positions. After long-dominant First Trust Company of St. Paul, once the city's financial powerhouse, faltered in the late 1980s, Mairs & Power was quick to tap it for experienced and talented staffers and many clients. The firm's mutual funds, limited to investors in just three states in the mid-1990s, are now available to them in all 50 states.

But we are getting ahead of our story. Let us begin years before the firm was born with how the forebears of the Mairs and Power families established an entrepreneurial tradition and came to Minnesota; what the city was like then and earlier; and how the railroad industry centered in St. Paul influenced the early investment style of the firm. We will describe the striking shift in the region's economy, from the bleak days of the 1930s to the vibrance that emerged in the 1960s; how it got through the economic struggles of the 1970s; how it adjusted to the turbulence in its industry; and how it established a national presence. We will trace this uncommon journey through its many twists and turns to the present day and look at how the firm hopes to guarantee its success long into the future.

Part I

THE ROOTS AND THE GEORGE JR. ERA

CHAPTER 1

The Entrepreneurial Culture of the Forebears

Both the Mairs and Power families share a common heritage and have their roots in the land of the Yankees—the Hudson River Valley, and upstate New York, Boston, western Massachusetts, and Nova Scotia. When the forebears of today's Mairs and Power families came to Minnesota in the last half of the nineteenth century, they brought with them commitments to entrepreneurism and trade, education, egalitarianism, and a Protestant religious conviction that so many of the people who were the original colonizers of the northeastern region of the United States had also valued.

The family roots for George Mairs III and his father, George A. Mairs Jr., lie in the small town of Argyle, New York, 50 miles north of Albany. In 1793, the Reverend George Mairs arrived from Ireland to take up pastoral duties at the United Presbyterian Church in Argyle, then a growing town with a population of more than 2,000. The congregation flourished under his watch. In 1823, one of his 11 children, Rev. George Mairs Jr., joined him and gradually succeeded him as pastor. Together, they ran "The Mairs Church," an influential institution in and around Argyle, for 58 years. When Rev. George Mairs Sr. passed on in 1841 at age 81, the *Washington County Post* hailed him in a lengthy obituary. "At the beginning of his settlement, the surrounding country was uncultivated, and existed only in the wildness of nature. He was for years the father, the counsellor, the legislator of that district. He watched over its rising prosperity with the warmest interest and embarked in every measure calculated to advance its moral and spiritual prosperity . . . with sound judgment and the fervor of his capacious heart."[1]

THE MAIRS FAMILY'S JOURNEY TO MINNESOTA

A nineteenth-century publication provides insight into the Mairs family genealogy. It identified both father and son as abolitionists and suggested that the younger Mairs built an underground railway hideaway into the chimney of his home to accommodate enslaved people escaping the South during the Civil War.

A child of the younger minister, James Walker Mairs (1836-1893), married Amelia Ann Dyer (1841-1912) about 1870. James and Amelia relocated from Schenectady, New York, which is west of Albany, to St. Paul. James had run a grocery store in Schenectady and, according to Amelia's will, the family continued to own property there after they moved to St. Paul. James and Amelia had three children, a girl and two boys.[2] George Alexander Mairs, born in 1873, was the youngest child. No documentation exists that explains why James and Amelia Mairs came to St. Paul, but Amelia's brothers were already in the city, where they owned and operated the Dyer Music Store located initially at Seventh and Jackson streets and then later in a much bigger building at 148-150 East Third Street (now Kellogg Boulevard) in downtown St. Paul.[3]

Rev. George Alexander (1843–1930), seated right, a celebrated Presbyterian minister in New York City, was the namesake for George Alexander Mairs (1873–1944), seated left, George Alexander Mairs Jr. (1901–1983), standing rear, and George Alexander Mairs III (1928–2010), the very young boy held by Rev. Alexander. This photo is undated, but it was probably taken in 1929 or 1930. Photo courtesy of Rob Mairs.

An obituary for George Alexander Mairs (born 1873), published in the *St. Paul Pioneer Press* in 1944, reported that he came to the city in 1895 from Schenectady when he was 23 years old and that he had been an officer and director of the W. J. Dyer Bro. music store in St. Paul.[4] The 1895 *St. Paul City Directory* identifies him as employed at the Dyer store as a travel agent. In 1898, George A. Mairs married Leontine Paradis (1875-1956), whose residence before her marriage was in St. Paul's Lowertown neighborhood.[5]

The Mairs family ties to the senior member of the Dyer family, William J. Dyer (1863-1925), eventually became financially significant for George A. Mairs. When George's mother, Amelia, died in 1912, she bequeathed to him 25 shares of preferred stock in the W. J. Dyer & Bro. Company. When his uncle, William Dyer, died in 1925, he left another 10 shares of Dyer preferred to George. The total value of these shares was $3,500 in 1912—the equivalent of roughly $95,000 today, adjusting for inflation.[6]

George Alexander Mairs Jr., the son of George A. and Leontine P. Mairs, was born in 1901. Although his parents were not wealthy relative to the members of the family of railroad baron James J. Hill, they were solid members of St. Paul's middle class. Only a few years after the death of William Dyer in 1925, George A. Mairs Jr. would establish the investment firm that in the mid-1950s became known as Mairs & Power.

An undated photo of a youthful Leontine Elizabeth Paradis (1875–1956), who lived in St. Paul and married George A. Mairs in 1898. Photo courtesy of the Mairs family.

THE POWER ANCESTORS AND MINNESOTA'S EARLY DAYS

The other name in the Mairs & Power firm that of Power has as interesting a family history as does George A. Mairs. Family stories identify two Power brothers who came to the land that became the United States from Liverpool before 1700. According to Diane Power, the archivist for the family, many believe the Power family originally came from Ireland but documentation is lacking. Much is known, however, of the family history since the mid-1700s.[7]

The Power family member whose name is perpetuated in the firm of Mairs & Power was George Center Power Jr. His roots go back to the Berkshires in western Massachusetts and the Hudson River Valley and later, to Minnesota's founders. Thomas Power was born is Rhode Island or eastern Massachusetts in 1753. His father moved the family to Adams, in western Massachusetts, in 1768. Thomas and his family moved on, to Hudson, New York, in 1786. He served with a Rhode Island unit in the Revolutionary War.[8]

Thomas's son, John, was a prominent merchant and boat operator on the Hudson River. John's son, William, became the first station agent in Pittsfield, in western Massachusetts, for the Boston & Albany Railroad. In 1849, the oldest of William's nine children, 17-year-old James Buel Power, left Pittsfield for opportunities in the then-emerging railroad industry. By the early 1860s, he and his family were in St. Paul. James went on to an illustrious career in railroading, agriculture, and education in Minnesota and North Dakota. For a time, he was a land agent for James J. Hill. Eventually, in 1878, he purchased a large cattle farm located southwest of Fargo in the Dakota Territory (the northern portion of the territory became the state of North Dakota in 1889) and plunged into experimental farming.

The farm, Helendale, became widely known for its scientific achievements in grain production and livestock breeding. With the purchase of Helendale Farm, Power helped to originate "bonanza" farming in the Red River Valley—very large, efficient, profit-focused farms that made use of the latest machinery, cheap and abundant land, growing Eastern markets, and emerging railroads. The earliest of the bonanza farms dotted the land along or near the Northern Pacific Railroad's tracks as they darted west from the Red River Valley through North Dakota. A booklet about Helendale, commissioned by George C. Power III (the son of George C. Power Jr. of Mairs & Power),

"Dakota" by Carl Gutherz (1844–1907). French artist Gutherz painted this scene of plowing on Helendale Farm in Dakota Territory, southwest of Fargo, in 1884. The 6,000-acre Helendale Farm was established by James Buel Power in 1878 and was one of the first bonanza farms in what later became North Dakota. Photo courtesy of the Institute for Regional Studies, North Dakota State University Archives, Fargo.

noted that James B. Power generally embraced the advanced farming methods of the bonanza farmers, but he dealt more with community-wide concerns than many of them did.

James B. Power was the second president of the North Dakota Agricultural College (now known as North Dakota State University), served a term in the state's House of Representatives and was one of the six original inductees into the North Dakota Hall of Fame. George Power of Mairs & Power was his great-grandson.

George Power's mother, Anna Rice Dawson, was the daughter of Maria Rice and William Dawson. Maria's father, Edmund Rice, born in 1819 and raised in Vermont, lived in Michigan for 11 years, then came to St. Paul in 1849. Rice, a lawyer, was president of three different railroads at various times from 1857 to 1877, served in both houses of the Minnesota Legislature, and was elected as St. Paul's mayor in 1881 and again in 1885. His brother, Henry Mower Rice, was instrumental in establishing the Minnesota Territory in 1849 and, eight years later, in enabling Minnesota to become a state. He was one of the state's first two U.S. senators. Maria's father-in-law, William Dawson, was St. Paul's mayor from 1878 to 1881.

THE DYER AND MCLEOD FAMILIES

The history of the Mairs family is closely tied to those of the Dyer and McLeod families in St. Paul. Ultimately, the leaders of these two families, William Dyer and Angus McLeod, helped George Jr. start his business. Both men, originally from the Northeast, were ambitious achievers who resettled in St. Paul, built successful retail businesses in the city's downtown, and joined the ranks of the city's most prominent citizens. Dyer, born in Boston in 1841, came to Minnesota as a music teacher in Faribault and to open a music store there. Two years later, he moved to St. Paul to open a much larger store. His business prospered. At various times, his three brothers worked at the store, which became one of the leading music stores in the Midwest.[9]

When George Mairs Jr. married Angus McLeod's daughter, Jean, in 1925, the newlyweds tightened the family ties with the McLeods. Angus McLeod was born in 1859 near Halifax, Nova Scotia, which developed as a port city with extensive shipping ties to Maine and Boston. McLeod began his career as a carpenter and contractor in Halifax. He was a

Angus McLeod (1859–1924) was born in Nova Scotia, Canada, and emigrated to the Twin Cities, where he became a St. Paul real estate developer and retailer. He and two partners established the Emporium Mercantile Company, which built the Emporium Department Store. Lee Brothers photo from 1921. Photo courtesy of the Minnesota Historical Society.

An undated photo of George A. Mairs Jr. Photo courtesy of the Mairs family.

A 1937 portrait in pencil of Jean McLeod Mairs by artist Carl Bohnen (1888–1977). Photo courtesy of the Mairs family.

professional cyclist who took part in races in Canada, the Twin Cities, and possibly elsewhere. In 1881, he came to Minneapolis where he organized the Angus McLeod Co., a construction contracting business. He and three partners built the Emporium, a downtown St. Paul department store that opened in 1902.[10]

DEFINING THE YANKEE HERITAGE

John Rice (no relation to Edmund Rice), a University of Minnesota geography professor, described the new arrivals from the Yankee region in an essay that was part of the Minnesota Historical Society's 1981 book *They Chose Minnesota: A Survey of the State's Ethnic Groups*. They were members of white European families who came to the state directly from abroad or in two steps: first, to the northeastern part of North America that is now mostly part of the United States; then on to Minnesota. "They differed from the newer immigrants who were part of the Great Atlantic Migration of the nineteenth century in at least two respects," Rice wrote. "First, their culture was founded primarily, though not exclusively, on the cultures of the British Isles. Second, after the Revolutionary War, the regional subcultures of Colonial America [New England, Middle Atlantic and Southern] began to come together west of the Appalachian Mountains to form a distinctive national culture."[11]

Rice goes on to say that by the start of the nineteenth century, few Yankees had ventured beyond the shores of Lake Erie. But after 1830, they came in a "deluge" and by 1860, "nearly half of the Yankees then living had left New England." When more fertile lands became available, "these New Englanders flocked to Wisconsin and Minnesota in droves. They were enthusiastically joined by [New] Yorkers, until in 1860 just over half of the total northeastern-born population of Minnesota was made up of these Yankees 'one step removed.'"

Rice wrote that these new arrivals—New Englanders and New Yorkers, who he also describes as "Old-Stock Americans"—laid the groundwork for the future state of Minnesota.[12]

As he prepared to start his investment business, George Mairs Jr. had to benefit from his family ties with William Dyer and Angus McLeod, self-made men with extensive experience in business. Their downtown stores were highly visible exemplars of commercial success, admirable models to reshape so they would work in the investment business. They also offered rich repositories of experience and advice on how to start and sustain a profitable enterprise in a highly competitive environment.

We don't know how much George Jr. learned from these caches of expertise, or in what ways, but it's difficult to imagine him not taking advantage of these opportunities. His father had become a senior manager at the Dyer store before George Jr. graduated from high school. His father-in-law, Angus McLeod, and Angus's brother, George, were widely known for their popular department store. The McLeods and William Dyer, joined by his brothers, had other business interests as well.

William Dyer was a tenor soloist and choir director when he came to St. Paul. His music store grew with the city. He built a four-story structure downtown. It featured state-of-the-art sound booths and other new technology, a staff that sold everything from records and sheet music to grand pianos, organs, and a complete line of musical instruments including many imported from abroad. It became a must-stop for visiting musicians. Dyer built close ties with church

A photo of the interior of the W. J. Dyer Bros. Music Company store, 21–25 West Fifth Street (between Wabasha and St. Peter streets), in downtown St. Paul, about 1900. The photo captures some of the size of the store and the extent of its music-related inventory. Photographer Anderson. Photo courtesy of the Minnesota Historical Society.

and school music programs. His St. Paul store was comparable to the leading Midwest music stores in Chicago, Milwaukee and Cleveland and, according to the Minnesota Historical Society, "was said to be the largest music store west of Chicago."[13]

Dyer's life was widely chronicled when he died in 1925. He drew particular attention from the St. Paul-based *Northwestern Bulletin-Appeal*, a weekly newspaper circulated to the small African-American communities in the Twin Cities. In a tribute featuring his picture, near the top of the front page, the paper eulogized him for creating a business "built largely on its reputation for handling dependable high-grade lines of goods, square dealing and personal contact. Dyer was a man of deep religious conviction and lived a life of constructive usefulness. He was known to every noted musician in the country." It was an extensive memorial that suggested Dyer placed a high value on developing a significant base of loyal African-American customers, unusual for a white-owned store at the time.[14]

St. Paul's downtown was bustling at the turn of century. Angus McLeod, sensing that the heyday of downtown department store retailing

The June 27, 1925, edition of *The Northwestern Bulletin Appeal* newspaper in St. Paul carried a front-page announcement of the death of William J. Dyer along with his photo. Photo courtesy of the Library of Congress.

was approaching, joined with partners J.T. and W.S. Kennedy and P. McArthur to build the Emporium. In her book about Minnesota department store retailing—*Thank You for Shopping*—Kristal Leebrick described the Emporium as a 35,000-square-foot store that featured 22 departments and employed 150 salespeople.[15]

"The ladies, in particular, will find much to interest them," declared the store's opening day ad in the *St. Paul Globe*. "Our styles are new, original and exclusive. Our store, with its various departments, stocked with beautiful, unique and useful articles, offers exceptional advantages to those who do not wish to waste their valuable time going about from store to store in a fruitless search of odd articles."

Seven months later, the new store had a second opening of its expanded "'beautiful daylight store,' which was now double the size when it first opened," Leebrick noted. She cited excerpts, touting amenities, from the Emporium's July 1917 *News from the 'Fresh Air Store' Newsletter*; overnight Kodak film delivery service; Columbia Grafonola talking machines that enable listeners to hear great bands and orchestras, opera singers, comedians, and world-famous artists over and over again at less than the cost of hearing them once in person.

McLeod moved to St. Paul and quickly joined the ranks of the city's business and civic leadership, becoming chair of Macalester College's Board of Trustees. By the early 1920s, the store had expanded to many times its original size. When McLeod died in 1924, the *Pioneer Press* declared that the Emporium was the crowning achievement of his career. McLeod and William Dyer were also deeply engaged in charitable

St. Paul's *Globe* newspaper for March 1, 1902, featured this lengthy announcement of the opening of The Emporium Department Store on East Seventh Street. Photo courtesy of the Library of Congress.

This 1917 photo by photographer Charles P. Gibson gives some sense of the vast size of St. Paul's Emporium Department Store. Photo courtesy of the Minnesota Historical Society.

activities. McLeod was president of the board of trustees of the Union Gospel Mission. Dyer was president of the Children's Home Society for 13 years.[16]

THE ROLE OF THE RAILROADS

Transportation first built and then drove commercial activity in St. Paul from its earliest days until the middle of the twentieth century. The city, situated just adjacent to the confluence of the Minnesota and Mississippi rivers (the site of Fort Snelling) and at the head of navigable water on the Mississippi until early in the twentieth century, was founded before Minneapolis and was the commercially dominant twin in the nineteenth century. In 1858, the year Minnesota became a state, more than 1,000 steamboats docked in St. Paul, the state capital. Only after Minneapolis harnessed the waterpower at the Falls of St. Anthony for lumber and flour milling did the younger twin surpass its older neighbor in population and commercial activity.[17]

Neither St. Paul nor Minneapolis, however, would have achieved such dominance in the Upper Midwest but for the Indigenous peoples who had populated the future state of Minnesota for centuries prior to the arrival of Euro-Americans. Native Americans first created the trade relationships and transportation routes upon which these great commercial centers were built. The numerous steamboats and railroad trains relied heavily on these routes and patterns of trade and transport that the native peoples had established in the region long before the invention of the steam engine.

Entrepreneurially minded men such as Edmund Rice were first drawn to St. Paul by business prospects initially tied to steamboat traffic. Later they seized financial opportunity by investing in the railroads. Although this early railroad building in Minnesota came a generation after the first trains in the Northeast began running, Minnesota hastened to catch up because its citizens immediately saw the advantages that the railroads had over steamboats and wagons. By 1880, the state had 3,100 miles of track.[18]

Edmund Rice is sometimes described as the father of railroading in Minnesota. Soon after he settled in St. Paul, he became the town recorder. In 1857, he was named president of the fledgling Minnesota & Pacific Railway Co. That year, the Minnesota & Pacific received a land grant that allowed it to earn more land if it would build rail lines connecting important river cities. In 1862, after several years of complex legal and financial maneuvering, another railroad—the St. Paul and Pacific, also led by Rice—laid the first track in the state over a 10-mile stretch linking downtown St. Paul and St. Anthony, near Minneapolis.

The four authors of *The Great Northern Railway* (Ralph W. Hidy, Muriel E. Hidy, Roy V. Scott, and Don L. Hofsommer) described meticulously the rise of the Great Northern, which was the creation of James J. Hill. They wrote that no other railroad shaped the landscape and society of the territory that runs from the Upper Mississippi River Valley to Puget Sound like the Great Northern did. As happened so often with the early railroads in Minnesota, the original owner often gave way to new owners, particularly after a period of financial distress in the state. In the 1870s, James J. Hill and his partners acquired ownership of the railroad that Edmund Rice and others had established. Reorganized first as the St. Paul, Minneapolis and Manitoba Railroad (in 1878) and later, in 1889, as the Great Northern, Hill's leadership and tight control over the railroad's finances resulted in its completion in 1893 of a transcontinental road running from St. Paul to the Pacific coast.[19]

Called by some the "father of railroading in Minnesota" because of his early involvement in three Minnesota railroads, Edmund Rice was an important political and civic leader in the state. He was also related to the Power family of St. Paul. This is an 1855 portrait of Rice painted by Eastman Johnson. Photo courtesy of the Minnesota Historical Society.

The authors opened their book about the Great Northern with an extended salute to Edmund Rice. "He suffered illness in lonely hotel rooms, rebuffs from bankers and disappointments when expected contracts did not materialize," they wrote. Nonetheless, he persevered to emerge as "a remarkable railroad pioneer" who helped set the stage for the achievements of Hill and the Great Northern.

Hill consolidated various railroads, laid more track, built depots, and developed related interests as he assembled his Great Northern empire. The decades-long railroad boom, so much of which was centered in St. Paul, drew a massive flow of immigrants directly from Germany, Ireland, Sweden, and other European countries or in a two-step flow from these countries to another part of the U.S. and then on to St. Paul. The city's population tripled, to 133,000 in 1890 from 41,000 in 1880. St. Paul would add another 102,000 residents, many of them immigrants, between 1890 and 1920.[20]

The building of railroads in the last half of nineteenth century slowly fostered a national market economy for consumer goods; consequently middle-class families in St. Paul and elsewhere in the Upper

This 1912 photograph of James J. Hill, left, and his son, Louis W. Hill, captures two of Minnesota's foremost railroad leaders. James Hill was a railroad pioneer whose Great Northern Railway went from St. Paul to the west coast. Louis became president of the GN in 1907 and chairman of the board in 1912. Photo courtesy of the Minnesota Historical Society.

Midwest were no longer dependent on buying goods that were produced locally. The buyers at the Dyer Music Store and the Emporium ordered goods from elsewhere that they judged shoppers in St. Paul would want. Even though these goods were produced in places such as New York City or Chicago, the railroads made it easy for the retailer to get them and sell them at an affordable price that was also profitable for the merchant in St. Paul.

George Mairs Jr., while studying at the University of Minnesota in the aftermath of the Great Crash of 1929, was calmly taking the measure of this environment and carefully refining his plans to enter the investment business.

This is a view of the railroad yards and St. Paul skyline adjacent to the Mississippi River and the Union Depot as seen from Dayton's Bluff in about 1925. The photograph captures the substantial volume of rail traffic in the 1920s and the close proximity of the nine railroads serving the city and the warehouses of the Lowertown neighborhood.

Here a locomotive is heading west from Chestnut Street in downtown St. Paul pulling a string of freight cars behind as it slowly makes its way upgrade toward Minneapolis. Photographer Helmut Kroening made this photo in 1932. Helmut Kroening Railroad Transportation Photographs, 1917–1947 (Album 2, page 69). Photo courtesy of the Minnesota Historical Society.

CHAPTER 2

St. Paul Slogs through the Depression

In broad daylight, on a steamy day in June 1933, members of the Barker/Karpis gang kidnapped William Hamm Jr. as he left his office at the family brewery on St. Paul's East Side. Hamm was one of the city's most prominent business leaders. His interests included the Emporium, the downtown St. Paul department store that the Hamm family had purchased from George Mairs Jr.'s father-in-law nearly a decade earlier. Seven months after the Hamm kidnapping, the Barker/Karpis gang struck again, kidnapping Edward G. Bremer, president of the Commercial State Bank in St. Paul. He was the son of Adolph Bremer, who owned the city's other major brewer, Schmidt.[1]

The kidnappings sent chills through St. Paul's business community. In April 1936, *Fortune* magazine picked up on the Hamm and Bremer sagas and a litany of other travails to publish a blistering takedown of the business climate in the Twin Cities. The magazine reserved its harshest comments for St. Paul, literally writing an obituary for the city. The kidnappings had made the front pages of newspapers across the country; yet more black eyes for a city whose people and institutions had already been pounded by the mounting stress of the Great Depression.[2]

The Depression took a heavy toll on St. Paul in the 1930s. The city's best-known business, the Great Northern Railway, suffered steep revenue declines and red ink. So did many other businesses. Decades later, the Ramsey County Historical Society's magazine assessed the early damage. In 1932, some 15,000 men were without a job in St. Paul, one in every five of the city's families. Widespread unemployment and homelessness had settled in not only in the city, but also in many other parts of the state.[3]

Until then, churches, sectarian agencies—Catholic Charities, Jewish Family Welfare, and the Union Gospel Mission—along with private nonprofits—the Salvation Army, Volunteers of America, the Wilder Charity, and United Charities—had been able to keep up with the rising cries for help in St. Paul. But the federal assistance programs initiated under President Franklin Delano Roosevelt and his New Deal had not yet taken hold. The massive costs of providing relief to the needy in St. Paul were beginning to outrun the capacity of those organizations to meet the need for more support. The City Council was spending more on welfare than it was receiving in real and personal property taxes.

And that was just part of the story. St. Paul had gone into the Depression saddled with a reputation as a wide-open town that tolerated corruption. Many of the problems were embedded in what came to be seen as the "O'Connor System." Mary Lethert Wingerd described the arrangement in her 2001 book, *Claiming the City*, about the history of St. Paul. Upon taking office in 1900, Police Chief John O'Connor worked out a scheme to control crime while allowing its practitioners to operate freely so long as they followed three rules: check in at police headquarters within 12 hours of arriving in the city; provide "appropriate gratuities" to the police; and "behave themselves" when inside the city limits.[4]

The city's judiciary cooperated, making St. Paul a safe harbor for gangsters by consistently refusing to extradite them to other cities for prosecution. Elaborating on that point, Wingerd noted that in 1932, 21 percent of the nation's bank robberies occurred in Minnesota, but not a single one of them was in St. Paul. "Newspaper accounts of the crimes frequently noted that the robbers were 'last seen heading for St. Paul,'" she wrote.

Prohibition, which had become effective in January 1920 after passage of the Eighteenth Amendment to the U.S. Constitution, fit like a hand in a glove with the O'Connor System. Wingerd noted that perhaps the single issue that St. Paul's citizenry agreed on nearly unanimously when Prohibition began was opposition to this law. That was not surprising. "The amendment prohibiting the sale and production of alcohol had dealt the city's economy a potentially crippling blow,"

These bullet holes in the plate glass window of the Third Northwestern National Bank in Minneapolis that resulted from a robbery in December 1932 are evidence of the serious criminal activities that occurred during the Great Depression. Photo courtesy of the Minnesota Historical Society.

Wingerd wrote. "The trade in liquor and beer, from the prosperous turreted breweries to the hundreds of saloons scattered across town, was the source of critical income and jobs, and the consumption of alcohol was an integral part of the immigrant city's cultural fabric. St. Paul residents responded to this economic and cultural assault in predictable fashion: they ignored the law. Though Prohibition was openly flouted in cities and towns all across the nation, St. Paul was particularly well prepared to take its insurgency to an extreme."

Two years after the law was enacted, Michael Gebhart, O'Connor's successor as police chief, estimated that at least 75 percent of the city's residents were either distilling whiskey or making wine or beer. Speakeasies flourished. Alcohol spurred new social ties that pulled neighbors closer to one another. "Many other entrepreneurial St. Paulites created a small-scale cottage industry out of moonshining to supplement inadequate incomes," Wingerd wrote.[5]

DISTRESS IN THE BANKING SYSTEM

Much of the nation's banking system was near collapse in the weeks before FDR was inaugurated, on Saturday, March 4, 1933. Depositors rushed to the banks to pull their savings out. The bank runs led to "holidays"—temporary closures of the banks—in nearly half of the states. Two days after he took office, President Roosevelt declared a national bank holiday. In Minnesota, Governor Floyd B. Olson, a former Democrat who was the first Farmer-Labor politician to be elected to the state's highest office, had declared on March 2 that there would be no bank holiday in Minnesota; his administration reversed itself the next day. Chaos prevailed.

In his book *Banking in the Great Northern Territory*, Richard Slade wrote that Saturday, March 4 was a "banking nightmare." In his history of the First National Bank of Minneapolis, Gordon Malen recounted how a throng of angry and befuddled customers gathered at the bank's entrance. "They were all screaming and demanding their money," one of the bank's executives said, "and I almost got myself killed, or so it seemed." *Commercial West*, the Twin Cities-based trade publication that covered the banking industry for the five-state Upper Midwest region, called Roosevelt "a hard-hitting dictator president."[6]

So went the start of FDR's "First 100 days," when his administration and the new Democratic Congress actively intervened in the private sector to stabilize the economy. They began by rushing through the Emergency Banking Act. This legislation authorized the immediate reopening of sound banks, ordered the reorganization of others, and took other steps to fortify the system.[7]

FDR called for federal regulation of the securities industry. *Commercial West* reported that reaction of Twin Cities stockbrokers was mixed. "If government keeps hog-tying business . . . all of us will have to step down and out and let government do the business of the nation," one broker said. Another disagreed, saying "the sooner this whole matter is cleared up and the new regulations are in effect, the better it will be."

Advocates of the bank holiday argued that it worked. On the first day of trading after it ended, the Dow Jones Industrials leaped 15.3 percent—to this day, the greatest single-day percentage gain ever. In May, *Commercial West* reported that of the 555 state-chartered banks operating in Minnesota when the holiday began, 467 had reopened; the rest were being consolidated, reorganized, or liquidated. The publication found sharply improved business conditions throughout the region. In June, J.F.T. O'Connor, the U.S. Comptroller of the Currency, came to Minnesota to declare victory. "Ten black days," he said of the bank holiday in an address to the Minnesota Bankers Association.

"Every bank in the nation closed. Uncertainty, doubt, bewilderment was written in every face, but confidence and courage came to the rescue. It is over. We have succeeded."[8]

Even before the bank holiday, the federal government was moving toward a far greater role in regulating the financial sector. In March 1932, the U.S. Senate's Banking Committee opened an investigation into the causes of the 1929 stock market crash. Initially, the committee foundered. Two chief counsels were fired for being ineffective. A third quit after the committee failed to give him the subpoena power he had sought. But public anger was growing over the behavior of leading investors and speculators. Ferdinand Pecora, an assistant district attorney for New York County, took over as the banking committee's chief counsel. The committee, which became known as the Pecora Commission, convened hearings that generated many headlines. Its investigations exposed a wide array of abuses. Congress enacted a series of laws regulating the financial sector, including the Federal Securities Act and the Glass-Steagall Act in 1933 and the Securities Exchange Act of 1934. These laws led to the establishment of the Federal Deposit Insurance Corp. and the Securities and Exchange Commission.[9]

PATCHING UP A BAD IMAGE

The Hamm kidnapping had occurred about a week before the comptroller's talk to the Minnesota bankers. The FBI had one of the kidnappers, Alvin Karpis, at the top of its most-wanted list. Three days after the kidnapping, authorities captured him. He was tried in St. Paul. J. Edgar Hoover, then the FBI's chief, escorted him into the courthouse. Nate Bomberg, who chronicled crime for the St. Paul dailies for years, covered the trial. "Nate was streetwise and had a photographic memory, and an encyclopedic mind," Donald O'Grady wrote in his history of the *Pioneer Press* and *Dispatch*. "He knew both the good guys and the bad guys. As he walked from the car, Karpis looked over the crowd of newsmen and spotted Bomberg. 'Hi Nate,' he said, and walked on. Hoover and his agents looked Bomberg over very carefully."[10]

But times were changing. "With the end of prohibition, the city's nice, well-behaved gangsters turned on the city that had sheltered them," *Fortune* magazine noted. The piece suggested that the end of Prohibition had blown a hole in the O'Connor System. That

The FBI captured celebrated gangster Alvin "Creepy" Karpis in New Orleans in 1936. Here the handcuffed Karpis, front, enters the Federal Courts Building in St. Paul (now Landmark Center) escorted by federal agents to be tried for his involvement in the Hamm and Bremer kidnappings. Found guilty, Karpis served 26 years in the prison at Alcatraz. Photo courtesy of the Minnesota Historical Society.

arrangement—essentially a silent handshake between business, labor, and government leaders with gangsters to keep the peace in St. Paul—had sharply contrasted to the scene in Minneapolis. That city had witnessed violent confrontations during the 1934 Teamsters' strike. Yet *Fortune* stuck with its stinging indictment of St. Paul. While the leading citizens of Minneapolis were terrified by labor-management strife in their city, the magazine declared that "St. Paul's important people were dining quietly in their homes on Summit Avenue, discussing the happenings across the river with interest but no grave concern."

Fortune's critique stressed the heavy blow the opening of the Panama Canal dealt to the Twin Cities, particularly St. Paul. The canal made it cheaper to ship goods by water than by rail. The article went on to thrust a dagger into St. Paul. "Consciousness of St. Paul's decadence is never mentioned aloud by her citizens," the magazine wrote. "But the consciousness is there. It lies in an unmistakable inferiority complex betrayed by the conspicuous scorn of bustling Minneapolis. It is the tight-lipped contempt of an embarrassed invalid for a twin who insists on having a hell of a time."

Fortune summarized its look at the Twin Cities as "an examination of Minneapolis and an autopsy of St. Paul," which it called "cramped, hilly, stagnant," and filled with narrow streets. The article also included a watercolor painting of the State Capitol in St. Paul, which showed dark tenements in the foreground that the caption described as slums.

Many in St. Paul's business community were outraged. They called *Fortune*'s spread "untrue, distorted and malicious." Richard Lilly, president of St. Paul's First National Bank, began organizing a boycott of the magazine. Albert W. Lindeke, a prominent business leader who was a broker at the St. Paul office of Chicago-based Harris, Burrows & Hicks, disputed *Fortune*'s statement that St. Paul was one of the most slum-infested cities in the country. Lindeke argued that the city had seen no major bank failures since the Depression began; that the lack of open confrontation between business and labor in the city reflected sound labor-management practices rather than collusion with City Hall; and that the magazine had ignored much manufacturing and construction activity in St. Paul.

Lindeke argued that the strength of the city's banking sector had helped to finance $68 million of public and private construction projects during the Depression. Three months later, *Fortune* published a lengthy response to Lindeke's retort and other criticisms, in what it called a "reappraisal that acknowledged a controversy." The magazine's editors corrected and clarified several points, acknowledged that the tenements in its painting were not slums and apologized "to anyone who may have been hit by a warped shaft."[11]

FORTUNE STANDS ITS GROUND

But *Fortune* did not back away from its negative portrayal of the Twin Cities. Its harsh portrait of St. Paul noted that the troubles of the 1930s had not spared the city's best-known business: the Great Northern, founded by fabled "Empire Builder" James J. Hill. Nearly four years earlier, in December 1932, *Fortune* had hailed the railroad, in what became known to collectors as its "Great Northern issue," declaring that the company "is cherished by railroad security owners for the soundness of its financial structure." The Great Northern, the magazine said, had come through the 1920s as one of the country's best-managed railroads.[12]

Richard C. Lilly (1884–1959) was a civic leader in St. Paul and a business associate of Albert W. Lindeke, who took issue with *Fortune* magazine's 1936 critique of the city. When Lilly's Merchants National Bank merged with St. Paul's First National Bank in 1929, Lilly became president of First National, a position he held until his retirement in 1945. Photo courtesy of the Ramsey County Historical Society, St. Paul.

Many years before he became the president of the Great Northern Railway, William Kenney suggested the railroad use the mountain goat, which flourished at Glacier National Park in Montana, as its emblem. The design of the emblem went through multiple iterations before the railroad settled in 1936 on the one seen here. Reproduced courtesy of the Burlington Northern Santa Fe Railway.

The magazine reported then that the Great Northern had never been in reorganization or receivership, that it had a "remarkable necklace" of four hotels and eight groups of chalets at scenic Glacier National Park, and that it had generated an uninterrupted flow of dividends for 42 years. But by 1932, the Depression was bearing down on the once-prosperous cluster of business activity the Great Northern had generated for St. Paul.

Nationally, trouble had been brewing at the nation's railroads for years. The industry peaked in 1916 with 254,000 miles of trackage, but then the federal government defined the business as essential to the war effort following the U.S. entry to World War I and took over the nation's railroads. In 1921, the industry returned to private control, but by then new forms of transportation were signaling the end of the railroads' monopoly status. U.S. motor vehicle registrations rose from 3 million in 1916 to 23 million in 1929 as millions of Americans rushed onto newly built roads; private auto passenger-miles soared to 175 million, five times greater than rail passenger miles. Intercity bus service boomed.[13]

Later, the trucking business would take vast amounts of freight from the railroads. Eventually, carriers such as Northwest Airlines in St. Paul would combine forces with the automobile to deal a near-fatal blow to once-burgeoning rail passenger service. In 1928, the year after Charles Lindbergh electrified the world with his solo nonstop

Rail passengers are seen in 1936 hurrying along one of the platforms of St. Paul's Union Depot heading toward the building's concourse and lobby. Photo courtesy of the Minnesota Historical Society.

flight from New York City to Paris, the Great Northern's passenger department warned: "Expansion of airplane service, with dependable year-round schedules, is beginning to have its effect." The railroad responded by arranging for two of its passenger trains to connect at St. Paul with Northwest's flights between St. Paul and Chicago.

Ominously, in its 1936 critique of the Twin Cities, *Fortune* also described troubling developments at the Great Northern. In February 1932, the railroad stopped paying dividends. In the first nine months of that year, the financial bellwether of St. Paul reported a $12.3 million loss vs. a deficit of only $916,000 in the comparable 1931 period. Business conditions had suddenly gone from bad to awful in the Great Northern's sprawling territory, which stretched from Minnesota to Seattle and Portland on the Pacific Coast.

As *Fortune* told it, shipments of ore from the Iron Range had dwindled to a trickle. Prices had nosedived for the lumber, wheat, steers, lettuce, apples, and berries that in ordinary times filled the boxcars headed east to the big cities of the industrial Midwest. Similarly, the owners of the orchards, ranges, farms, and berry patches that dotted the landscape from the Twin Cities to the Pacific Northwest lacked the cash to buy the radios, cars, iceboxes, and ice cream separators that typically kept the westbound boxcars well-stocked.

The authors of *The Great Northern Railway* wrote that in the 1920s, the railroad had fared better financially than its peers except for the Union Pacific. They went on to report that when William P. Kenney became its president on January 1, 1932, the railroad's financial structure, so much of which was built on debt, had become perilous. In 1933, an official from the Interstate Commerce Commission "lightly tossed off" a suggestion that the Great Northern could solve its financial problems by declaring bankruptcy. Kenney refused to consider the idea.[14]

FEDERAL GOVERNMENT BACKSTOPS RAILROADS

That year, the railroad worked with a syndicate of New York banks and the federal government's Reconstruction Finance Corporation (RFC), to refinance its short-term debt. But the Great Northern's historians called that move a small accomplishment compared with the financial hurdle that loomed just ahead. In 1936, $106 million in bonds would come due, hanging over the railroad "Like Damocles' sword."

William Kenney (1870–1939) was president of the Great Northern Railway from 1932 until his death in 1939. Photo courtesy of the Minnesota Historical Society.

Jesse H. Jones was an entrepreneur and Democratic politician from Texas, who headed the Reconstruction Finance Corporation for President Franklin Roosevelt from 1932 to 1939. He also served as secretary of Commerce (1940–1945). Harris & Ewing Photograph. Courtesy of the Library of Congress.

The RFC had been established in 1932 by President Herbert Hoover as a temporary government financing device that could soon repair the nation's faltering bank credit system. FDR envisioned a much greater role for the agency. He named Jesse Jones, a powerful Southern Democrat, to head the RFC. Jones, a real estate and banking entrepreneur from Houston, was sometimes described as the second most powerful man in the country. FDR called him "Jesus Jones."

Jesse Jones offered to refund the $106 million in maturing GN bonds. A syndicate led by New York banks countered, but Jones responded with a better offer, which the Great Northern accepted. Arthur Curtiss James, a wealthy railroad investor who was the Great Northern's largest shareholder, called the 1936 refunding "the finest piece of work I have ever seen of a similar nature." The *Wall Street Journal* concluded that "probably none of the country's leading steam carriers experienced a more dramatic change in fortunes over the past year than the Great Northern Railway." In the end, the railroad's historians concluded that Kenney's refunding of the railroad's debt and reduction in interest charges were his finest achievements.

Banking expert Herbert Spero analyzed the RFC's railroad financing activity. He found that the amount the agency authorized for the Great Northern in 1936 was so large that it moved the St. Paul-based railroad to the top of the list of all 75 of the railroads winning approval for financing by the RFC from its inception in 1932 through June 30, 1937. In 1932, the RFC approved $362 million in loans to railroads; by 1939, it had authorized another $1.4 billion for them. Critics saw the RFC's help for railroads as bailouts for an industry that didn't do enough to maintain its infrastructure. Supporters said it helped a critical industry get past the hard times of the 1930s and eventually, to play a vital role in World War II by shipping military equipment and troops across the country and to ports on both the East and West Coasts. They noted that this time, unlike during World War I, the federal government didn't take over the railroads.[15]

BREAKING THROUGH THE CLOUDS

Like the country, St. Paul's Great Northern soldiered on during the 1930s, under the leadership of William Kenney. A traffic and marketing specialist. Kenney assigned financial expert Vernon P. Turnburke

This photo from about 1931 is of Ralph Budd (1879–1962), left, who was then the president of the Great Northern Railway, with Arthur Curtiss James (1867–1941), a wealthy businessman who was at one time said to be the largest owner of railroad stock in America. Photo courtesy of the Minnesota Historical Society.

to help him steer the company through the Depression. Kenney was the Great Northern's president from January 1, 1932, until his death on January 24, 1939. Under him, the deficits shrank, from a record $13.4 million in 1932 to $3.2 million in 1933 and $1.4 million in 1934. In 1935, the railroad went back into the black with a $7.1 million profit. It would remain solidly profitable year after year, until it merged with the Burlington Northern and the Chicago Burlington & Quincy railroads in 1970 to create the Burlington Northern.[16]

St. Paul, too, worked its way through the Depression. Some of Albert Lindeke's counterpunches against *Fortune* hit home. While construction had screeched to a halt in most of the country, a building boom continued well into the 1930s in St. Paul. "More building construction took place in the 13 years beginning about 1923 than during any comparable period, before and since," developer Jim Stolpestad wrote for the Historical Society's magazine in 2014. Three early-1930s projects reshaped the city's skyline: the First National Bank's 32-story skyscraper, opened in 1931 and topped by a huge, fire-engine red "1st" sign visible from many parts of the city; the St. Paul City Hall and Ramsey County Courthouse, considered a masterpiece of art deco architecture, in 1932; and the U.S. Post Office and Custom House in 1934.[17]

Some of the city's most significant employers got through the 1930s without cutting jobs. The Seeger Refrigerator Company, strengthened by a popular new model of its Coldspot Refrigerator, expanded twice and went to three shifts operating around the clock. 3M, lifted by Scotch Tape and other new products, averted layoffs by cutting the work weeks of its hourly employees from 50 hours to four-day, 32-hour weeks in the worst months. Two other large employers, West Publishing, which

The *Spring-Summer 1935 Sears Catalog* carried this advertisement for the Coldspot Super Six Refrigerator, which was manufactured for Sears by the Seeger Refrigerator Company on Arcade Street in St. Paul. Shoppers could purchase the Coldspot 6, which had an interior storage space of 6.20 cubic feet, with $5.00 down and an $8.00 per month payment. The total cost of the refrigerator was $134.50.

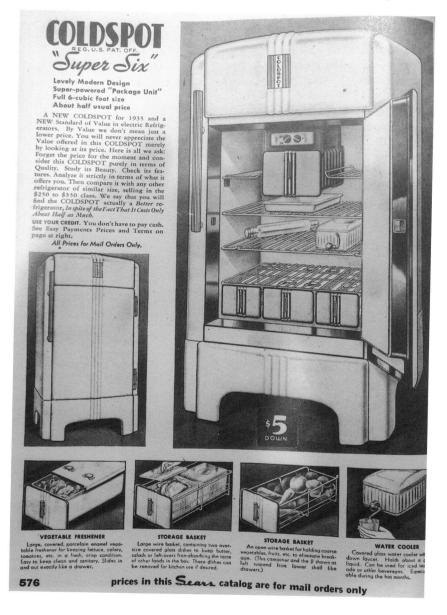

produced lawbooks, and crane manufacturer American Hoist and Derrick, also averted job cuts by trimming their workers' hours. (Across the river, Minneapolis Honeywell Regulator made a list of the nation's 10 best-performing stocks of the 1930s.)[18]

The construction boom collapsed in the mid-1930s. Yet the new landmarks that were its legacy and a feeling of pride about the city by many of its residents reinforced their belief that St. Paul was different—a place with an identity distinct from that of Minneapolis. So distinct that Minneapolis was viewed almost as a foreign country by many St. Paul residents. Bonnie Mairs, one of George Mairs III's cousins, remembers that time. One day, she and her grade-school classmates hopped on the train to Minneapolis for a birthday party at a downtown restaurant. "That was the first time I'd been there," she said. "Who in St. Paul ever went to Minneapolis?"[19]

And some new entrepreneurs looking to a better day, such as George Mairs Jr., helped to shield their families and the city from the hard times of the 1930s. As Teedie Frankenbach, one of his six children, would note many years later about her youth: "We never knew there was a Depression."[20]

CHAPTER 3

The Birth of Mairs & Power

George Mairs Jr. was a busy man with a mission, and the means to accomplish it, when in 1931 he founded the investment firm that would become Mairs & Power. The economy was in terrible shape. Prices of all manner of securities had crashed in 1929. Investors were spooked. Conventional thinkers felt the times were not right to start a new business; George took the opposite view.

His confidence was understandable. Since at least 1927, he had been buying and selling securities. He produced a 115-page thesis on the complexities of owning and trading stocks and bonds to cap his advanced studies at the University of Minnesota, which awarded him a graduate degree in economics in December 1930. His thesis advisor, economist Arthur W. Marget (1899–1962), a teacher and researcher at the University from 1927 to 1941, was on his way to wide recognition for his professional achievements. In 1938, Marget published the first of two volumes of his best-known work, *The Theory of Prices*. He went on to a successful career in government service, including being named to the Federal Reserve's Board of Governors in 1950.[1]

The 1930 *St. Paul City Directory* identified George as treasurer of the Gyro Club, a St. Paul social organization whose members held important jobs at businesses in the city but did not show an occupation for him. He may have been a full-time student at the University that year.[2] In 1930, he joined Macalester College's prestigious Board of Trustees, which included some of the city's foremost business leaders, when he was just 29 years old.[3]

George apparently had ample personal wealth to draw on, including shares of the assets his parents inherited from the estate of William J. Dyer, the founder of the W. J. Dyer & Bro. Music Store, and some of the resources amassed by his father-in-law, Angus McLeod,

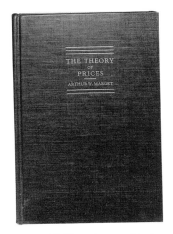

Arthur W. Marget assembled his ideas on monetary theory in his *Theory of Prices*. Volume 1 published in 1938; the second in 1942. Together they amount to more than 1,400 pages. Photo courtesy of the University of Minnesota.

who was a co-founder of the Emporium Department Store. McLeod passed on in 1924; Dyer died the following year. George also had brief experience working at a large company, Northern States Power. And as noted in the opening chapter of this history, he had ready access to the considerable business expertise available at both the Dyer and Emporium stores in downtown St. Paul. Given all of this, it seems highly likely that by the mid-1920s, he had begun to develop a sense that he was destined to go into business on his own.

In 1931, George opened his business, "George Mairs Jr., Investment Counsel," on the 10th floor of the Pioneer Building in downtown St. Paul. He had just one employee, a secretary. In an interview, Teedie Frankenbach, one of the six children in George's blended family, recalled visiting her father's office. Conspicuously absent, she said, was a stock ticker, the machine typically prominent in the offices of traders and stockbrokers. They and often their customers used the tickers to track rapidly fluctuating prices of securities. The timing of George's investing would be based more on fundamental analysis as opposed to the speculation facilitated by a ticker, which he must have seen as a pricey frill.[4]

A brief newspaper report described him as "one of the few investment counselors in the West." George explained that the investment counselor "furnishes information and advice on matters of investments much as a lawyer looks after a client's legal affairs. He studies the investment field, noting the conditions that are affecting investment and observing the probable tendencies." He apparently sensed something else in the air that could work to his advantage. It was becoming increasingly clear that the stock market might not recover quickly from the crash of 1929. Many people who still had money no longer felt comfortable leaving it in the hands of institutions such as the banks, trust companies, or Wall Street brokerage firms. Unlike many of them, George didn't need a lot of clients; instead, he sought to secure and keep the accounts of a small number of families of means in and around St. Paul. They would come to put more value on personal relationships with local advisors they knew and trusted. Independent advisors like George Mairs Jr.

Teedie would take the streetcar downtown, then meet her dad there to get a ride home. "It was a very small, modest office," she said. "He had the same secretary for years. It was just the two of them." Despite

"THE PRESENT TIME

is particularly propitious for having an investment list analyzed for advantageous switching of commitments to suit changed conditions."
—*Chicago Journal of Commerce, Feb. 3, 1932.*

GEORGE A. MAIRS Jr.

Investment Counsel

1024 PIONEER BUILDING

Analysis—Supervision   No Securities for Sale

his unexceptional office, the Pioneer Building was an address of distinction (it still is, redone as upscale housing). An architectural gem, it was built in 1889 as the home of the St. Paul *Pioneer Press*. The building featured a 16-story atrium, flanked by two open-cage elevators and a spiral staircase.[5]

Just half a block away stood the Railroad and Bank Building, built in 1916 by the Great Northern Railway founder James J. Hill. That structure, the largest office building in the Twin Cities until the IDS Tower opened in 1972 in Minneapolis, served as the headquarters for three of the city's most important business institutions during much of the twentieth century: the Great Northern, the Northern Pacific Railway and, until its new home opened a block away in 1931, the First National Bank of St. Paul.[6]

PIONEER PRESS, BUILDING
ST. PAUL, MINN.

Chicago architect Solon Beman designed the Pioneer Building at Fourth and Robert streets in downtown St. Paul (1889). When it opened, it was St. Paul's tallest building. Four additional stories were added in 1909. The office of George Mairs Jr. was on the 10th floor. Tinted postcard photo courtesy of the Minnesota Historical Society.

NEW GREAT NORTHERN BUILDING, ST. PAUL, MINN.

The Railroad and Bank Building, which was the headquarters for both the Great Northern and the Northern Pacific railroads along with the First National Bank, was designed by Chicago architect Charles Frost. It opened in 1916 at Fifth and Jackson Streets in downtown St. Paul. Tinted postcard photo courtesy of the Minnesota Historical Society.

While few financial records from George's early days of investing have survived, enough are available to sketch a reasonably accurate picture of that period. Monthly ledger entries from August 1927 through January 1929 chart his securities trading activity, most likely managing his own family accounts. These entries show that except for one month, he was largely swinging from buying stocks to selling them, starting in March 1928. That likely was a savvy move because many stocks were by then approaching their precrash highs.[7]

GRADUATE THESIS: DOOR INTO A CAREER

George designed his graduate thesis to help vault him into a career of picking securities. His comments about that time at the University clearly indicate that he worked closely with his advisor, economist Arthur Marget, as he proceeded. For the project, George analyzed the investment practices of the Continental Insurance Company of New York and St. Paul Fire and Marine Insurance Company (nearly 30 years later, the St. Paul insurer would become part of the Growth

Fund's first portfolio and ultimately, one of the Fund's most enduring holdings.) He sought to discern whether and how large investors were using investment theory to make decisions about buying and selling securities, how successful they were, and how private individuals made good investments. After perusing the investment results at 25 of the nation's largest fire insurers, he chose the St. Paul insurer and Continental because they were among the most ably managed; yet they had radically different investment policies.[8]

His principal conclusion was that over the previous 25 years, a portfolio containing both stocks and bonds generated more income than one made up mainly of bonds. His thesis was punctuated with provocative observations in tune with the tumultuous times. He noted the steep declines in many stocks since the crash—Montgomery Ward, down from $149 to $20; International Telephone down from $149 to $25; Cash Register, Simmons, Radio, and dozens of other pre-crash favorites selling at fractions of their former prices. "Even if one does intend on holding for 20 or 30 years, there is no sense in buying stocks at the crest of a cycle, when by waiting a year one can get the same stock for a third or less," he wrote.

He was critical of the St. Paul company for an overemphasis on municipal bonds, and of Continental for relying too much on preferred stocks. He hailed Continental for maintaining a complete statistical department to analyze securities. His journey took him deep into the ups and downs of the stock market in the 1920s, and the role of that decade's fast-changing technology in powering the rise of new companies and the decline of others. He noted the promise of new technologies just beginning to blossom, such as transoceanic telephone communications, television, and speedier air transportation.

"While average stock prices began the 'new era' deflation about 13 months ago, certain stocks have been in a liquidating movement as far back as 1916," he observed. "The radio and high-priced housing ruined the piano business." He cited an article showing that all but four of 20 high-grade industrial stocks in 1900 had seriously deteriorated by 1925. He warned that a good investment today may not be good tomorrow. Earlier deflation is conspicuous in sugar, shipping, fertilizer, and textiles shares, he wrote, and "it is quite probable that industrial supremacy in the next upward business phase will be along different lines than in the 1925–1929 bull market."

Arthur W. Marget (1899–1962) was born in Massachusetts, served in the army in World War I, and received his Ph.D. in economics from Harvard. He taught at the University of Minnesota for 15 years and was George Mairs's thesis advisor. Photo courtesy of the *Minneapolis Morning Tribune.*

Overall, Rob Mairs, now president of Mairs & Power, would conclude many years later that George's views as spelled out in his graduate thesis set forth the original framework for the contemporary firm's style of fundamental, intense securities analysis.[9]

FOCUSING ON BONDS

Today's leaders at Mairs & Power believe George Jr.'s financial successes in the 1930s stemmed largely from wise investments in bonds, particularly railroad bonds. Charles ("Todd") Driscoll, whose parents Fletcher and Abigail Driscoll retained George Jr. in the mid-1930s to manage a portfolio of their securities, preserved details about the portfolio along with their letters from and to George. This information shows how important advising clients on investments in bonds issued by public utilities, railroads, and municipalities was to his business. Fletcher Driscoll was in the real estate business in St. Paul; his wife inherited a share of the wealth left by Abigail Wheeler Thompson, who owned a 50 percent stake in St. Paul's *Pioneer Press* and *Dispatch* newspapers when she died in 1923. The Driscolls' records suggest that George's other early clients may have been St. Paul families with similar financial assets. Later in this chapter, we will describe the Driscolls' portfolio and how George managed it.

George's secretary, Margaret Long, was charged with keeping him current on any concerns of his clients when he was away. She wrote a letter to him—undated but likely in early July 1932—when George and his wife, Jean, were vacationing in Bermuda. Several of the clients mentioned in the letter were likely St. Paul residents. The letter noted the status of a handful of securities that George managed for his clients. One client was anxious to sell 300 shares of National Investors stock, which had been falling.[10]

National Investors had three affiliated trusts, each of which reported results separately. Each had differing amounts of the same 25 blue-chip stocks. On July 1, 1932, the *New York Times* cited a report from National Investors that each of the three trusts had reported sharp six-month declines in the value of their portfolios as of June 30 and disclosed that the combined trusts had moved out of stocks to the point where they were nearly 50 percent in cash. (On July 8, 1932, the

Dear Mr. Mairs:

I received your letter this morning and am glad to hear that you are having such a wonderful trip.

I haven't received the book, but will take care of it as soon as it comes. I'll keep the stamps, too. I had my check for the 15th already, but there isn't much left.

I will copy the Dow letter this afternoon and mail it as soon as I have finished it. There have been no important calls, but Larry has had trouble about Mrs. Routtell's National Investors. She is holding her 308 shares waiting instructions to sell from you. Larry just called and said he bought 15 Kennecott at $34\frac{1}{8}$ for her and a New York Central 4s, 1998 at 63 for Mrs. Holmes. The bid for Mrs. Sandison's B & O is about 3 points lower than the market, but Larry is keeping it in. Everything else is cleared up.

Enclosed you will find a check from Mr. Cincera for only $200. Your two bills on the Ruff estate are also enclosed, but come to $225. There is a pencil change evidently by Mr. Cincera. Sign and return if the check is all right, if not you better write him and explain.

This is the first page of Margaret Long's letter to George Mairs Jr. when he was on vacation in which she reports clients' concerns regarding stocks and bonds that he was handling for them. Although the letter is undated, internal evidence indicates it was likely to have been written in July 1932. Photo courtesy of Mairs & Power.

Dow Jones Industrial Average, which had reached its peak of 380 on September 3, 1929, hit a Depression-era low of 41.)

In 1934, George began teaching finance courses at Macalester. He taught two courses—principles of investment and business finance—alternating them from one semester to another. In a February 1934 interview with the college's *Mac Weekly* newspaper, he explained: "If we could get no more across than to show a student that no matter how good a security may be, it must be watched, we would accomplish something exceedingly practical." He went on to say that he would teach students how to choose investments wisely, how to monitor them, and how to set up investment programs customized for the needs of specific individuals. The thing that has caused more losses than anything else during the last setback is dependence upon prejudiced advice. We try to show people how they can tell investment from speculation."[11]

"THESE PEOPLE ALL KNEW EACH OTHER"

Railroad bonds were far from the only securities assembled by George Mairs Jr. in his early portfolios. Among the other securities mentioned by Margaret Long in her letter to him in Bermuda: Chicago's Stevens Hotel (a stock that soon imploded) and Kennecott Copper. There had to be many other stocks as the 1930s progressed. But given the deep reservoir of knowledge about railroad finance at Great Northern's headquarters, less than a five-minute walk from George Mairs's office, it's virtually certain that he was well aware of its financing practices and knew its financial decisionmakers.

That bonds, particularly railroad bonds, would become an important part of George Jr.'s business is no surprise. Bondholders ranked ahead of shareholders in bankruptcy reorganizations, which were a particular concern during the Depression; bonds are the investment of choice for many securities investors in deflationary times. Thus many investors preferred the security of bonds to the risk of stocks in the 1930s (and today).

According to the *SBBI Yearbook*, which assembles comparative data on the performance of securities based on the work of Ibbotson Associates founder Roger Ibbotson, long-term corporate bonds returned 6.9 percent annually in the 1930s vs. -0.1 percent for large-cap stocks. In contrast, during all other decades since the 1920s other than 2000–2010, large-cap stocks outperformed corporate bonds. Many railroad debt issues ended up performing relatively well in the 1930s. And as noted in the preceding chapter, some railroads including the Great Northern were buoyed by the financial assistance offered by the Reconstruction Finance Corporation, which was committed to strengthening the railroads during the Depression.[12]

Bob Garland, now retired, joined the Great Northern in 1959 and rose to become vice president and controller of the Burlington Northern in 1976. He cited another factor that helped George Mairs Jr. "These people all knew each other," Garland said. "St. Paul isn't and wasn't such an awfully big place. The potential investors and their investment advisors and the railroad, insurance, banking, manufacturing, wholesale and retail owners, and executives all lived in the same neighborhoods, belonged to the same churches and clubs, and served as directors of the same organizations." Garland, an amateur historian who wrote a history of the St. Paul Rotary Club, offered an example. In the mid-1940s, when George Mairs Jr., was an active member of the club, George Hess Jr., then the Great Northern's comptroller, was the club's president.[13]

Up From Tragedy: The Rise of the Blended Family

This is the story of how profound mourning over two tragic deaths gave way to joyful triumphs of the blended family led by its surviving spouses: George Mairs Jr. and Louise Power. George's wife and Louise's husband were struck down in the prime of their lives. Jean McLeod Mairs died in November 1936 at age 33, of pneumonia. Her widowed husband was left to care for four children under 10 years old. Robert Ellsworth Power died in September 1928, from a ruptured appendix. He was 36. At the time, the couple had a 15-months-old son and Louise was carrying their second child.

But by May 7, 1938, the grief had turned to happiness. Louise and George were married. She brought her two children to the marriage; he bought his four. They would flourish, initially at the family's stately residence on Summit Avenue in St. Paul, helped by the strength of the

Depression-resistant business that George Mairs Jr. founded. All the children would go on to establish their own families and lead successful lives. One of them,

A portrait of the blended family of Louise Power Mairs and George Mairs Jr. in 1936. Seated from left to right are Nancy, Bobby, Jean, Angus, Teedie, and George III. Photo courtesy of the Mairs family.

George III, would carry forward his father's business. "Our minister once said that mom and dad put together our families so you couldn't see the seam," said Teedie Frankenbach, the last survivor among the six children. "They merged," added Dusty Mairs, who later married George III. "They were lucky people to find one another."[14]

Robert Power: A Promising Life, Cut Short

A death in the early stages of a marriage can decimate the dreams of the surviving spouse for years. Robert Ellsworth Power and Louise Ritchie were married in a widely noted ceremony at the House of Hope Presbyterian Church in St. Paul on January 2, 1926. Robert was well on his way to a successful career in banking. He and Louise were about to raise a family with broad support from a strong network of family and friends.[15]

Robert was the third of four sons of George Center Power (1858–1912), a leading St. Paul banker. His nephew (also named George Center Power Jr., 1914–1995) would eventually become "the Power" of Mairs & Power. Robert attended St. Paul Academy and Williams College in western Massachusetts. An obituary in the *Brooklyn Eagle* reported that he had worked for three Twin Cities financial institutions—the Stockyards National Bank, the Bank of St. Paul, and the Minneapolis Morris Plan (Morris Plan banks were established in 1910 to make loans to lower and middle-income borrowers). During World War I,

Robert Ellsworth Power (1891–1928) died unexpectedly in New York City. Photo courtesy of the Power family.

Power served as a lieutenant in the Coast Artillery. He went overseas with an army artillery unit in October 1918. Four months later, he was discharged. In August 1921, he joined the office of the U.S. Comptroller of the Currency as a bank examiner. The 1920s were a time of great stress for many rural banks in the Upper Midwest. *St. Paul City Directory* for 1925–1927 shows him living at 62 South Dale Street, a short walk from the Ritchie residence where Louise was raised.[16] According to newspaper clippings, Louise and Robert resided there, after they were married.[17]

In all likelihood, Robert Power's superiors in the comptroller's office sent him to St. Paul in or about 1925 to monitor the then-precarious conditions of the many country banks in nearby agricultural regions hit hard by economic troubles. He would return to the private sector soon, to take up a bright, new opportunity. The *Brooklyn Eagle* story said he left his bank examiner job in November of 1927 and was named manager of the Flushing branch of the National City Bank in Queens, N.Y., when that office opened seven months later (National City eventually became part of Citicorp, today the nation's third largest bank). The couple's first child, Robert (Bobby), was born on June 9, 1927. Soon after Robert died, Louise and her son returned from New York City to St. Paul to live with her parents. Her second child, also named Louise (Teedie), was born on January 12, 1929.

Louise Power: Worldly Writer

Louise, born in 1903, was the youngest of the four children of Harry and Elizabeth Ritchie. The family lived at 46 Crocus Place in Crocus Hill, which was, like Summit Avenue, home to many of St Paul's most prominent families. Harry Ritchie, a physician with an office in downtown St. Paul, was one of the country's leading plastic surgeons. Louise became a talented writer with a worldly perspective. In 1922–1923, she kept a detailed diary of the six-month overseas trip she and Alice Lee, her roommate from Vassar College, had taken. Alice was the daughter of noted public relations pioneer Ivy Lee. Her father tapped into his contacts with the Rockefeller family to arrange guided tours and meetings with influential personalities throughout Asia for Alice and Louise. Louise's family preserved her diary of that trip in a 40,000-word manuscript. Thirteen years later, Louise would put that experience to good use, producing another lengthy journal. Many years later, Louise joined a prayer group that met weekly. She wrote spiritual poetry. After she died in 1981, her family published a collection of her poems.[18]

The wedding of Louise and Robert drew much attention from the elite of St. Paul society. Among the attendants were Alice Lee; Caroline Clark, daughter of West Publishing CEO and president Homer P. Clark; and Margaret Weyerhaeuser, daughter of Frederick Weyerhaeuser, the lumber baron and close associate of James J. Hill.[19]

The Jolt: News of the Death of Jean Mairs

Louise Power's daughter Teedie, seven years old at the time, still remembers the phone call her mother received on November 8, 1936. It was a Sunday, five days after Franklin Delano Roosevelt won his second term as president. The caller told Louise that Jean McLeod had passed on. Louise and Jean had forged a deep friendship, possibly after first meeting at their families' church, House of Hope. The report of Jean's death at such an early age shocked and saddened her family and friends.[20]

Jean McLeod, born in 1903, was the last-born child of Angus and Jean McLeod, who had two other daughters and a son. She went to St. Paul Central High School and began dating George Jr. while she was still in high school. George, who was two grades ahead of Jean, graduated from the all-boys high school on Summit Avenue that was then part of St. Thomas College (decades later, the college became the University of St. Thomas; the high school is now

St. Thomas Academy, still an all-boys school but no longer part of the university).[21]

Jean and George both went to colleges in Pennsylvania, Jean to Wilson College, an all-women's school in Chambersburg, and George to Lafayette College, a "Little Ivy" school in Easton that at the time was the largest Presbyterian men's college in the country. Jean and George corresponded frequently, and it is likely that they visited one another often; Wilson College was just 150 miles west of the Lafayette campus. According to a Wilson College Yearbook, Jean was the class treasurer in her first year there, in the choral club, and a member of Omega Theta, which was a literary society that met monthly. Its members studied poetry, drama, novels, and short stories. She was also a member of the Dramatic Club and the Biology Club, and was on the board of Pharetra, a literary journal that published short stories, poems, and other writing done by students.[22]

After graduating from Lafayette in 1923, George returned to St. Paul to live with his parents. Angus McLeod, Jean's father and a co-founder of the Emporium Department Store, died in February 1924. Jean inherited at least $7,000 from her father after he died, shortly before she and George were married.[23] On December 29, 1925, just four days before Robert Power and Louise Ritchie were married at the House of Hope Church, George Mairs and Jean were married at this same church. Their marriage, like that of Robert and Louise, was a much-celebrated event. Mrs. C. Marshall

JEAN McLEOD
St. Paul, Minn.

Freshman Chorus; Choral Club (2); Class Treasurer (1); Omega Theta (1); Phi Chi Psi (2, 3), Secretary (3); Dramatic Club (2, 3); "Pharetra" Board (2); Biology Club (3).

Of a' the airts the wind can blaw,
She dearly loves the West,
For there this bonnie lassie lives—
Our lassie frae the West.

Oh, blaw, ye westlin' winds, blaw soft
Among the leafy green.
Wi' balmy gale, frae hill and dale,
Bring hame the thoughts o' Jean.

Jean McLeod in the 1925 annual published by Wilson College. Photo courtesy of Wilson College.

Muir, wife of the newly appointed pastor at the House of Hope, co-hosted a tea in Jean's honor. Sometime after they were married, Jean planned to sail to Scotland to attend a Sunday School conference, according to a news clipping preserved by Wilson College. The clipping is not dated, but it seems

Louise Ritchie Power in an undated photo holding her young son, Bobby, at a relative's summer home on the Rhode Island coastline.

likely that this was in 1926—before Jean and George Jr.'s first child was born.[24]

At first, Jean and George lived in a modest, newly built home at 2145 Fairmount Avenue in St. Paul. Their first child, Nancy, was born on January 29, 1927. By 1928, they had moved to much larger quarters at 1504 Summit Avenue. George III was born on June 15, 1928; Jean, on September 18, 1930; and Angus, on September 12, 1933.

The Five Minnesota Moms

A good way to understand the social world in which the Ritchie, Mairs, and Power families and their peers moved is to follow the journey that Louise, Jean, and three other St. Paul mothers took early in 1936. That is possible because, much as she had chronicled her globe-girdling trip with Alice Lee, Louise wrote a 31-page journal of the five mothers' trek to Taos and Santa Fe. In 2005, her story became the basis for a reenactment of the journey that was staged at the New Century Club in St. Paul.[25]

The five St. Paul mothers had just come through a seriously nerve-rattling Minnesota winter. The temperature fell below zero for a record-breaking 36 straight days. As Louise wrote, the brutal weather, the restless voices of the five mothers' combined crew of 18 children, and the nagging cares of their households gave birth to a radical adventure: their road trip to New Mexico to get away from it all.

Comfortable economic circumstances had cushioned them from the hard times of the Depression. Still, the five mothers shared one trait with the less fortunate. They watched their pennies. Each of them had a tight budget, just $64, for three weeks of gas and oil, food, hotels, and incidentals.

As Louise told it, the New Mexico trip came out of a meeting the five mothers convened at the home of Anne Stringer, wife of attorney Philip Stringer. In addition to Louise, Jean, and Anne, the group included Peggy Jackson, whose husband, Archibald, would later become president of St. Paul Fire & Marine, and Polly Bancroft, whose husband was an executive at the company. (Years later, St. Paul Fire & Marine's stock became one of the original holdings, and among the most enduring, in the Mairs & Power Growth Fund.)

Back and forth they went, weighing the pros and cons of a getaway. "Honestly, girls, we are crazy," Polly Bancroft declared. "Rich would have a fit if he even suspected we were vaguely thinking about it. But I don't care. Let's plan it anyway." Jean wasn't so sure. "I believe George would love to have me go on a trip if I really wanted to go. But I couldn't bear to leave the children. Angus is so little [two years old]." Then Peggy Jackson threw caution to the wind. "Now girls, this is ridiculous," she declared. "When I was a little girl, mother told me that if I wanted a worthwhile thing bad enough, I can always get it. It will do our husbands and children good to get along without us."

And so, driven by the spirit of adventure that would consume Polly's granddaughter, explorer Ann Bancroft two generations later, the five mothers crafted a plan to drive to Santa Fe. Anne Stringer's sister lived there. The latter part of

One of the St. Paul newspapers published this photo in early 1936 with the following information: "On a pleasure jaunt to Santa Fe, N.M., by motor are these five young mothers, left to right, Mmes. Archibald Jackson, George Mairs Jr., Richard Bancroft, Philip Stringer, and Robert Power. They plan to spend a few days in Des Moines en route." Photo courtesy of the Mairs family.

their route followed the Santa Fe Trail. After arranging to leave their children in the care of their husbands, relatives, friends, and hired help, they crammed themselves and their luggage into Louise's second-hand 1935 Ford and hit the road. Louise captured the moments. "For the five Minnesota mothers, at last, at last, in a Ford, knew only this. They were off," she wrote. "Around the corner, down the hill, over the High Bridge, past the golf course. Faster, faster. Even the little Ford, so shining black, so sleekly running after its thorough overhauling, seemed as excited as they, and the laughing and chattering mounted with the miles that flew beneath the car."

Late that afternoon, at Des Moines, Jean took her turn driving. "Poor Jean, she had the worst of that day's ride because she took the wheel as dark came on and the road that had been straight dipped up and down and the trucks of Iowa corn that had been a constant source of amusement by day became decidedly otherwise at night. We swept around the corner in a small town not realizing that we had taken the wrong turn until the car lights fell on a sign: 'Dead end.' Thundering behind us came a huge truck which had apparently followed our taillight off the highway. Like a small terrier annoying a bulldog, we turned with a gleeful yap and made for the highway while the truck, with screeching gears, turned clumsily about." At 9 p.m., after covering 450 miles, they checked into the historic Roubidoux

Hotel in St. Joseph, Missouri, and took up their assigned duties for the trip. Louise would tend to the car. Jean would pay the bills. Polly would get the lodging. Anne would handle the tips. Peggy would buy the postcards and send the telegrams back home.

In Kansas, they encountered dust storms. "The colors were changing," Louise wrote, "and not even the blood red sun setting squarely at the end of the highway could soften the murky gray of a country over which sand had shifted for months and months on end." Later, as they approached Trinidad, in Colorado just north of the Raton Pass, the mood shifted. They turned on the car radio. "Miraculously, wave on wave of a Tchaikovsky Overture poured forth, matching note for note each new mountain that rose majestically before our enchanted eyes." Soon they were in Taos, where they met up with Anne's sister. Jean, taking in the sights of centuries-old Native American settlements and the mountains beyond, remarked: "Maybe this country doesn't really belong to the white man at all. I have never felt more like such an intruder." The mothers returned to St. Paul under budget.

Nearly 70 years later, in a reenactment of the trip, the New Century Club noted the premature deaths of Jean and Robert Power. The epilogue closed with a joyful ending—the marriage of the two surviving spouses, George Jr. and Louise, and the coming together of the six Mairs and Power children into a single family.

George Mairs Jr.: Quiet, Deep Community Engagement

George A. Mairs Jr. was born May 28, 1901, in St. Paul, the first of two sons of George A. and Leontine Mairs. As he continued his romance with Jean, he graduated from Lafayette College with a major in finance and a minor in accounting. Not surprisingly, given his father's career at the W. J. Dyer & Bro. Music Store, he was in the glee club and the band. He was also in the school's literary society, and on the cross-country squad. George wrote for the *Lyre*, Lafayette College's literary and humor magazine. His senior page said this of him: "When people go west, the only city worth seeing is St. Paul. The largest city for its size is St. Paul." Then, in an apparent reference to Jean, his page went on to note that "the prettiest girl comes from St. Paul."[26]

"And so," the page continued "day in and day out, our George rambles on. Out of the West came he, to mingle with us, poor worms. . . . and to say that our class and the college as a whole has profited from his pilgrimage, is to say the least. Clever and witty, he has attained much renown for his work on the *Lyre*. But this has been only one of his talents. He is also musically inclined, and his presence in our famous band was keenly felt and much of the success of the instrumental clubs in the past two seasons has been due to his efforts."

After graduating from college, George returned to St. Paul to work as an engineer at St. Paul Gas & Light. It was a time of rapid technological change, with larger electric utilities snapping up gas and light companies. Northern States Power absorbed St. Paul Gas & Light. George became a salesman, and later an engineer, at NSP.[27]

Family members and friends have described George Jr. as frugal yet generous, reserved, focused, and ambitious. He became deeply engaged with religious and civic organizations, and at Macalester College. Angus McLeod had been the chair of the Macalester Board of Trustees from 1918 to 1921. George Jr., who had joined the board in 1930, was an active trustee there for 45 years, and then an emeritus trustee until his death in 1983. He was the treasurer at both the House of Hope, where he taught Sunday School for more than 30 years, and at the Ramsey County Sunday School Association. He served on the boards of the Union Gospel Mission and the St. Paul Council of Churches and led a Boy Scout troop at House of Hope.

George was a member of the St. Paul Charter Commission, the American and Minnesota Statistical Societies, the International Professional Men's Institute, and the Civil War Round Table. He visited Civil War battlefields, filled his home with books about Abraham Lincoln, and ultimately donated his collection of books about the war to Macalester. The school gave him an honorary degree, noting that he established "the first investment counsel firm in the Upper Midwest" in 1931. George Jr. was an incurable auto aficionado, a music lover, and an avid golfer. Once he got a mention in the newspaper for sinking a hole-in-one

George Mairs Jr. served on the Board of Trustees of Macalester College for 53 years beginning in 1930. In May 1977 Macalester awarded him an honorary degree. Photo courtesy of the Mairs family.

on what was then the 157-yard fifth hole at the Somerset Country Club.[28]

The Blended Family Comes of Age

An offbeat document memorialized the creation of the enlarged household on Summit Avenue. It took the form of a succinct, atypical invoice sent to George by his attorney and close friend, Philip Stringer, when he and Louise were married. "1/2 dozen children at $12.00 per dozen . . . $6.00," it read. Stringer had billed George for legal work to handle the adoptions of the six children, each one for a dollar. George and Louise had arranged complementary adoptions. He adopted her two children; she adopted his four. Thus the blended Mairs family was born, an alliance that would foretell the business marriage that later rebranded the investment counseling business of George Mairs Jr. as Mairs & Power.[29]

Soon after George and Louise were married, they moved the family to

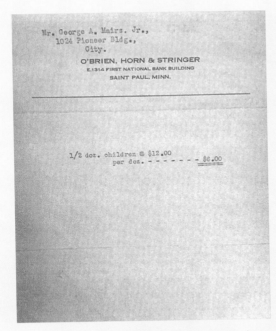

Mr. George A. Mairs. Jr.,
1024 Pioneer Bldg.,
City.

O'BRIEN, HORN & STRINGER
E.1314 FIRST NATIONAL BANK BUILDING
SAINT PAUL, MINN.

1/2 doz. children @ $12.00
per doz. - - - - - - - $6.00

In 1938 attorney Philip Stringer, a close friend of
George Mairs Jr., arranged for George to adopt the
six children that made up George's and Louise's
blended family. This is the invoice that Stringer sent
Mairs for his services in the adoption process. Photo
courtesy of the Mairs family.

temporary quarters in the Ritchies' home
so workers could add new bedrooms to accommodate the larger family at their home
on Summit Avenue. George and Bobby set
up a model train layout in their bedroom
on the new third floor. Later, students from
the Macalester campus, just two blocks
away, became occasional boarders. In 1944,
after George Jr.'s father died, his mother,
Leontine, moved in with him and Louise.[30]

The children spent their summers at
the family cabin in Wisconsin, on Bass
Lake 30 miles east of St. Paul. The Mairs
and Stringer families had built modest

cabins there in the mid-1930s, on adjoining
property. The family outgrew the cabin,
so George Jr. himself took on the task of
building a one-room house for George and
Bobby. "We kids dug the hole for the foundation," Teedie recalled. Her father also
tended to a large "victory garden" there,
one of millions of vegetable and fruit gar-
dens planted across the country to increase
the food supply and boost morale during
World War II.[31]

George Jr. sold the cabin at Bass Lake
in the 1950s. "We had really outgrown it,"
Teedie said. "No phone. No social life. No
actual town." At that time, George and
Louise focused their cabin activities at the
Ritchie cabin, built by Louise's parents in
1925 in the Encampment Forest, a heavily
wooded development that hugs Minnesota's North Shore at the point where the
Encampment River tumbles into Lake
Superior. The development, near Two
Harbors, got its start after Twin Cities
interests purchased a 1,575-acre tract
there in 1921. Today, it includes about 50
cabins. The Ritchie family was one the
first to build there. The families of many
of Minnesota's leading businesses have
followed suit over the years. Eventually,
that included the Budd family, which
produced two CEOs (Ralph Budd and his
son, John Budd) who led the Great Northern Railroad for more than three decades.
Typically, the families lived their lives
without pretentiousness or show. On the
other hand, census reports show that they
often had live-in servants.[32]

Members of the Mairs, Power, Driscoll, and other families are present in this group portrait that was probably taken in the early 1940s. The setting is Hazel's Den Farm, then owned by Hazel and Charlie Power, near Center City, Minn. The man on the far left is Fletcher Driscoll Sr. and his wife, Abigail, is the third person from the right. Known to George Mairs Jr. as "Dotch" and "Abbie," they were among Mairs's early clients. George Mairs Jr. is the sixteenth person from the left and right next to him is his wife, Louise Power Mairs, and to her immediate left is George Mairs III. Missing from the gathering is George C. Power Jr. At the time this photo was taken, he was likely in military service. Charlie Power had acquired this 215-acre farm in 1925 and named it after his wife. In 1948 they sold the farm to a foundation headed by Richard C. Lilly, which then sold it to a charitable hospital that operated the farm as a sanatorium for alcoholics. Today that hospital is known as the Hazelden Betty Ford Foundation. Photo courtesy of the Power family.

The financial achievements of the firm founded by George Mairs Jr. funded the educations of the children in the blended family, and those of many of their relatives, and launched them on fruitful lives. Starting in 1945, the six children of the blended family left for college at eastern schools: Nancy, Jean, and Teedie for Mount Holyoke, where they graduated. George and Bobby went to Yale; Angus to Amherst. The three girls went on to raise families in eastern states.

Nancy had a long career as a grade-school teacher and in community service in Baltimore. Jean became an ordained Presbyterian minister in Pittsburgh. Teedie raised four children; her husband, Charlie Frankenbach, ran a successful insurance agency, which represented St. Paul Fire & Marine, in Westfield, N. J. The three boys settled in the Twin Cities. Bobby transferred from Yale to the University of Minnesota, where he graduated. George III switched from Yale, too, to graduate from Macalester. Angus graduated from Amherst. Bob had a 40-year career as an executive at St. Paul Fire & Marine (now part of the Travelers Companies); today his son, Rob Mairs, is the president of Mairs & Power. Angus was a stockbroker for 40 years. George III would go on to a 57-year career at Mairs & Power, including heading the firm for the better part of a generation after his father eased into retirement. The six children had 19 more children. The 19 had 32 more.[33]

Rejecting the Trappings of Wealth

George Jr. set the template for his descendants' lifestyles. He had no interest in conspicuous displays of wealth. "Over much of his career, my father's compensation probably did not much exceed that of a senior vice president" at the First National Bank in St. Paul, George III would say nearly a generation after his father's death. Instead, he established a pattern of giving, donating to Macalester, House of Hope, the Boy Scouts, and other institutions. His philanthropy was very private, as was typical in his era. Much later, Mairs & Power would boost considerably its giving as the firm generated more wealth.[34]

In 1967, George Mairs Jr. drew attention—presumably unwelcome—from legendary *St. Paul Dispatch* columnist Gareth Hiebert. For 32 years, Hiebert covered St. Paul like a blanket, documenting the foibles and follies of the city's residents under the pen name of Oliver Towne—meaning "All Over Town." Under the headline "Curious George," Hiebert offered a glimpse into George Jr.'s obsession with cars and, perhaps more notably, his character. His column described how George—determined to get a sneak preview of new car models before they were unveiled to the public—had discovered one of the obscure areas around the city where these models were secretly stashed away before delivery.[35]

At dusk one evening, George drove his car through an open gate into a fenced-in area, and spent an hour checking out details on half-a-dozen 1968 models. Then, as he sought to drive out his car out of the lot, Hiebert reported that he discovered to his horror that the gate had been "shut and padlocked, marooning him and his car inside." The only way out? "I figured it unwise to call the police and explain the situation," he said, recounting his actions. "I decided to come back at dawn and try to drive my car out after the gate was opened—without being seen." As the sun rose and he approached the lot, he recognized the night watchman sitting in his car outside the lot. "George, with pride in hand, confessed what happened. The guard opened the gate and let him get his car and drive away without any questions." Oliver Towne concluded: "His honest face paid off."

"They were not flashy people," Teedie Frankenbach said of the blended family. George Jr. died in 1983, two years after Louise passed on. Shortly before his death, his son, George III, would write this of the firm his father founded: "Our satisfaction was derived from moderate compensation, plus the recognition that we alone controlled our destiny. The trappings of wealth had little allure for us."[36]

A LOOK AT ONE CLIENT'S PORTFOLIO

George and Fletcher Driscoll had known one another since at least the 1920s, when both men were active in Gyro, the St. Paul social club. After the trust that held the Driscoll securities expired in mid-1930s, they shifted the management of their inherited securities to George (later, George Power would handle their accounts for many years). Family records show that Mairs-Shaughnessy & Company, which traded stocks and bonds for clients, executed many of the trades of the Driscolls' securities that George Jr. recommended. James L. Mairs, a principal at Mairs-Shaughnessy who died in 1940, was George Jr.'s brother.

The Driscoll family's records show that their portfolio at George's firm was almost totally invested in bonds rather than stocks in 1938 and that railroad bonds were a significant part of the holdings. Detailed letters that George sent to the Driscolls show that he was closely monitoring the securities in the portfolio. The family's records show two inventories of valuations for each of the securities in the portfolio, the first on November 15, 1938, and the second on February 15, 1939. The total value of the securities in the portfolio on the first date was $100,595. The first accounting lists 71 securities—66 bonds valued at $94,725 and 5 stocks valued at $5,870.[37]

The second inventory shows 76 securities—71 bonds valued at $92,690 and 5 stocks valued at $5,056. Municipal bonds accounted for the largest share of the portfolio's value on both dates. Generally, investors saw them as attractive because of the vast Depression-era spending on public works projects. But their share of the portfolio's value fell to 43.8 percent on February 15 from 49.1 percent on November 15. The value of railroad bonds increased to 22.5 percent from 19.8 percent. Public utility bonds rose to 26.8 percent from 23.6 percent.

The earlier inventory listed the bonds of 18 railroads and train depots; the latter one had 17. Both lists included bonds of the Great Northern and Northern Pacific, and other large railroads such as the Baltimore & Ohio, the Milwaukee Road, and the Union Pacific. The November 15 inventory valued the stake in the Great Northern—a single bond—at $987.50. The February 15 accounting listed three Great Northern bonds, valued at $3,183—the highest amount for any of the 71 securities in the portfolio then. The value of the securities in the portfolio fell to $97,746 from $100,595, but this value would have dropped to $95,551 but for the purchase of two additional Great Northern bonds. At George's recommendation, the portfolio had gone to three of the St. Paul-based railroad's bonds from one.

ACQUIRING GREY HAIR

Still, George's December 1, 1938, letter to the Driscolls led off with a cautionary note. He wrote that uncertain business conditions led to a constantly changing market for Great Northern's bonds. Hence, he could not recommend that be they be viewed as "a permanent investment." Instead, he observed, "we will acquire grey hair and different securities from time to time." Put another way, the move to buy more Great Northern bonds carried a certain amount of risk, probably as did another key shift over the three months: a move out of New York Central bonds. The two inventories showed that the portfolio sold out its position in the New York Central's bonds, decreasing the value of the railroad portion of the inventory by roughly the same amount as the larger Great Northern stake increased it. George was rebalancing the Driscolls' portfolio to raise the likelihood of a better long-term return on their investment.

The Driscoll family's records also showed that by August 15, 1940, the overall makeup of the portfolio had shifted somewhat, from bonds to stocks. At that point, stocks had grown to about 20 percent of the overall valuation, almost four times their share at the end of 1938 (the rest was in bonds both times). On January 27, 1939, George wrote a letter to the Driscolls suggesting they consider buying stocks. Prices of attractive stocks were falling then, creating opportunities to buy them at bargain prices. He offered to draw up a list of promising stocks. The Driscolls promptly wrote back, taking up his offer. Meanwhile, George was becoming more concerned that the shaky condition of some municipalities could impair their capacity to pay their debtors.

Municipal bonds were easily the most heavily weighted sector in the Driscolls' portfolio in the late 1930s. As is the case today, interest received from municipals was exempt from both federal and Minnesota income taxes, but as the decade ended, their share was plunging. In just six months, from November 15 of 1938 to May 15 of 1939, it fell to 31 percent of the portfolio from 49 percent.

George may have been advising the Driscolls on matters other than just securities. On January 25, 1940, he gave them advice on how to handle their income taxes. The salutations of his letters illustrate his close, longtime friendship with the Driscolls. He sometimes addressed Fletcher and Abigail by the names their closest friends called them: "Dotch and Abbie." The Driscolls often wintered for a month or more in Florida during the 1920s and '30s. In the winter of 1938–1939, they had invited George and Louise to visit them in Daytona Beach, but George apparently was too busy with business and family matters. "In another year or so, Louise and I might break away for a short trip South, but it isn't in the picture this year and probably won't be next year," he wrote to the Driscolls on December 22, 1938.

A month later, he wrote that a measles epidemic had temporarily sidelined five of the six Mairs children, but that their cases were mild. "The kids are looking forward to the [St. Paul Winter] Carnival parade tomorrow afternoon and I am sorry that you can't watch it with us," he wrote, "but I guess that is the only compensation I can think of for remaining in this part of the country for this season of the year." In summary, George's communications with the Driscolls illustrate his knowledge of the securities markets, his attention to detail, and his commitment to stay in close contact with them. They also suggest that despite his small office, a bare-bones operation, they trusted him to manage their investments.

SIZE OF BUSINESS BY 1943

The federal government didn't require investment advisors to file annual reports with the U.S. Securities & Exchange Commission until passage of the Investment Advisors Act of 1940 and the State of Minnesota didn't license investment advisors until 1941. The firm may have been exempt from filings until it changed its legal status from a partnership to a corporation in 1961. In any event, no annual reports could be found with the federal or state government prior to 1958, when the Growth Fund began filing annual reports.

The earliest regulatory document Mairs & Power preserved was a report dated July 13, 1943, that George filed with the securities division of the Minnesota Department of Commerce. Operating as a sole

80 Investment Advisers				
File No	Name - Address	Licensed	Year	Expires
9a = #27	Mairs, George A Jr	7-15 =	1941	7-14-42
	Pioneer Bldg St. Paul, Minn	7-15 -	1942	7-14-43
	E-901 First Natl Bk Bldg			
	L #27	7-15-	1943	7-14-44
		7-17-	1944	7-16-45
	L #47	7-17	1945	7-16-46
	L #61	7-17	1946	7-16-47
	L #79 =	7-17	1947	7-16-48
	L #94 =	7-17	1948	7-16-49
	L #111 =	7-17	1949	7-16-50
	L #127 :	7-26	1950	7-25-51
	L #142	7-26	1951	7-25-52
	L #157	7-26	1952	7-25-53
	L #175	7-26-53		7-25-54
	L #175 Cancelled 11-16-53 In #2			
	Lic #210	11-16	55	11-15-56
	Lic 319	10-10-	61	10-9-62
	Mairs & Power, Inc. corp.			

This handwritten record documents George Mairs Jr.'s license as an investment advisor in the state of Minnesota. His was the 27th license issued in 1941. The subsequent listings show his renewals of the license. The licensing of investment advisors in Minnesota followed the passage of the federal Investment Act of 1940. Photo courtesy of the Minnesota Historical Society.

proprietorship, he disclosed that he had 35 clients, all individuals, and managed $2.5 million of their money. His annual fees were 3/8ths of 1 percent of the market value of bonds and ½ of 1 percent of the market value of stocks. He had $1,350 in cash, $635 in accounts receivable, no accounts payable, and more than $25,000 in a personal investment account. "I take almost all of the reputable statistical services, magazines, newspapers and so forth," he said in the report. "No recommendation is passed on to a client until I have studied and approved it."[38]

About that time, George Jr. hired Tillie Schunicht to run his office. Like George, she was there for the long run. In 1968, she was named "assistant secretary/assistant treasurer." Nine years later, when she was 76, she retired. Ron DeSellier, who had joined the firm in 1973, described her phone-answering voice as legendary: "an almost squeaky, cinematic uniqueness no one could ever forget." She lived with her sister in Rush City, 55 miles north of St. Paul, and took the train to and from work.[39]

Late in 1946, George C. Power Jr., then 32 and 13 years younger than George Mairs Jr., joined the firm. The following year, the firm moved to larger quarters in the First National Bank Building. Late in 1951, George Mairs III, George Jr.'s son, then 23 years old, joined the business. Soon, the enterprise's days as a sole proprietorship with George Jr. running the show would give way to a new time—the era of The Three Georges.

Part II

THE THREE GEORGES

CHAPTER 4

The Pivot: Saying Goodbye to Fear

In 1954, George Mairs Jr., then 53 years old, decided it was time for a change. He had operated his business as a sole proprietorship—"George A. Mairs Jr., Investment Counsel"—for almost a quarter of a century. In 1946, he had hired George Power. In 1951, his son, George Mairs III, joined the firm. Now the time had come to bring the other two Georges into a partnership.

This was a signature moment for the firm. We don't know what led the founder to change the firm's name and bring George Power in as a partner. But George Jr. believed in trusted relationships, such as his deep liaison with Power. And he had to know that shifting to a partnership structure would help his firm play the long game, avoiding fleeting salary incentives and commission schemes. His son claimed some influence in his father's decision to promote Power and rebrand the firm, as noted in the profile of George Power accompanying this chapter.

Being a decisive leader, George Jr. did not hesitate.

He executed a partnership agreement wherein he gave up half of his equity in the firm. Under the agreement, George Power, 40 years old, got a 35 percent stake; George III, age 26, got 15 percent. Soon, all three would become equal partners, with each holding a third of the company. They produced a promotional brochure—"What Is Investment Counsel?"—to seek new clients.[1]

When this portrait of George Mairs Jr. was taken in 1950, he was an experienced investment counselor who had guided clients through the difficult years of the Great Depression and World War II. Photo courtesy of the Mairs family.

THE MOOD SHIFTS

These were foresighted moves; 1954 turned out to be a pivotal year for the financial community. As Wall Street historian John Steele Gordon noted in his 1999 book *The Great Game: The Emergence of Wall Street as a World Power*, the economy had boomed during World War II thanks to the colossal military spending it took to win the war. Unemployment had fallen to 700,000 by 1944, just 10 percent of what it was in 1940. Factory workers were taking home ever-fatter paychecks, but they didn't have many options for spending them thanks largely to wartime rationing.[2]

The federal government promoted "Series E bonds"—war bonds used to finance the titanic battles with Germany and Japan—with massive marketing campaigns. Hollywood stars such as Greer Garson, Bette Davis, and Rita Hayworth, and cultural icons like Norman Rockwell all were rolled into this effort. "Any Bonds Today?" became a patriotic jingle stamped into the national psyche. Americans could easily buy these bonds through payroll deduction plans or at their local bank. They were dealing with safe, familiar institutions. No brokers, no middlemen, no commissions. Everyone knew in advance what the return would be if they held the bonds to maturity—a bond that cost $18.75 could be cashed in for $25 after 10 years through the magic of compound interest. No risk, and a specified reward.

Many Americans hesitated until the early 1950s to shake off their lingering fear that the economy, lacking the staggering stimulus of producing the ships, planes, tanks, jeeps, weaponry, and infrastructure needed to win the war, would sink back into a Depression again. Then, in 1954, the stock market woke up. It took 25 years, but the Dow Jones Industrial Average finally got back above its 1929 high of 381. This index would break above 400 that year and by the end of the decade, it would be pushing toward 700. The New York Stock Exchange's average daily trading volume, which had lacked a pulse for years, topped 2 million shares in 1954 for the first time since 1933. By 1959, annual volume would exceed one billion shares.

Soon Americans would unleash a hurricane of spending on cars, houses, clothing, and all manner of other consumer goods. A popular Broadway Musical, *The Pajama Game*, captured the mood almost perfectly. The plot played out at the Sleep-Tite Pajama Factory, where union workers were battling for a seemingly small hourly wage increase. The lyrics to the song, *Seven-and-a-Half Cents*, reflected the rising aspirations of the workers for more material goods and services.[3]

With pencil and pad in hand, the workers figured out that a seven-and-a half-cents-an-hour wage increase, over five years, would add up to $852.74—enough to buy an automatic washing machine, a year's supply of gasoline, carpeting for the living room, a vacuum instead of a broom, even a 40-inch television screen. Over another five years, they would have that much again—enough for a trip to France, a motorboat and water skis, a charge account at the neighborhood bar. Maybe even a foreign car and a Scrabble Board with letters made from gold.

Twenty years on, the grand total reached $3,411.96—enough to be a sultan in a taj mahal and buy a pajama factory. The head of the union's grievance committee and the factory's boss fell in love. The workers got their wage increase. The show's lyricist was engaging in a bit of hyperbole, of course, but the words and the music blended well, delighting audiences, night after night. The original production, which opened on Broadway on May 13, 1954, ran for 1,063 performances.

George C. Power Jr.: Putting Clients First

George C. Power Jr. was born in the heart of the Greatest Generation, and he lived up to its name.[4] He graduated with honors in 1935 from Carleton College with a degree in history. He was drafted into the army in 1942 and rose to the rank of captain before he was discharged more than four years later. Late in 1946, he joined the firm that George Mairs Jr. founded. Veterans were streaming into the work force as the nation shifted to a peacetime economy after years of Depression and war. A promising new era, favorable to growing businesses, had arrived.[5]

Power quickly won the trust of a handful of clients. They spread the word. Soon, the few became the many as he built up a large base of individual accounts. Some of his earliest clients, and many who followed, were older women living in St. Paul. Their late husbands had always handled the family finances. Typically, these women had scant experience in managing money; so they turned to George for help. He responded, defining his advisor-client relationships as enduring personal friendships. He stopped by to visit with them on his way home from work, even took their silver downtown to deposit it in their safe deposit boxes.

By the early 1950s, George Power was also handling some of the administrative work at the firm. At the end of 1953 or early in 1954, George Mairs Jr. made George Power a partner and rebranded the firm as Mairs & Power. These were moves that George III, who had then been at the firm for two years, advised his father to make. "At the outset of my employment I was impressed that George [Power] was really the chief operating officer assuming broad responsibilities in this firm, which permitted my father to spend more time in civic activities," George III wrote decades later in a one-page memoir. "After two years in this, I suggested to my father that the firm be named Mairs & Power in order to recognize George Power's vital role in the organization." Today, the individual accounts (managed separately from the mutual funds) are arguably George Power's primary legacy at the firm. These accounts represent nearly a third of the assets managed by the firm.

"He had unbelievable social skills," said Todd Driscoll, whose family assets were managed by Power for decades. "His clients trusted him because he played bridge with them. He did the kinds of things that are unheard of today. He was

Mr. Congeniality."[6] Power's daughter, Peggie Klema, remembers the time when she and her husband were tempted to buy a house about two miles from where she grew up. The house turned out to be the former home of one of her father's clients. "He loved to meet with his older clients and compare stories and mutual friends from the good old days in St. Paul," she said.[7]

While we don't know how many individual accounts Mairs & Power had by 1958, when the firm started its first mutual fund, we can assume the number was substantially more than the 35 it had in 1943—and that George Power brought in many of these new accounts. Mutual funds emerged as a logical next step, a way for Mairs & Power to serve some of its clients more efficiently, but these funds didn't account for the majority of the firm's assets under management until the mid-1990s. That is when the Growth Fund surged thanks to the stock-picking prowess of "The Third George"—George Mairs III.

A Bridge between the Other Georges

So while the "The First George" founded the company and took it through the Depression and World War II in good shape and his son, George Mairs III, would much later see it through bursts of growth; "The Second George"—George Power, working so closely with individual clients—provided the bridge between the two eras.

Power had a wide circle of friends. In the spring of 1994, he invited 250 of them to a party at the Minnesota Club in St. Paul

GEORGE A. MAIRS, JR.

ANNOUNCES THAT HE HAS BEEN JOINED IN PARTNERSHIP WITH

GEORGE C. POWER, JR.

THE ORGANIZATION IS NOW KNOWN AS

MAIRS AND POWER

INVESTMENT COUNSEL

EAST 1002 FIRST NATIONAL BANK BUILDING

SAINT PAUL 1, MINNESOTA

When George Mairs Jr. decided to make his investment firm a partnership with George C. Power Jr. in 1953, the firm mailed announcements such as this one to its clients and friends to tell them of the change. Photo courtesy of Mairs & Power.

to celebrate his 80th birthday. Choirmaster Philip Brunelle and performers from the Minnesota Opera entertained the crowd. George loved gardening, travelling, the arts, entertaining and his church. He was a generous donor to many good causes.

George and his wife, Jeanne, had two children: George C. Power III, born in 1945, and Peggie, adopted in 1949 when she was four weeks old. His commitment to the Children's Home Society began in 1949. He gave annually to the Society and helped it establish a planned giving program. He

was a strong backer of DARTs, a non-profit that offered services to seniors. This organization established The George Power Initiative to help the elderly stay in their homes so they could remain close to family and friends. He served on the boards of the Dodge Nature Center and the Friends of the St. Paul Public Library. His son established a fund at St. Paul's Wilder Foundation to honor him and his wife, Jeanne. His grandfather had been one of the six Wilder family friends who filed the original articles of incorporation establishing the Wilder Charity, which eventually became one of the country's largest operating foundations.

He attended St. Clement's Episcopal Church in St. Paul, five blocks from the home where he grew up. He was in the choir, a lay reader and chalice bearer, vestryman and senior warden at the church, a member of the Episcopal diocesan finance committee and a board member of the University Episcopal Center. Banking and finance were part of his pedigree. His paternal grandfather—also named George C. Power—was the president of the Second National Bank of St. Paul. When he died in 1912, at age 54, bankers from across the state flocked to his funeral. He had risen in Minnesota banking during a period of great economic growth, starting in the 1870s, and served on the executive committee of the Minnesota State Bankers Association.

His grandson was born and raised in St. Paul, graduated from St. Paul Academy in 1931 and began his investment career in 1933, when he had a summer

Tuesday, December 8

1953

Counselor Names Partner

Mr. Power   Mr. Mairs

George C. Power Jr. has been named a partner by George A. Mairs Jr., investment counsel, it was announced today.

The firm is now known as Mairs and Power, Investment Counsel, with offices in the First National Bank bldg.

Mr. Power has been associated with the firm since 1946. He was formerly with the investment research department of the First Service Corp. and holds a B. A. degree from Carleton college.

One of the local St. Paul newspapers carried this brief report of the new partnership between George Mairs Jr. and George C. Power Jr. Photo courtesy of the Power family.

job at the Northwestern National Bank in Minneapolis.[8] One of his roles there was to value collateral for customers who had purchased securities before the 1929 stock market crash.

From 1937 until 1942, he worked at First Service Corp., which was affiliated with First Trust Company in St. Paul and other banking units that were part of one of the state's two large bank holding companies (Northwestern National was part of the other bank holding company). At First Service, he gathered, interpreted, and presented information about earnings and dividends of corporations, industries, and securities; gave investment advice to clients; and supervised four statistical clerks in compiling information. He took 24 semester hours of business administration courses at the University of Minnesota from 1938 to 1941 but did not go on to get a degree there.

The Army: Rising Through the Ranks

Power was a 28-year-old bachelor in May 1942, six months after the Japanese attack on Pearl Harbor, when the army called. He did his basic training at Camp Grant in Illinois and then was sent to Medical Administrator Officer Training School at Carlisle Barracks in Pennsylvania. In March 1943, while stationed in the Aleutian Islands, he broke both of his heels getting off a troop ship in Alaska and spent six weeks recovering in the hospital. After recovering, he attended additional training in civilian personnel management at Fort Washington, Maryland.

George Center Power Jr. in his army uniform in 1943. At the time, he was a first lieutenant in the medical corps. Photo courtesy of the Power family.

George was then assigned as an administrative officer at the Army Service Forces Regional Station Hospital at Camp Crowder, Mo., where he supervised military and civil personnel in all the wards and clinics at the base hospital. He enjoyed this experience so much that he considered a career in hospital administration. The critical nature of his military assignment as a hospital administrator apparently convinced his superiors to keep him in the service for almost a year after the war ended. "The Army was in no hurry to let him go," his son said. He was finally discharged on July 31, 1946, with the rank of Captain, and then went on reserve status, serving as the detachment commander of the army's headquarters medical units of the organized reserve at Fort Snelling until 1953.

He probably met Jeanne Rogers in Rockford, Il. when he was on leave from his station at nearby Camp Grant. George and Jeanne were married in February of 1944. George had known George Mairs Jr. socially before he came to the firm and, in fact, they were "shirttail relatives" (George Jr.'s second wife, Louise, was George Power's aunt). So, a few months after Power left active duty, George Mairs Jr., apparently anticipating postwar growth, invited him to become the first investment professional there other than himself. Soon after he became a partner, he got a 35 percent stake in the firm.

Power's experience in supervising medical units in the army, and his own family's traditions, led him to leadership roles at hospitals in St. Paul. In 1962, he was elected president of the St. Luke's Hospital board. His great-grandfather, William Dawson Sr., had been a founder of the hospital; his grandfather, William Dawson Jr., was on its board. In 1972, St. Luke's and the Miller Hospital merged to form the United Hospital. Power played a key role in orchestrating the merger.

In 1971, he became the United Hospital's first board chairman. He served on the United board until 1992, including many years as its chairman. In 1988, the United Hospital Foundation honored him with its Service to Humanity Award. "George Power's dedication to the field of health, which started in the Army, had survived the test of this great merger," the foundation said. Jeanne, a nurse, was also involved at United and taught nursing courses at St. Mary's Junior College. A Type 1 diabetic, Jeanne died in 1981, when she was 63. It was an ironic twist, given that so many of her husband's original clients were women who outlived their husbands.

In 1995, a few months before George Power died, he took his family to Sanibel

This photo from about 1945 presents four generations of the Power family. Seated on the left is Maria Rice Dawson, the great-grandmother of George C. Power III, who's resting in her lap. George C. Power Jr. is standing behind them and to his left is the infant's grandmother, Anna Dawson Power, and on the right is the child's mother, Jeanne Rogers Power. Photo courtesy of the Power family.

Island in Florida for a vacation. His health was declining then, but he continued to come into the office almost up to the day he died. "He could talk to anybody, and talk at their level," his son said. "He was a good man, a brilliant man, fair, caring and generous," his daughter added. Peter Robb, who subsequently assumed management of most of George's accounts at Mairs & Power, commented: "George always said your friends become your clients, and your clients become your friends."[9]

WALL STREET HEADS TO MAIN STREET

Then there was good-time Charlie Merrill. Throughout the 1920s and '30s, he had been known for his deal-making, partying, and rocky marriages (three of them), all of which provided rich fodder for the tabloids. But in the end, Merrill would be remembered as the person who, more than any other, realized that the stock market could not prosper unless it broadened its reach to take in America's middle-class and did more to recognize the companies of the future instead of being so wedded to established companies that had seen their best days.

Merrill, who founded Merrill Lynch in 1914, was a contrarian harshly critical of the speculative binges of the late-1920s stock market. He laid out his views in real time, as the frenzy was occurring. This, as opposed to near-universal hindsight of the many who spoke out against the speculators *after* the 1929 crash. Nineteen months before the market collapsed, in a March 1928 advisory, he had urged his clients to get out of the stock market. (That was also the month when George Mairs Jr., then 27 years old, became a net seller of stocks instead of a net buyer.)

Ever since he started his firm, Merrill had been fascinated with the emergence of chain store retailers despite Wall Street's dismissal of them as a fad. As the stagnant stock market of the 1930s settled in, Merrill switched his attention from his own investment firm to the grocery chain in which he held a controlling interest: California-based Safeway Stores. But when the 1940s began, he renewed his interest in the stock market and Merrill Lynch. He shaped elaborate plans to turn Merrill Lynch into a nationwide powerhouse that would bring massive numbers of Americans into the stock market for the first time.

Merrill Lynch opened offices across the country. Apparently, one of the early branches was in St. Paul. In 1942, the firm recruited James M. Wallace, who had worked at Paine Webber's office downtown, to open a branch in the city. The office was in the First National Bank Building, on the very same floor that Mairs & Power occupies today. By the time Charlie died in 1956, there would be 122 branches across the country and his firm's "Thundering Herd" slogan, depicting Merrill Lynch's bullishness on the stock market, was on its way to becoming as American as baseball, apple pie, and Chevrolets.

An undated photo of Charlie Merrill. Photo courtesy of Getty Images.

Charlie Merrill lowered customers' costs by dropping the fees his firm had passed on to them for collecting dividends. He eliminated the commission surcharges many brokers has been charging clients. Many years later, such visionary moves would prevail as the industry finally abandoned its fixed commission system. Merrill put brokers on a salary instead of a commission, so they would be less incentivized to churn their clients in and out of stocks and focus more on long-term performance. He introduced company-wide training programs to strengthen ethical standards and higher levels of professionalism. He stressed fundamental securities analysis. That emphasis lined up well with the work of investor and academician Benjamin Graham, who became known as the father of modern securities analysis. John Steele Gordon noted that when the New York Society of Securities Analysts was founded in the 1930s, it had just 20 members. By 1962, it had 2,700.

By the mid-1950s, all of this was building trust with investors. Many of them had turned a deaf ear to the stock market for years. Others were new to the market. In the first biography of Charlie Merrill—*Wall Street to Main Street*, published in 1999—financial historian Edwin J. Perkins described Merrill as the financial services industry's most innovative entrepreneur of the twentieth century. Many of Merrill's moves were the same strategies Mairs & Power pursued from its founding in 1931.[10]

CUSTOMIZING THE APPROACH

On a far smaller scale than Charlie Merrill had commanded, the firm's modest three-fold brochure was bringing in new accounts. The brochure laced into the concept of "the average investor," agreeing with a financial magazine that had recently termed such a person a "non-existent monstrosity."

"Investment advice of this type may be likened to prescribing the same remedy for every patient with a headache, regardless of its cause," the brochure explained. "Aspirin will provide temporary relief for a number of ailments, but it is no substitute for thorough examination and diagnosis by a trained physician." It went on to liken investment counsellors to doctors and lawyers who tailor their advice to fit the special needs of their patients and clients.

The brochure outlined a four-point process for serving clients: a complete analysis of the client's sources of personal finances in order to shape a portfolio of securities based on (1) their appropriate level of risk; (2) continuous supervision of the portfolio, drawing on the best research to balance the goals of asset growth and security; (3) quarterly reports showing the costs, valuations, earnings, and dividends of clients' securities; and (4) tax planning. The brochure noted that the firm does not buy or sell securities, derives its income entirely from clients' fees, and benefits clients by providing them with a bundle of services at a lower cost than they would pay if they purchased the services separately.

The firm's fee was one-eighth of 1 percent of the market value of the securities being supervised. The brochure made no mention of a minimum fee or a requirement that clients sign a contract for the firm's services. Instead, it said the value of the firm's services "depends upon mutual understanding and satisfaction." This underscored Mairs & Power's emphasis on trust and close communications between the firm and its clients.

In the mid-1950s, Mairs & Power was still entirely in the business of managing the private accounts of individuals and companies. Among them was Tradehome Shoes, which had been co-founded in 1921 by Al Mains. In 1954, Tradehome started a profit-sharing plan for its employees. Don Mains, son of Al Mains and a longtime co-owner with his father and brother-in-law, said that initially Tradehome rejected having large brokerage firms manage the plan's money. Instead, the company hired a local savings and loan association to manage the plan. Then the three owners met with George Mairs Jr. He suggested that Tradehome "try out" Mairs & Power for two years. If the owners were dissatisfied, they could drop the firm and recoup all the fees they had paid.[11]

Tradehome stuck with Mairs & Power. Today, the company, based in the St. Paul suburb of Cottage Grove, is the firm's longest-tenured private account. "They were not interested in generating fees," said Don Mains. "They were looking after us." In 1956, Tradehome had 13 stores and $300,000 in its profit-sharing plan. At the end of 2020, the company noted on its Web site that it had become employee-owned with 120 stores in 22 states and $30 million in its profit-sharing plan. Today, Mairs & Power's private accounts still represent roughly 40

The front cover of the trifold brochure *What Is Investment Counsel?* that the three partners in Mairs & Power—George Mairs Jr., George C. Power Jr., and George Mairs III—circulated to their clients in the mid-1950s. Photo courtesy of Mairs & Power.

This was a view of the 32-story First National Bank Building in St. Paul in 1952 looking up from the bluff of the Mississippi River. The 10-story, "1st" sign at the top of the building, when illuminated at night, could be seen for miles. Photo by Walter Trenerry. Photo courtesy of the Minnesota Historical Society.

percent of the assets it manages. These accounts come from many loyal clients who stuck with the firm in good times and bad.

MUTUAL FUNDS EMERGE

In 1957, Mairs & Power was seriously weighing a major diversification beyond supervising private accounts: starting a mutual fund. Matthew P. (Matt) Fink, a longtime president of the Investment Company Institute (the principal trade association for the mutual fund industry), recalled the early development of mutual funds in his book *The Rise of Mutual Funds*, first published in 2008. Fink described his book as the second overall history of the industry; the first was Hugh Bullock's *The Story of Investment Companies*, published nearly half a century earlier. The first true (open-ended) mutual fund, where shares were bought and redeemed from the fund itself at net asset value, didn't appear until the creation of the Massachusetts Investment Trust in 1924.[12]

Until 1940, fund shares were sold by independent brokers unaffiliated with fund sponsors. That year, Congress passed the Investment Company Act, which established a legal and regulatory framework for mutual funds. Minneapolis-based Investors Syndicate, which had been contemplating entry into the field since 1932, responded by establishing the Investors Mutual Fund in 1940 to become the first firm to both sponsor and sell funds. In 1949, Investors Syndicate was renamed Investors Diversified Services—IDS. By 1950, there were still only about 100 mutual funds, but they were becoming more prevalent.

By the end of 1958, the IDS Investors Mutual Fund and a Massachusetts Investment Trust fund had become the first two mutual funds to top $1 billion in assets and the IDS family of funds was one of the country's five largest mutual fund complexes. In 1959, *Time* magazine declared in a cover story that mutual funds "have taken the specialized world of Wall Street and put it within reach of every man with enough money to buy a fund share . . . the shares are bought by maids and wealthy dowagers, by doctors and factory workers, by labor unions and clergymen. No amount is too large . . . or too small. Ten years ago, most people had never heard of mutual funds; now, the term is a household word." By 1960, mutual fund assets had risen to $19 billion, up from $1 billion in 1940.[13]

IDS became famous for its widely dispersed sales force, which touted the firm's mutual funds to expose customers to additional financial services. For years, the first advertising motorists would see as they approached Midwestern towns was an IDS sign promoting its funds and other financial services. According to Ameriprise, the Minneapolis firm that inherited the IDS family of mutual funds and runs them today, IDS's Investor Mutual Fund became the largest balanced mutual fund in the world in the 1960s. John Elliott Tappan (1870–1957) founded the Investors Syndicate, which eventually became IDS, in Minneapolis in 1894. His biographers (business historian Kenneth Lipartito and Carol Heher Peters, Tappan's great-granddaughter) describe him as a champion of bringing investing opportunities to America's emerging middle class, much as A. P. Giannini and Charlie Merrill did.[14]

PRELUDE TO THE GROWTH FUND

Attorney Ed Stringer recalled the circumstances that would soon lead Mairs & Power to launch its Growth Fund. Stringer served on the firm's fund board for nine years after he left his seat on the Minnesota Supreme Court in 2002. His family has been close to the Mairs family since the 1930s. His father, Philip Stringer, was the Mairs & Power

attorney when it considered establishing a mutual fund. In a 2020 interview, Ed Stringer explained that Mairs & Power was getting many requests from potential clients, but often their assets were too small for the firm to manage profitably. A mutual fund would solve that problem by offering efficiencies to the firm while also accommodating clients with fewer assets. Clients could choose whether to go into the fund or maintain a private account at Mairs & Power, outside of the fund. "It was a win-win situation for everybody," Ed Stringer said.[15]

Mairs & Power's principals had discussed the idea of a mutual fund with Wells Farnham, one of George Mairs Jr.'s contemporaries. Farnham had grown up in the Twin Cities and maintained many Minnesota ties. During the early 1940s, both leading principals at the Chicago investment firm of Stein Roe left for wartime assignments; Farnham stepped in for them and the firm became known as Stein Roe & Farnham. George Jr. also discussed the idea with Stanley Platt, a Minneapolis investor he had known for years. George III was urging his father to start a fund. And Mairs & Power had to be studying the successes that nearby IDS had been experiencing with its mutual funds.

Ed Stringer pointed to a phone conversation his father had as part of setting up the fund to illustrate the firm's legendary frugality. George Jr. was seeking to register the Growth Fund with regulators. Philip Stringer's roommate at the Yale Law School had become a Wall Street lawyer. Philip suggested that George call his friend, to get advice on registering the fund. "Let's get him on the line and we'll talk about how we can get registration set up," Philip Stringer told George, who then made the call. When the conversation got around to the question of how much the legal fee would be, the answer—$20,000 or more—was not satisfactory. "You could hear a gasp on the phone from George," Ed Stringer recalled. "We did it instead, for $500."

In their typical low-key manner, the three partners at Mairs & Power announced the formation of the firm's Growth Fund with this description in the January 1959 issue of the magazine published by the St. Paul Athletic Club.

The Growth Fund was organized on January 8, 1958. Its shares were first offered 10 months later. On December 31, George Jr. reported that the Fund had 49 shareholders, assets of $184,006, and net income for the year of $2,011. About 13 percent of the assets were in U.S. Treasury bills and a number of the stocks in the fund were blue chips such as IBM, Sinclair Oil, General Electric, and Caterpillar Tractor. Back then, there weren't many Minnesota stocks to choose from. Soon, there would be plenty of them. "We had never intended this to be a regional fund," George III would tell *Barron's* 44 years later.

THE ROLE OF THE CREDIT CARD

1958 would also be remembered for the birth of the modern credit-card era, a sea change for the financial services industry. This facilitated more consumer spending, which in turn fueled the stocks of the companies that were providing the goods and services that consumers desired. More of these stocks began turning up in the Growth Fund. Single-purpose or single-retailer charge cards offered by department stores, such as the Dayton's cards held by thousands of shoppers in the Twin Cities, had been around for years. In the 1950s, it seemed like a rite of passage that everyone who drove a car needed at least one oil company credit card to gas up. But those were not multiple-purpose cards. Instead, Bank of America, created by another legendary financial services entrepreneur who some said ranked with Charlie Merrill, brought credit to just about everyone by introducing the all-purpose credit card.

This mammoth, and yet in some ways still-nimble financial institution, had been founded by A.P. Giannini, the son of an Italian immigrant. Giannini started the Bank of Italy in 1904 largely to make money available to immigrant farmers in California's Santa Clara Valley. His bank grew explosively as Americans flocked to the Golden State. The bank renamed itself as the Bank of America, but by some measures it became the Bank of the World. By 1945, it was the largest bank on the planet.

Financial journalist Joe Nocera would lead off his 1994 book *A Piece of the Action: How the Middle Class Joined the Money Class,* with a description of the Bank of America's "Fresno Drop." Nocera explained that 1958 was when the Bank of America "dropped its first 60,000 credit cards on the unassuming city of Fresno, California." The move would soon usher in a new age of instant credit, easily and eagerly tapped in the 1960s by a burgeoning cohort of middle-income American households.[16]

By the late 1950s, critics had begun to question the growing consumer mentality in the country. In 1957, Vance Packard wrote *The Hidden Persuaders*, a slashing assessment of the psychological techniques that advertisers were wielding to convince customers to buy material goods. Marketers fought back, decrying the book as sensationalism. In 1958, economist John Kenneth Galbraith followed up with *The Affluent Society*, arguing that the accumulation of material wealth was not the best measure of economic and social well-being. The emergence of books such as these from a former Madison Avenue marketer and a distinguished Harvard professor signaled just how much the outlook and buying habits of Americans had changed during the growth years of the 1950s.

Cautiously, the Three Georges began inching into Minnesota stocks, which were becoming plentiful courtesy of the rapidly expanding local over-the-counter market. This was a time of more sophisticated and diverse investing opportunities. On the other hand, opportunities were growing among the new stocks for buyers who

In 1973 the U.S. Postal Service issued a 21¢ commemorative stamp honoring Amadeo Pietro Giannini (1870–1949), the founder of the bank that became known as Bank of America.

Beginning with the "Fresno Drop" in 1958, multi-use credit cards began to change the way consumers paid for products and services across the U.S. Today Visa and MasterCard are two of the most widely used cards.

did their homework and analyzed prospects carefully. In 1960, the Growth Fund picked up Norwest Bancorp; in 1961, First Bank Stock Corp. By the end of 1961, it had 204 shareholders, $1.1 million in assets, and net income that year of $12,694.

A NEW LEGAL STRUCTURE

In 1961, with an eye to the future, Mairs & Power was incorporated. A memo from George Mairs Jr. cited two reasons for the decision. First, incorporation would enable the firm to set up a profit-sharing plan. Second, the move would make it easier to bring in more partners.[17]

In November of that year, Mairs & Power launched its second mutual fund—the Income Fund, later renamed as the Balanced Fund—with a public offering. The concept was to offer a diverse mix of stocks and bonds. At the end of the year, this fund had assets of $192,717 with net income for the year of $5,532. Bonds accounted for $106,412 of the assets and stocks $83,691. The bond portfolio consisted largely of oil and gas companies, railroads, public utilities, pipeline companies, and financial firms. The stocks were mostly oil and gas companies, utilities, and railroads.

Mairs & Power introduced its first mutual fund, the Growth Fund, originally called the Mairs and Power Fund, toward the end of 1958. As can be seen from this Growth Fund stock certificate, the Fund was initially organized under the laws of Minnesota. Photo courtesy of Mairs & Power.

In 1961, the Mairs & Power Growth Fund was joined by a second mutual fund, the Income Fund, later renamed the Balanced Fund (1997). Photo courtesy of Mairs & Power.

As the first half of the 1960s wore on, the Growth Fund began attracting more retail investors. Often, these were non-professional investors with modest amounts of money looking to buy a package of securities that offered better returns than traditional options such as bank or credit union savings accounts, Series E savings bonds, or whole-life insurance policies.

By the end of 1966, the Growth Fund was starting to take on a "Minnesota tilt." Minnesota stocks accounted for 9 of its 38 holdings, up from 4 in 1958. The value of these stocks was up to 21 percent of the value of the Fund, from 14 percent in 1958. The Growth Fund's assets stood at $2.42 million on December 31, 1966; the Income Fund's assets were $788,900. It would be the late 1960s—more than the 1950s—when equity mutual funds would boom. That included the Growth Fund, but in its own special way: by tapping into the rising opportunities to invest in promising companies with headquarters in Minnesota.

CHAPTER 5

A Garden Blooms in the Backyard

Gradually, the business climate in Minnesota flipped from darkness in the 1930s to dawn by the late 1960s. The Mairs & Power Growth Fund recognized this shift and became a barometer of how much the state's economic prospects had changed.

And as successful Minnesota companies were spurring a surge in the Growth Fund's assets, Eugene Fama, a bright, young economist at the University of Chicago, was undertaking extensive research into the movement of stock prices. His work eventually led him to develop "the efficient market hypothesis," which came to be widely embraced by economists, business school professors, and many investors. Fama's work launched him on a long and successful career on the Chicago school's venerable campus. Eventually, he became internationally acclaimed, winning a Nobel Prize for economics.[1]

Put in its simplest form, the efficient market theory postulates that all information about securities is already incorporated into prices, thus there is no way to beat the market. Passive investors tend to believe this theory. Typically, they are content to "buy the market" through index funds or other investment vehicles that reflect the movements of the entire market as opposed to stock-picking based on fundamental analysis and familiarity with the managements and cultures of specific companies.

Shortly before he died in 2010, George Mairs III looked back respectfully at the efficient market theory. Then, in a single lengthy paragraph, he rejected it insofar as it applies to Mairs & Power. He explained that his firm had a special advantage: long-standing knowledge of Minnesota companies based in part on personal relations with

In 2013 Professor Eugene Fama of the University of Chicago, along with his colleague at the University, Lars Peter Hansen, and Yale economist Robert Shiller, was awarded the Nobel prize in economics for research that helps explain "how and why prices of stocks and bonds change over time." Photo courtesy of the Booth School of Business, University of Chicago.

their managements. "Most of these companies were poorly covered by Wall Street, in part because of their location but also because of the unique nature of many of these companies which made them difficult to analyze," he wrote.[2]

"Minnesota is generally regarded as a high-tax state, which citizens have accepted" because of the state's high quality of life. "High business taxes have made this a difficult environment for companies, particularly ones subject to commodity pricing. Therefore, companies that have survived and thrived in the state generally produce unique products or services. Partners at this firm continue to stress strong ties with managements that generally require somewhat frequent visits."

BECOMING MINNESOTA-CENTRIC

He might have added that by the late-1960s, a rich garden of choice stocks was flowering in the Growth Fund's own backyard: the pickings had gotten considerably better in Minnesota. Since the end of the previous decade, scores of companies in the state had gone public. Most of them flamed out in one way or another, but some didn't. Instead, they became profitable, grew, and prospered. As 1967 arrived, a six-year run of growth began at the Fund, greatly enabled by an increasing focus on Minnesota companies that had gone public. Thus began the era when the Fund developed its preference for Minnesota stocks. Each year, at the end of January, George Mairs Jr. reported the Growth Fund's performance to its shareholders. The results from 1966 to 1972 were inarguably strong:

- In 1967, the Fund's net asset value per share rose 41 percent vs. a 20 percent gain for Standard & Poor's 500 Index.
- In 1968, the net asset value climbed 19 percent vs. 8 percent for the S&P 500 and 4 percent for the Dow Jones Industrials.
- In 1969, the stock market had a rough year. Yet the net asset value fell only 9 percent. The S&P 500 dropped 11 percent and the Dow fell 15 percent.
- 1970 was an exception, with the overall market ending its longest decline since World War II in May. The Fund's net asset value fell 4 percent vs. gains of 0.1 percent for the S&P 500 and 4.8 percent for the Dow.

- In 1971, the net asset value of the fund rose 21.6 percent vs. increases of 10.8 percent the S&P 500 and 6.1 percent for the Dow.
- In 1972, the Fund's net asset value rose 21.8 percent vs. rises of 15.6 percent for the S&P 500 and 14.6 percent for the Dow. In his January 31, 1973, report to shareholders, George Mairs Jr. cited a recent Standard & Poor's comparison that ranked the Growth Fund's performance as the 16th best among 400 funds over a prior 5-year period. The Fund's net asset value had risen 52.7 percent during this stretch vs. increases of 22.4 percent for the S&P 500 and 12.7 percent for the Dow.

Over the six years that ended on December 31, 1972, the assets of the Growth Fund climbed nearly seven-fold to $15.0 million from $2.3 million. The number of shareholders rose to 1,473 from 393. The Fund's share of all stocks that were based in Minnesota increased to 40 percent (19 of 48) from 24 percent (9 of 38) and the Minnesota stocks' market value doubled to 41 percent of the Fund's value from 21 percent.

At the outset of this period, in July 1967, George Power wrote a Market Outlook piece for the St. Paul Athletic Club's magazine. In it, he suggested that stocks likely would be a good hedge against inflation in the years to come. Power was on to something. Inflation had been a minimal problem in the 1950s and the first half of the 1960s. But by 1967, President Lyndon Johnson's "guns and butter" policies—sizable federal spending for both the Vietnam War and his Great Society programs—were by some accounts building the foundation for what would become the virulent inflation of the 1970s. In the first half of the 1960s, annual inflation rates ran under 2 percent. In 1966, the rate skipped up to 2.9 percent; in 1967, 3.1 percent; in 1968, 4.2 percent; in 1969, 5.5 percent. Insofar as the Growth Fund was concerned during this time, Power's prediction turned out to be prescient—at least through 1972. Inflation, as measured by the Consumer Price Index, rose 29 percent over 1966–1972, while the net asset value of the Growth Fund rose 109 percent to $15.29 a share from $7.31.[3]

Mairs & Power almost never advertised for its funds, with one consistent exception: tiny ads in the local dailies that described them as "no-load" funds. This characteristic differentiated them from "load" funds.

When this 1984 photo was taken, Deluxe Check Printers (now Deluxe) used computers to check the accuracy of individual check orders in its plant. Mike Zerby photo, *Star Tribune,* copyright 1984.

"Load" meant that the seller of such a fund levied a sales charge or commission, typically about 7.5 percent of the price buyers paid for their purchase, to compensate the broker who handled the sale. By 1970, no-loads were still accounting for just 11 percent of long-term mutual fund sales, according to mutual fund historian Matt Fink. The Growth Fund was a no-load from the start, in 1958, when it was among a relative handful of pioneering no-load funds. Fink notes that by 1977, the big fund groups, led by Vanguard, were switching to direct sales of no-loads.[4] By 2001, no-loads accounted for 58 percent of all equity fund sales, and today most mutual funds are no-loads. Brokers evolved into fee-based financial planners, and consumers became more astute shoppers.[5]

During this period, the firm's razor-thin staff still consisted of only the directors (the three Georges) plus one or two support workers. At a June 22, 1970, meeting of Mairs & Power, the directors considered broader advertising and direct mail solicitation. They rejected the idea, evidently feeling the firm was faring so well that there was no need for more marketing. According to the minutes of the meeting: "After some discussion, it was decided that these methods did not appear to be particularly productive, except for sale of shares in Mairs & Power Growth Fund, and that personal contact on the part of the members of the firm still seemed to be the best method of securing new accounts."[6]

FUND'S COMPANIES POSITIONED FOR TAKEOFF

Some of the Minnesota stocks the Fund added in these years went on to become strikingly successful investments for Mairs & Power. Deluxe Check (today known as Deluxe), which the Fund first purchased in 1966, was the nation's leading check printer for years. It was the Fund's largest holding in seven of the years between 1971 to 1986. The Fund sold the last of its Deluxe stock in 2001.

In 1969, the Growth Fund made its initial purchases of Medtronic and Economics Laboratory (Ecolab). Both stocks went on to become enormous successes for the Fund (see Table 1 in chapter 12). At the end of 2020, Medtronic was the Fund's fourth largest holding and Ecolab its fifth largest. In 1970, the Fund initially purchased Toro, a stock that had first gone public in the Twin Cities over-the-counter market. This stock, another big success for the Fund, remains in its portfolio today as its 10th largest holding.

As these companies grew up and prospered, so did the Growth Fund. Medtronic was founded in 1949 by Earl Bakken and his brother-in-law, Palmer Hermundslie, at their medical repair shop in a garage in northeast Minneapolis. Bakken worked part-time at the University of Minnesota. In 1957, Dr. C. Walton Lillehei, a pioneer in open heart surgery at the University, had a patient die in surgery when a blackout knocked out the power. Lillehei asked Bakken to design a device that would lower the fatality rate during heart surgeries. Bakken came up with the world's first transistorized, battey-powered, wearable heart pacemaker.[7]

The Growth Fund's initial purchases of Medtronic stock in 1969 marked its first stake in a holding that would see immense growth in value over the next half century. Today, Medtronic has become the world's largest medical devices company, with annual sales of $28.9 billion and 105,000 employees in 140 countries.

Analysts from Piper Jaffray & Hopwood produced reports, preserved in in Piper's archives at the Minnesota Historical Society, on some of these companies. The reports, almost certainly perused by the Three Georges, provided information that supplemented the familiarity that Mairs & Power's partners had already gleaned through face-to-face meetings with the top managers at these companies. George Mairs III's appointment books show three appointments with or presentations from Medtronic, in January of 1969 and March and August of 1972.[8]

"Toro has interesting longer-term prospects," analyst Kenneth W. Scully wrote in a Piper report issued

Medtronic founder, Earl Bakken, left, in 1986 with Medtronic executive Winston Wallin, who's holding one of the company's early pacemakers. Jeffrey Grosscup photo. Photo courtesy of the Minnesota Historical Society.

This is Medtronic's Model 5800 Pacemaker from about 1957. A pacemaker is an artificial device used to stimulate the human heart muscle and to regulate its contractions. Photo courtesy of the Minnesota Historical Society.

in January of 1963. "Besides continuing to strengthen its position as a leading manufacturer of high-grade grass-cutting equipment, the company is increasing its importance as a producer of snow removal machines, golf course vehicles, and lawn sprinkling systems."

Toro's roots go back to 1914, when a predecessor company began producing farm tractors. In 1945, David Lilly and two other veterans who were friends from Dartmouth College, purchased the company. Toro had just 50 employees then. Lilly, who died in 2014, was the son of Richard Lilly, the longtime president of the First National Bank of St. Paul. Toro's new owners, sensing a postwar boom in demand for its principal product—lawn mowers—reorganized the company and mapped out an ambitious expansion program. Sales quintupled, rising from $1.4 million in 1946 to $7 million in 1950.

David Lilly served as Toro's president from 1950 until 1968 and chairman until 1976, when he joined the Federal Reserve System as a governor of the central bank's board. When his term expired, he returned to the Twin Cities to become dean of the University of Minnesota's Carlson School of Management. Later, he served as the university's vice president for finance and operations. In 1962, Toro had sales of $21 million. In 2020, its sales were $3.38 billion, and the company had a presence in 135 countries.[9]

The Toro Corporation got its start manufacturing farm equipment and lawn mowers. This photo from 1962 shows Toro's assembly line for snow blowers, a key part of that growing firm's plan to expand its product lines. Dwight Miller photo, *Star Tribune,* copyright 1962.

Merritt J. Osborn, initially a salesman, founded Economics Laboratory in 1924. A stain in a hotel carpet convinced him that a rug cleaning compound could be developed that would get rid of such stains instead of having to remove the carpet. He set up shop in an office in the basement of the Endicott Building in downtown St. Paul, hired a former St. Paul Winter Carnival princess as his secretary and assistant, and began producing an array of cleaning products. During World War II, the company developed one of the first germ-killing detergents and distributed it to U.S. military forces so they could sterilize their mess kits. The Osborn family gave up management of the company in 1978 and the company changed its name to Ecolab in 1983.

In 1965, when Piper's Ken Scully put out a report on the company, its annual sales were $48.5 million. "Cleanliness is of utmost importance in sections of many industries," Scully wrote. "As a specialist in sanitation, Economics Laboratory is a part of a dynamic industry.

Following service in World War II, David Lilly (1917–2014), left, with key executives Robert Gibson, middle and E. S. Conover, was the president of the Toro Corporation for nearly 30 years. He retired from Toro in 1978. Dwight Miller photo, *Star Tribune*, copyright 1962.

Merritt J. Osborn (1880–1960) founded Economics Laboratory (now Ecolab) in 1923 and over time it became one of the nation's leading manufacturers and distributors of detergents and cleaning chemicals for restaurants, hotels, hospitals, and commercial dishwashing. In this 1935 photo, Osborn is seated in the center of the front row with his sons E. B. on his right and Steve on his left. E. B. began his career in sales and in 1950 succeeded his father as the firm's president. Photo courtesy of Ecolab, Inc.

With prospects favoring further gains in profits, the common [stock] has attraction for investors seeking equities with appreciation potential." By 2020, Ecolab employed nearly 40,000 workers in more than 170 countries. It reported nearly $12 billion in annual sales of hygiene, water, and energy products.[10]

These Minnesota companies and others became the core of the state's unusually large contingent of Fortune 500 companies we still see today. They and the service entities that supported them—law and accounting firms, bankers, educators, and vendors—helped Minnesota's economy diversify from one based on material resources, primarily lumber and forestry, iron ore, and agricultural goods, that had dominated in earlier generations. As the farms became more mechanized and less in need of labor, skilled farmhands poured into the Twin Cities area to take good jobs in the region's bustling factories.

Beginning in the late 1960s, Ecolab had its corporate headquarters in the 20-story Osborn Building in downtown St. Paul. In 2017 Ecolab moved to the nearby building previously occupied by Travelers Inc. Today Ecolab's former building is known as the Osborn 370 Building, which operates as an entrepreneurial hub for tech startups. The offices of Mairs & Power Private Capital Management are in this building. Photo courtesy of the Minnesota Historical Society.

THE GO-GO YEARS

Nationally, a very different picture was playing out. In addition to growth, volatility and controversy also came to characterize much of the mutual fund industry. Fund assets had nearly doubled, to $35 billion during the first half of the 1960s and, as writer John Brooks noted, "the great rising giant of American finance, the mutual fund industry, had come out with honors." The stock market had suddenly gone into a steep decline in May 1962. Mutual funds, cash-heavy, and still conservatively managed, stepped in to stabilize trading.[11]

Yet as 1966 began, a paradox became evident. Mutual funds, which had for the first time turned the American stock market into a market dominated by institutions, were in some cases also reinventing the power and celebrity of individuals who symbolized the stock market in and before the 1920s. Brooks would label this new age "The Go-Go Years"—a time that ran from late 1965 until it began to fizzle out in 1968. The Go-Go Years would be represented most of all by Gerald Tsai.

Tsai had been hired by Fidelity Investments in 1952. He launched a fund there in 1957, Fidelity Capital Growth. Tsai bought stocks then deemed much too speculative for a mutual fund. He typically turned over his portfolio at annual rates exceeding 100 percent—meaning stocks in the portfolio were typically held less than one year—churning stocks to chase short-term performance and boost fees. (In contrast, the Mairs & Power Growth Fund's turnover rates have been unusually low, almost always in single digits, and the fees have been minimal). Fidelity Capital Growth, riding the highest-flying stocks of the mid-1960s bull market, rose nearly 50 percent on a turnover rate of 120 percent in 1965. Then, when Fidelity head Edward Johnson passed Tsai over and chose his son, Ned Johnson, as his successor, Tsai left to start his own fund.

Tsai's Manhattan Fund opened in February 1966. It quickly raised $250 million—10 times the amount Tsai had initially sought. Financial writer Joe Nocera called his fund's fees "egregiously high . . . an 8.5 percent upfront commission plus a stiff annual management fee. No one cared. There were several other funds with track records every bit as good as Tsai's. It didn't matter. Gerald Tsai was the mutual fund manager everybody wanted—the man with the golden touch."[12]

Brooks, who wrote for the *New Yorker*, profiled other stars of the new cult of performance: Bernard Cornfeld, whose Overseas Investment Services became a $2.5 billion global empire notable for evading regulators; Frederick Mates, whose Mates Fund reported an asset gain of nearly 100 percent in its first year; Fred Carr, whose Enterprise Fund reported a 117 percent increase in value in 1967. All of them ran into trouble once the stock market turned bearish.[13]

The market, like the country then working through racial and cultural unrest and upheaval, was a tumultuous place in 1966–1972. The Dow Jones Industrials neared 1,000 every year during the last half of the 1960s, but never broke through that level during that decade. In December 1968, the index peaked at 985. Then it fell 36 percent to 631 by May 1970. The low understated the overall decline, since the average was propped up by the so-called "Nifty Fifty" large-capitalization stocks.

The Nifty Fifty stocks, all traded on the New York Stock Exchange, came to be revered for their size, stability, and earnings growth in the

Gerald Tsai was a highly successful mutual fund manager whose style eventually came to symbolize the cult of short-term performance that drew much attention in the mid-to-late 1960s. Patrick McMullan photo, Getty Images.

William L. McKnight (1887–1978) began working at the Minnesota Mining and Manufacturing Company (3M) in 1907 and rose steadily through the ranks to become the company's president in 1929. His career at 3M spanned 59 years. McKnight guided the company from the brink of bankruptcy to its position today as a large multinational corporation by diversifying its product lines. Art Hager photo. *Star Tribune*, copyright 1951.

late 1960s and early '70s. Investors shoveled money into them, driving their shares up to as much as 50 times earnings, far above long-term averages. They came down to earth when the market turned bearish in 1973–1974. 3M was Minnesota's only Nifty Fifty stock.[14]

Through it all, mutual funds generally prospered. By 1970, the fund count was up to 361 funds with $48 billion in assets. Ninety-four percent of them were equity funds. The promise of more growth for the funds drew new competitors from outside the fund industry. Insurers moved into the field by creating variable annuity funds, acquiring existing mutual funds or, as giant insurers Connecticut General, John Hancock, and Mutual of Omaha did, by starting up their own funds.[15] By 1970, insurers accounted for roughly 15 percent of all mutual fund assets. Fund families—groups of funds operating under one banner that managed ever-larger pools of assets—were becoming more common. Yet financial giant Merrill Lynch refrained from getting into the fund business because Charlie Merrill disliked mutual funds. The firm finally entered the field in 1971, 15 years after Merrill died, when Donald Regan became the firm's CEO and chairman.

CHARLIE MERRILL'S BLIND SPOT

In the early 1950s, Merrill had dismissed out of hand an elaborate plan drawn up by Regan, then one of the firm's rising stars, to take Merrill Lynch into mutual funds (Regan would go on to become Ronald Reagan's first treasury secretary and later his chief of staff). Merrill's aversion to mutual funds helped keep the field wide open for much smaller firms, such as then-tiny Mairs & Power, to enter the business in 1958. For George Mairs Jr. and his two partners, handling administrative work for the funds was less time-consuming than dealing with many of their separately managed accounts.

Edwin Perkins, Merrill's biographer, explained that much of Charlie Merrill's disdain for mutual funds arose partly from his familiarity with the closed-end funds that grew in the early years of the twentieth century. Since the closed-end funds traded on the stock exchanges like other securities, their prices could vary widely, swinging significantly higher or lower than the underlying value of the securities in the funds. Prices for the closed-end funds soared in the late 1920s, contributing to speculation that led to the 1929 market crash. Charlie

Merrill had even drawn up a proposal for a closed-end fund, but—fortunately from his perspective—he dropped the idea when the stock market failed to recover in 1930.[16]

Merrill came away from that experience with a permanent distaste for mutual funds. But the fund managers who arose, first at the Massachusetts Investors Trust and later after the Investment Company Act (1940), did not view the closed-end funds as true mutual funds. They championed open-end funds which, unlike the closed-end funds, promptly redeemed their customers' shares at the fund's portfolio's current liquidation value.

Perkins also explained that Charlie Merrill felt his brokers, armed with superior securities analysis and other support from the company, could do at least as well as fund managers in deciding what stocks their clients should buy, hold, or sell, and when. Yet Merrill feared that the funds would become so popular that they would end up taking substantial business from Merrill Lynch. This was his view, even though some of the open-end funds were load funds charging high fees.

Biographer Perkins agreed with others who called Merrill's resolute opposition to mutual funds a serious mistake. "In one of the few instances in his long and distinguished career, Charlie Merrill simply failed to consider what type of service might be in the best interest of certain groups of serious investors," Perkins concluded. "Instead, he placed the welfare of the firm—his partners and loyal employees—on a higher plane than the dictates of those impersonal market forces so clearly identified as paramount two centuries earlier by political economist Adam Smith. Consequently, the firm was slow to recognize the legitimate appeal of mutual funds to small accounts, and in time, to more substantial investors with vast sums available for permanent investment."[17]

PLAYING ON A BIGGER FIELD

Edwin Perkins noted that by 1996, Merrill Lynch was offering its customers 200 different mutual funds with a combined portfolio value of more than $230 billion, thanks largely to its strong retail distribution network. Its entry into the field provided another example of how, in the late 1960s and early 1970s, the mutual fund industry was becoming increasingly dominated by financial services giants. The

When this photo was taken, Merrill Lynch had offices across the U.S., including this one in the Triangle Building in San Jose, Calif. In 2008, Bank of America bought Merrill Lynch. Photo courtesy of Shutterstock.

very aggressive practices of the gunslinging money managers of the Go-Go era presented a culture unimaginable at Mairs & Power, but the emergence of such Goliath-like players in the fund industry suggested that the firm would need to remain vigilant, focused, and successful in order to survive as an independent entity.

By 1972, as noted earlier, Mairs & Power's Growth Fund was living up to its name. But despite the rapid growth of the Fund, the separately managed accounts outside of the Fund and its much-smaller sister, the Income Fund, still accounted for roughly two-thirds of assets managed by the firm. That year, the Dow Jones Industrials finally topped 1,000. In his letter to Growth Fund shareholders on January 31, 1973, George Mairs Jr. summarized how good the preceding year had been for the Fund's shareholders, then offered an upbeat vision for the year ahead.

"We remain optimistic regarding the economic outlook for 1973 and anticipate strong growth trends throughout the year," he wrote. "Of particular significance to the investment outlook is a prospective rise in corporate earnings, perhaps approximating the 16 percent advance experienced in 1972." Many others were making similar forecasts, but those predictions would not come to pass. Instead, 1973 would usher in an era of tough new challenges for Mairs & Power and for the entire financial services industry.

Part III

THE GEORGE III ERA

CHAPTER 6

The Struggles of the '70s

The year 1973 did not go down as a time of plenty at Mairs & Power, contrary to the vision that George Mairs Jr. presented in his January letter to the shareholders of the firm's two mutual funds. Instead, 1973 ushered in a decade-long series of bouts with double-digit inflation, two harsh recessions, a pair of oil price shocks, and years of lethargy in the stock market. A new term, "stagflation," meaning a combination of a sluggish economy and persistent inflation, described this unsettling environment.[1]

The static 1970s—seen by economists as an era that covered the period from early 1973 to summer 1982—became a time when the Growth Fund went basically nowhere, at best. Its assets of $13.2 million at the end of 1981 were actually less than the $15.0 million of nine years earlier. And that was without adjusting for the rampant inflation so concerning for investors during those years. In defense of George Jr., almost nobody had foreseen such a scenario. And by the measure of the Growth Fund, Mairs & Power fared better than the market during the 1973–1982.

In 1973, the Fund represented $15 million of the $45 million in assets managed by the firm. Almost all the rest of the assets were in 130 separately managed accounts, largely for individuals and trusts. These accounts held many of the same stocks that were in the Growth Fund; so, the state of that Fund was a reasonable proxy for the state of the firm.

As this era began, the firm made a key hiring decision. In September 1973, with the stock market slipping into its worst bear market since the Depression and just two months before the 1973–1975 recession began, Mairs & Power hired a fourth investment professional, Ronald J. DeSellier, to join the Three Georges. DeSellier would go on to spend nearly 19 years at the firm, handling a wide variety of tasks.

About four years after he arrived, he became the first outsider—that is, a person not from the Mairs or Power families—to hold an ownership stake in the firm. As his responsibilities grew, his stake increased. By 1992, he owned 43.1 percent of the firm—just below George Mairs III's 44.4 percent stake. Shortly before coming to Mairs & Power, he began taking copious notes. That practice evolved into journaling, which he has kept up ever since. Keeping a journal has enabled him to readily draw on his experiences for fresh ideas and insights, he said, adding that "this is especially joyful when my friends admit they cannot argue with me because they know I have it all written down at home." He preserved many of the firm's records. Much of the story of the firm during 1973–1992 comes from extensive emails he provided for this project. Except for George III's brief description, many years later, of his time at the firm, the Three Georges left almost no personal accounts of their many years there.

CONTRASTING UPBRINGINGS

The rough-and-tumble circumstances that DeSellier was brought up in differed markedly from the more comfortable and genteel environment in which George Mairs Jr., his son George III, and George Power had been born and raised. DeSellier's ancestors on his father's side came to Canada from France in the 1600s, eventually reaching Michigan's Upper Peninsula and finally Minnesota's Iron Range. His mother's side's first-generation in America began with her father's arrival in Hibbing from Croatia in the early 1900s. DeSellier was born in Hibbing, in the heart of the Range, in 1941. Shortly thereafter, his family moved to Detroit.[2]

After his parents were divorced, when he was seven years old, he was passed from relative to relative, school to school—sometimes in Detroit, sometimes in Hibbing. Then came high school and junior college, while living with his grandfather in Hibbing. He left the Range for good when he was 20 years old. DeSellier spent a quarter at the University of Minnesota before he ran out of money, then took a job in the reservations department at Northwest Airlines (now part of Delta Air Lines). After two years there, the army drafted him. As he later put it, the clearly defined orderliness of military procedure suited him well and he gained an appreciation for even the smallest of details. Unlike many draftees who were sent to Vietnam the 1960s, he remained in the States, reaching a rank of staff sergeant, and working mostly at his battalion's headquarters. He was discharged after 22 months of active duty, returned to the University of Minnesota, and graduated in 1967 with a Bachelor of Science degree in Economics.

DeSellier's interest in investing grew from an introductory course in investing that he took during his senior year at the University. After graduating, he landed a job as an analyst at First Trust Company of St. Paul. In 1972, Angus Mairs recruited DeSellier to join the Minneapolis office of White, Weld & Co. as an institutional salesman marketing services to money managers. (Angus, George Mairs III's younger brother, had worked at Mairs & Power for at least six or seven years, leaving in about 1967 to go to White, Weld as a stockbroker.)

In January of 1973, George III, then an adjunct instructor at the University of Minnesota, invited DeSellier to speak to his class about his job. Nine months later, George III and George Power persuaded him to join the firm. By the time he arrived, George Jr. had pulled back from active engagement there. The slower pace at Mairs & Power gave DeSellier a chance to catch his breath, including time to complete the final leg of becoming certified as a chartered financial analyst. He forged many friendships in Minnesota's investment community and, in 1978–1979, served as president of the Twin Cities Society of Security Analysts.

DeSellier recalled that "all of the Mairs & Power accounts took a hit," during his early years at the firm. "Clients became gun-shy," he said. "There is a certain kind of toughness that can only be learned by fighting your way through a difficult period, and that's what we did. Frugal by nature and low cost by design, Mairs & Power weathered that period with only modest discomfort and when the tide turned, we were ready." Asked about reports that the tougher times led him and the two Georges to take pay cuts, he put it this way: "It was more the result of monitoring what was left in the checkbook at the end of the month and dividing whatever was there. When the market declined, the checkbook was less flush but never alarmingly so." The minutes from a meeting of the firm's directors on June 16, 1975, show that they voted to make no contributions to the firm's profit-sharing plan for the fiscal year that would end two weeks later. The minutes did not mention the size of prior years' distributions or whether they had been omitted in earlier years.[3]

Ronald J. DeSellier. Photo courtesy of Ronald J. DeSellier.

DIVERSIFYING THE CLIENT BASE

Mairs & Power tempered the adverse effects of the floundering stock market by diversifying its client base. In 1975, DeSellier and George Mairs III worked closely with one another to land the firm's first large Taft-Hartley union employee benefit plans. Taft-Hartley plans were defined benefit pension plan maintained by more than one employer, usually within the same or related industries, under collective bargaining agreements with a labor union. In 1974, Congress passed the Employee Retirement Income Security Act (ERISA), which required these plans to make significant operational changes. The legislation often led the non-investment consultants—the actuaries, administrators, and legal counsellors who were advising the plans' trustees—to recommend that they turn to professional money managers to handle their plans' investments.

DeSellier said St. Paul attorney Bob Faricy, the plan's attorney and one of the many 'friends of Mairs & Power,' directed the trustees to the firm. Then George laid out the basics to them: the history of the firm and its investment philosophy, its long-term view, low turnover, and how it was a small but stable operation responsive to clients' needs. "I was an Iron Ranger with the same kind of hardscrabble background so that they could ask me questions that they would never ask George III or ask in front of other trustees," DeSellier said.

Large construction projects such as the one seen here often employ workers representing a variety of trade unions. Photo courtesy of Shutterstock.

"The union trustees who sat on these boards were typically brash and accustomed to getting their way," DeSellier said. The consultants were proficient in their own disciplines, he said, but they lacked the firm's broader investment perspective. Also, the management and union trustees were often at odds with another but "we were able to create an informed focus on the one thing they could always agree on—the highest worker benefit for the lowest contributed amount." By the early 1990s, the union account would stand as the firm's largest for a time, easily exceeding the size of even the Growth Fund, and the firm had signed up a second large union account.

BACKBONE OF THE FIRM

Before DeSellier joined the firm and during his years there, George Power had by far the largest number of individual accounts, including many older women who, left with inheritances from their husbands, were inexperienced in and/or uneasy with handling investments. They sought advice and were attracted by Power's natural kindness and unusual dedication to his accounts. "These accounts were the backbone of the firm in the years before I arrived, and though they required a lot of back-office work, they were a solid and dependable revenue source in good times and bad." But DeSellier added that what began to show up in the mid-'70s was how much staff work was needed to generate each dollar of revenue in these accounts, compared to much less for the Funds and the employee benefit plans.

DeSellier and George III managed the equities, the mutual funds, and certain individual accounts. Almost by default, DeSellier also handled anything related to bonds. "Having little bond experience before I joined Mairs & Power, I became 'semi-expert' [on bonds] out of necessity." When he joined the firm, the plan was for him to help George Power with his long-standing accounts and to assist George III with his research and strategy. Power would continue to handle about 75 percent of the account relationships and George III about 75 percent of the research and strategy.

DeSellier said 90 percent of the firm's research then came from written reports and meetings with analysts from local and national brokerage firms that supplied the research in return for commissions on trades made on behalf of clients. "Knowing our universe of possible investments well, we didn't need special research input, and did not feel disadvantaged in any way by not getting it." When Goldman Sachs brought an analyst to town to see IDS, for instance, Goldman's local sales representative (from Chicago) would typically arrange a luncheon with the analyst for the smaller Twin Cities money managers. IDS got private meetings with the analyst first, since it provided the resources and connections needed to bring the analyst to the Twin Cities.

DeSellier described the remaining 10 percent of the firm's research as "in-person local"—visits to local companies, other contacts with their managers, and attending corporate annual meetings. Circulating in the community and doing a good job for existing clients were viewed as the most effective uses of time, he said. "The fact that our salaries were heavily dependent upon how much we did not spend during the year was certainly not lost on us."

THE BEARS RULE

Nationally, the unshakable bear market of the 1970s laid waste to large parts of the mutual fund industry. Matt Fink, the retired president of the Investment Company Institute (ICI), recalled the devastation in his 2011 history of the industry. Generally, the three previous decades had been prosperous times to be in the stock market, which drove immense growth in the mutual fund industry since the funds were heavily focused on equities. Nationally, shareholder accounts in funds had risen from fewer than 300,000 in 1940 to nearly 11 million in 1972. Looking back, an ICI paper in 1996 tracked the stagnation of the 1970s. The S&P 500 Index, which had reached a record high in December 1968, pushed briefly above the record early in 1973 but did not return to that level until late 1979. Broker-dealers, who had been the mainstay of the fund distribution system, turned from selling equity funds to selling hard assets.[4]

"As a result of the falloff in fund sales, for the first time in history, equity funds had net redemptions, month after month, year after year," Fink wrote. In 1973, the ICI moved its January conference, usually held at a sunny resort in the Caribbean Islands or Hawaii, to Williamsburg in Virginia to cut travel costs. Two months later, Donald

Pitti, president of Weisenberger Services, predicted that "the fund industry as we know it is likely to disappear." One fund executive even proposed that the trade group switch from reporting its data monthly to quarterly to reduce negative press coverage (that proposal died).[5]

The condition of the national economy did not spare Mairs & Power. In his final letter to Growth Fund shareholders on January 31, 1975, George Jr. would report seriously bad news. The net asset value per share of the Fund plunged 36.2 percent in 1974, worse than the declines that year of 27.6 percent for the Dow Jones Industrials and 29.7 percent for the S&P 500. "The drop in stock prices for the year was among the steepest of the century and the most severe since 1937," he noted. George Power reported much better news when he took over the letter a year later thanks mostly to a sharp rebound in the market, which had anticipated the end of the 1973–1975 recession, and a modest decline in inflation. The Fund's net asset value surged 33.7 percent in 1975, slightly more than the S&P but still below the 38.3 percent gain for the Dow.

But the persistent inflation and high interest rates of this era were a toxic mix for the stock market. In his book about the rise of the middle class, financial journalist Joe Nocera noted that inflation was almost non-existent, as measured by the Consumer Price Index, from shortly after the end of World War II until in 1967. In 1974, it exploded, reaching nearly 12 percent. Simultaneously, the 16-month recession that would linger until March of 1975—the longest since the Depression—was underway.[6]

TROUBLES MOUNT

All of this became the perfect storm in October 1973 when the Organization of Petroleum Exporting Countries (OPEC), angered by the U.S. decision to resupply Israeli military forces during the Yom Kippur War, launched a five-month embargo of oil exports to the U.S. Oil prices shot up and shortages of gasoline forced millions of Americans to queue up, day after day, in long lines at gas stations across the country.

Much of the economic trouble of the 1970s was due to high interest rates. As Nocera noted, Depression-era "Regulation Q" rules limited the interest rates banks and savings and loan associations paid to consumers for their deposits to around 5 percent. Yet, the banks and S&Ls could

Signs such as this one from January 1974 appeared with frequency during OPEC's five-months-long embargo of oil to the U.S. that began in October 1973. Many gas stations closed early, stayed closed longer, or ran out of gas, depending on how much gas they were allocated. Owen Franken—Corbis, Getty Images.

then turn around and invest that money in long-term securities that returned twice as much as they were paying their depositors. It was a version of the old "3-6-3" adage that so benefited these financial institutions—pay 3 percent on deposits to consumers, loan out the deposits at 6 percent, and be out on the golf course by 3 p.m. The combination of high interest rates and towering inflation that prevailed during so much of the 1970s was smacking middle-income Americans.

Economist Arthur Okun dreamed up a new economic barometer to reflect the situation: "The Misery Index"—the seasonally adjusted unemployment rate plus the annual rate of inflation combination. The Misery Index was at its worst from 1974 to 1980, when it averaged around 16 percent a year.[7]

A new storm swept in during 1979, when the Iranian Revolution led to the decade's second oil price shock. The crisis in Iran culminated in the overthrow of the Pahlavi dynasty under Shah Mohammad Reza Pahlavi, and the replacement of his government with an Islamic republic under the rule of Ayatollah Ruhollah Khomeini, a leader of one of the factions in the revolt. The U.S. had supported the Shah for many years prior to 1979; thus, Iran's new leadership quickly cast the U.S. as an enemy of the new regime.

Once again, the new energy crisis disrupted shipments of oil from the Mideast, leading to higher prices and more long lines snaking in all directions from the gas pumps. The inflation rate spiked at a staggering 13 percent in 1979. It remained in double-digit territory through the end

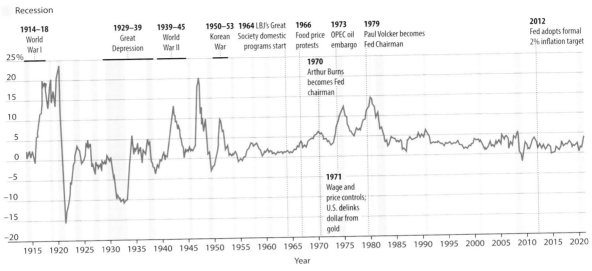

Figure 1

Inflation in the U.S., 1912–2020

Consumer Price Index, Monthly, Percentage Change from Previous Year

Recession

1914–18
World
War I

1929–39
Great
Depression

1939–45
World
War II

1950–53
Korean
War

1964 LBJ's Great
Society domestic
programs start

1966
Food price
protests

1973
OPEC oil
embargo

1979
Paul Volcker becomes
Fed Chairman

2012
Fed adopts formal
2% inflation target

1970
Arthur Burns
becomes Fed
chairman

1971
Wage and
price controls;
U.S. delinks
dollar from
gold

Year

Sources: U.S. Bureau of Labor Statistics and the St. Louis Federal Reserve Bank

of 1981 (see Figure 1). Then came a "double dip recession"—a mini-recession, in the first six months of 1980, followed by a brutal downturn that would run on for 16 months, from July 1981 until October 1982.

Congress finally phased out Regulation Q between 1981 and 1986. Until the surging inflation of the 1970s, this regulation didn't cause much concern at financial institutions. It helped them avoid offering accounts bearing higher interest-rates. Ultimately, though, such restrictions did a lot to transform the mutual fund industry by dispatching yield-chasing depositors and investors to an entirely new species that served as a hedge against inflation— the money market mutual fund. The first money market fund, the Reserve Fund, was started in September of 1972 by Henry Brown and Bruce Bent, former employees of TIAA-CREF (the Teachers' Insurance and Annuity Association-College Retirement Equities Fund).[8] Soon, wrote Matt Fink, "the advent of money market funds changed everything."[9]

When supplies of gasoline again ran short in 1979, some states adopted an odd-even gas rationing plan using the last digit on a car's license plate. This type of rationing worked, but it often resulted in long lines of cars waiting to fill up. Bettman, Getty Images.

In the 1970s, Honeywell in Minneapolis had a solid sales record, which helped Mairs & Power's Growth Fund to grow. Here Honeywell employees work on one of their firm's electrical products. Honeywell photo. Photo courtesy of the Minnesota Historical Society.

By 1980, money market funds accounted for 57 percent of the industry's $132 billion in assets vs. 33 percent for stock funds and 10 percent for bond and income funds. The bond and income funds fared well in the 1970s, with their assets rising fivefold to $14 billion and overall, mutual fund assets rose almost threefold from $48 billion in 1970. But the stock funds' total fell slightly from $45 billion to $44 billion. By 1980, the four largest fund groups—Merrill Lynch, Dreyfus, Fidelity, and Federated—were all major sponsors of money funds. IDS, which had been the largest fund group in 1970, had fallen to fifth by the end of the decade.

The money market funds invested in Treasury bills, jumbo certificates of deposit, and other high interest-bearing securities. This enabled them to pay returns steep enough for investors to keep up with inflation. The money funds were a direct response to the soaring prices, towering interest rates, and bearish markets that did so much to define the 1970s. Mairs & Power never started a money market fund. Looking back, Ron DeSellier brushed off the impact of the money funds on the firm. He explained that Mairs & Power's main competitors were other equity funds and that the firm could offer investors alternatives to its Growth Fund, such as its Income Fund and its separately managed accounts. Until late 1981, he and George III would engage in frequent brainstorming sessions to discuss portfolio-related issues. The firm's long-term view and the low turnover of the securities in its portfolios kept the need for new ideas manageable, he said. "We never felt pressed to be hyper-active just to show that we were doing something."

But DeSellier knew first-hand the stresses that Mairs & Power worked through during the 1970s. He managed the Income Fund during most of the 1980s. In his annual letter to its shareholders on February 2, 1990, he disclosed that the Income Fund "nearly disappeared" in the early 1970s when its partners decided to stop accepting new shareholders (in 1973 and 1974, its assets fell from $934,461 to $436,436, their lowest level in 11 years). But the suspension was short-lived. DeSellier went on to note that the Income Fund recovered when "the virtues of balanced investing were rediscovered" after the stock market unraveled in 1973–1974 and that the Fund had been growing ever since. Meanwhile, the Growth Fund outperformed one or both of the two major indexes in five of the seven years during the 1975–1981 period. Minnesota stocks frequently did well, including in one year or another, H.B. Fuller, Norwest, Medtronic, Dayton Hudson, Toro, Graco, Jostens, 3M, Deluxe, Honeywell, and General Mills.

To a considerable extent, the 1970s became a paradox for DeSellier and for Mairs & Power. Generally bad times, to be sure. Yet he and his two partners, George Mairs III and George Power, were easygoing and led rewarding lives outside the firm. Growth was fine, DeSellier explained, but better if it came produced by "non-marketing people like us." The three partners shared the view that marketing was, in DeSellier's words, a "somewhat distasteful" endeavor. There was no compelling need to aggressively chase after new business. The solid reputations of the Mairs and Power families would be enough to sustain the firm and attract more business. Most of the business walked in the door or was referred to the firm by its friends.

DeSellier missed the camaraderie he had enjoyed with contemporaries at White, Weld, but he was learning many facets of the investment business at a smaller

Mairs & Power first bought stock in St. Paul's H. B. Fuller Company in 1971. Founded by Harvey B. Fuller, right, as a manufacturer of wallpaper paste, the H. B. Fuller Company later branched out into making other kinds of adhesives. Elmer L. Andersen, left, bought the Fuller Company in 1941. This photo is from about 1937. Andersen went on to be elected governor of Minnesota in 1960 and returned to his former company following his gubernatorial service. Photo courtesy of the Minnesota Historical Society.

In 1982 the University of Minnesota awarded this medal to Gertrude Lippincott (1913–1996), a graduate of the University, for Outstanding Achievement in her career as a modern dancer, choreographer, and instructor. Jostens in Minneapolis, which is primarily known for manufacturing class rings, yearbooks, and Super Bowl rings, created this medal. Photo courtesy of the Minnesota Historical Society.

firm. His wife, who ran the Northwest Airlines international desk in downtown Minneapolis, received benefits that enabled the couple to take frequent vacations. Years later, he would liken his professional career to an unhurried country bike ride, stopping at his leisure for wine and sandwiches, in contrast to the years of pedaling at breakneck speed in the Tour de France that he would have faced at IDS or other larger and more aggressive firms.

THAT CELEBRATED MAGAZINE COVER

The 1970s limped to a close with one of the most famous business magazine cover stories of all time: *Business Week*'s August 13, 1979, story headlined "THE DEATH OF EQUITIES: How inflation is destroying the stock market." The magazine reported that at least seven million shareholders had left the stock market since the 1970s. "Only the elderly who have not understood the changes in the nation's financial markets, or who are unable to adjust to them, are sticking with stocks," *Business Week* declared. Others, often younger and seemingly wiser investors, were pouring their money into hard assets: gold, silver, diamonds, housing and other real estate, art, and commodities. Robert S. Salomon Jr, a general partner at Salomon Bros., put it bluntly: "We are running the risk of immobilizing a substantial portion of the world's wealth in someone's stamp collection."[10]

This foreboding vision seemed the reality for three more years. When *Business Week*'s story appeared, the Dow was sitting at 875. By August of 1982, it had fallen even more to a low of 777. Then everything changed. By August 13, 1989, the 10th anniversary of *Business Week*'s death sentence, the Dow had climbed to 2,684; By August 13, 1999, it was up to 10,974; On August 13, 2009, with the financial crisis still fresh in the market's mind, the Dow had slipped to 9,393. But by August 13, 2019, the 40th anniversary of *Business Week*'s cover, it was at 25,896—30 times its level when "The Death of Equities" story appeared. Market historians still look back on this headline as one of the most celebrated "buy signals" ever for stocks of all shapes and sizes.

Many things would soon change at Mairs & Power, too. The firm and its clients had survived the struggles and lingering legacy of the stagnating 1970s. It would still need to navigate through many ups and downs, and a smorgasbord of other challenges. For sure, there was no free ticket to survival in such an unforgiving business. But the nearly four decades of mostly bullish equity markets about to begin would provide many opportunities for Mairs & Power, showering enduring benefits on its growing roster of clients.

BusinessWeek magazine's celebrated "Death of Equities" cover of August 13, 1979.

CHAPTER 7

The Bull Arrives; an Industry Thrives

After steering through stormy seas for nearly a decade, Mairs & Power suddenly found itself in welcoming waters in the early 1980s. George Power, still the president of the firm's two mutual funds, cheerily dispatched the good news to their shareholders in his January 1983 annual letters. In 1982, the Growth Fund's net asset value had risen 34.6 percent, handily topping the performances of the Dow Jones Industrials (up 19.6 percent) and the S&P 500 (up 14.8 percent). That same year, Power reported that the Income Fund's total return (the combined effect of income and appreciation) was 28.5 percent—the highest since 1976.

Interest rates were falling. Inflation was easing. The economy was rebounding from a steep downturn. A long-awaited bull market had finally arrived. The firm replaced its committee investment decisions with more individual responsibility and autonomy. That led to DeSellier taking charge of the Income Fund, which proceeded to rattle off a string of good years. George Mairs III, who had already been picking stocks for some time, settled in for a long run at the Growth Fund.

In 1983, when founder George Mairs Jr. passed on, Mairs & Power crossed the $100 million mark in assets under management. Just $22 million of that was in the two mutual funds. The rest was in separately managed accounts, largely in the many individual accounts overseen by George Power and in two large institutional accounts: a union plan and an account for a fraternal order. The staff still consisted of only three professionals—George III, Power, and DeSellier, plus just three support staffers.

DeSellier said that he and both Georges met periodically to discuss strategy, with George Power acting as chairman emeritus, George III mostly as the chief executive officer, and himself as the chief operating officer. Over time, George III became more of a force in making key decisions. "Not privy to the private meetings they often had, I presumed George Power still had a voice when he felt forcefully about something, but I rarely saw him overrule George III," he recalled.

The three principals shared the same general approach to investing. As DeSellier put it: "Avoid the flash and dash of whatever was trendy, lean in against up markets, and nibble carefully in down ones, look for issues that will endure, and try to get on the compounding train whenever possible."

IMPROVING OFFICE PROCESSES

In 1985, Jean Reynolds, who had been the office manager, retired. The complexities of running the office were increasing, DeSellier said, adding that the firm needed a manager to take over the non-investment functions without the direct involvement of the partners, who were "for better or worse, investors and not administrators." DeSellier recruited Kathy Kellerman to succeed Reynolds.

Kellerman had wide-ranging experience doing tax work and record-keeping, dealing with compliance agencies, and handling a variety of other duties as a legal assistant at a large St. Paul law firm. She defined the job more broadly, developing written policies and accountability procedures, raising awareness of applicable regulations, and applying new technology effectively. DeSellier, who had been handling a growing amount of administrative work, was able to back away from much of it.

Until shortly before Kellerman came, virtually none of the office processes had been automated. Then, DeSellier shopped for and bought an IBM personal computer along with software for doing spreadsheets, database records, and word processing for just $10,000. That enabled the firm to handle much more office work without adding staff. Mairs & Power, however, was still posting transactions manually to handwritten ledgers well into the 1990s. In 1990, Michelle Maltby (now Michelle Lindenfelser), joined the firm to work with Kellerman (Today, Lindenfelser, now a portfolio administrator, is the firm's longest-tenured employee). DeSellier described Kellerman and Maltby as "the dynamos that for the first time made the office hum."

DeSellier's annual letters to Income Fund shareholders featured a folksy, informal style not typically seen in such communications. In his January 1986 letter, he acknowledged the favorable outlook for the year held by most professional investors but warned that it would be a time of not just opportunity, but also of confusion, crosscurrents, and highly volatile stock prices. "When you live near the Dragon, it pays to stay alert," he warned.

A typical desktop PC from the 1980s. IBM released its first PC in 1981. It had 16 KB of RAM, which could be expanded to 256 KB. The Model 5150 had a monochrome display, floppy-disk storage, DOS as its operating system, and cost $1,565. ShutterStock.

In January of 1989, he observed that the stock market's sharp climb in recent weeks was mindful of what Dennis the Menace once said to his close, personal friend, Joey ("We're lost, but we're makin' good time."). He recalled that author Bennett Goodspeed had once described a fanatic as "one who, when he loses sight of his goals, redoubles his efforts." In his 1991 letter, he explained that falling interest rates were complicating matters for the Fund: "If there is anything worse than high stock prices, it's low bond yields. Feeling a bit like the man who decided it was better to struggle with a sick jackass than to carry the wood himself, we have been slowly increasing the stock portion of the Fund's portfolio."[1]

Some of his reports to shareholders focused on financial education. Half of his 1986 letter was devoted to a page-by-page explanation of the annual report for the year just ended. In his last annual letter, in January 1992, he quipped that "total net assets have moved above $10 million, lifting us from the dreaded 'tiny' category into the 'very, very small' group; unlike some funds that have closed their doors to new orders because they have grown too large, we are still looking forward to having that particular problem."

CLIMB, CRASH, REBOUND

The stock market performed as if on steroids throughout the mid-1980s. The Dow topped 1,000 for the third time in 1982, this time never to look back. In January 1987, the index broke above 2,000 and by July, it reached 2,500. That level "was almost beyond imagination only 10 years earlier," financial historian John Steele Gordon wrote. Then suddenly, on October 19, 1987, the stock market crashed, with the Dow Jones Industrials plunging 508 points or 22.6 percent. That day would go down as "Black Monday," to mark the worst one-day percentage decline ever.[2]

Gordon described first impressions of the event as eerily reminiscent of the 1929 market crash. "In 1929, margin calls and short-selling had compounded the decline," he wrote. "In 1987, computer-program trading and funds managed by traders using a theory called 'portfolio insurance'—an economic oxymoron that supposedly eliminated risk while protecting reward—battered the market. It is little wonder that the press and many far more attuned to the ways of Wall Street anticipated a new Great Depression."

He cited three principal reasons why that didn't happen. First, investors were much more diversified than they had been in the late 1920s, with a much greater share of their wealth in real estate and other non-securities assets. Second, the reaction—more like a non-reaction—from the White House was reassuring. In the wake of the 1929 debacle, Herbert Hoover constantly told the public that Wall Street was a sound option for investors. His comments backfired, making investors more wary. Conversely, Ronald Reagan said little about the 1987 crash. "His laid-back, these-things-happen-from-time-to-time attitude" put investors' minds to rest. Third, and most important,

The October 20, 1987, headline in the *Philadelphia Inquirer* said it all regarding the New York Stock Market crash of that year. Photo by Hulton Archive, Getty Images.

the Federal Reserve immediately flooded the market by purchasing large amounts of government securities, thereby prompting a sharp decline in short-term interest rates and reversing the stock slide.

But Gordon noted that not all investment firms or individual investors came though the 1987 crash unscathed. Two large, old, and respected firms, E.F. Hutton and L.F. Rothschild, failed. So did more than 60 smaller firms. That underscored a long-term characteristic of the industry: constant churning that saw investment firms, including many that had been around for years, go out of business or get swallowed up by larger firms. The industry has provided a running portrait of "creative destruction"—a condition, famously defined by economist Joseph Schumpeter, wherein companies invariably rise and fall, then to be replaced by innovative and nimble newcomers.[2] White, Weld, where DeSellier worked for before joining Mairs & Power, was among them. Founded by wealthy Boston investors in 1895, it was sold to Merrill Lynch in 1978.[3]

At Mairs & Power, DeSellier said, life went on pretty much as usual. Throughout the 1980s, the firm circulated annual, two-page brochures, with unadorned covers that simply said "MAIRS and POWER Inc. Investment Counsel." The 1985 brochure, which summarized the firm's investment philosophy, performance, and salient facts about its operations and processes, said this: "Common stocks of well-managed corporations are stressed in individual accounts, while employee benefit plan accounts, generally more conservative because plan trustees are dealing with employee funds, use a mixture of stocks, bonds, and short-term investments to moderate the effect of stock market fluctuations. There is a strong tendency to stay true to an investment style that has served us well even though it may cause us to be out of phase with the market and our competitors from time to time."

The 1990 brochure, stressing a long-familiar theme, assured prospective clients that "absolutely no time is spent on marketing or promotion, which enables the firm to devote virtually 100% of its attention to the handling of existing client accounts." It went on to explain that "we aim for above average, but not necessarily spectacular investment performance," given that high-risk strategies are inappropriate for the kind of clients typically drawn to the firm. Throughout the 1980s, the firm urged its clients to take advantage of legal provisions, such as IRAs (individual retirement accounts) that would enable them to reduce their tax liability.

In his quarterly reports for 1987, DeSellier had been warning Income Fund shareholders that the stock market was overpriced. His first quarter report to them noted that stock prices had tripled since 1982 and consequently, the Fund was shifting to more bonds and fewer stocks. In his review of results for 1987, he described the crash as a return to reality "with a vengeance" and the inevitable result of "panic buying." George Mairs III was more circumspect in his Growth Fund summary, alluding to "October lows" and stressing that declines in inflation and in the value of the dollar boosted the prospect of rising earnings and dividends over the intermediate to longer term. In a general advisory to investors just after the year ended, Mairs & Power suggested that October's sharp retreat in equity prices left stocks underpriced.

ST. PAUL'S SATURDAY LUNCHES

Other developments in the 1980s paved the way for successes that would come later. One was the firm's intimate, ongoing ties with St. Paul's unusually close-knit business community, superbly reflected by the well-attended "Saturday lunches" held throughout the vicissitudes of winter at the Minnesota Club. Every Saturday from late fall up to early spring, a St. Paul area business would sponsor a reception and lunch at the club. The idea was to provide a networking venue that would enable executives to make connections that would help their businesses.

The sponsors included corporations whose stocks were in Mairs & Power portfolios: St. Paul Companies, Ecolab, the St. Paul affiliates of First Bank System and Norwest Bank, 3M, and St. Paul publisher Webb Co. All 400 members of the Club got invitations to the reception. The sponsors invited their best customers and suppliers, plus politicians and leaders of foundations, colleges and universities, and other institutions.

At one such gathering, sponsored by Webb in January 1983, the temperature outside was 14 below zero and the wind chill was 57 below. The luncheon attracted 280 attendees, including former Gov. Wendell Anderson. The Minneapolis Club, supported by a larger business community, had attempted to establish similar luncheons on several occasions. "They tried it and it was a miserable failure," said Robert Baker, a St. Paul historian.[4]

Business leaders in St. Paul founded the Minnesota Club in 1869 as a "gentlemen's social club." Clarence Johnston designed the Club's fourth building, which opened in 1915 and conveyed a sense of European elegance. Seen here in 1920, the Club experienced hard financial times in the 1990s and eventually Minnesota Sports and Entertainment bought this building and turned it into the offices for the Minnesota Wild professional hockey team and an event center known as 317 on Rice Park. Photo courtesy of the Minnesota Historical Society.

This sample from George Mairs's pocket calendar for January 1987 is interesting because it has a very readable notation for Saturday, January 24: "Minnesota Club." Photo courtesy of the Mairs family.

"I have an idea," George Mairs III told Malcolm McDonald, a seasoned St. Paul financial executive, at one of the Minnesota Club's Saturday gatherings. His idea was to invite McDonald onto the Mairs & Power mutual fund board, an invitation that McDonald readily accepted. "George Mairs came to these lunches all the time," McDonald said.[5]

Late in 1988, DeSellier signed up the employee benefit plan of a second large building trades union. The account was troubled and in disarray, he said, but the outside consultants who tended to its affairs were mostly the same group that Mairs & Power had been dealing with regarding another union account. "We were a known commodity to these consultants, offering the promise of stability and continuity to replace the often-chaotic history of this and other union accounts at that time, which would be good for the client and the consultants."

By June 30, 1991, one union account had become the firm's largest account, with $50.8 million in assets. The account for a fraternal organization was a close second, with $50.0 million; the Growth Fund was third, with $27.6 million. Both of the institutional accounts had been larger than the Growth Fund for several years, but

The construction of the light rail transportation line between the downtowns of Minneapolis and St. Paul took several years. This photo from 2013 shows workers leveling freshly poured concrete for the roadbed. Morris LePage photo. Photo courtesy of the Minnesota Historical Society.

the Fund passed them up after its surge in the mid-1990s. DeSellier said the assets under management number "was never a high visibility data point for us, as we focused on gross revenues almost exclusively." Then, as today, the firm's income came entirely from fees. By mid-1992, the two union accounts, while together still generating much less fee revenue than the firm's two mutual funds combined, were providing a rising share of the overall fee income.[6]

At first, the second union account was relatively small, but soon the union's leaders consolidated more of their scattered investment funds at Mairs & Power. On June 30, 1992, the three institutional accounts made up nearly half of the overall assets managed by the firm. These were primarily bond accounts.

In his later years at Mairs & Power, DeSellier kept detailed records of fee income, billable assets, and other data that enabled the firm to better understand its operations. Since he had introduced computer-generated spreadsheets and other back-office enhancements at the firm in the mid-1980s, his records were particularly descriptive after that time. In one spreadsheet and various emails that he sent to the author for this project, his data provided a snapshot of what Mairs & Power's business looked like in 1992: where its clients came from, the share of the firm's income generated by each of its categories of clients, and how the enterprise had changed since he joined the firm in 1973.

Much of the change had come courtesy of the two union employee benefit plans and a large fraternal association, none of which had been clients until after 1973. That year, the firm was managing $45 million, two-thirds of it in the separately managed accounts and rest in two mutual funds. The average size of the separate accounts was $230,000. "Probably all but a handful of these accounts were trusts and individual accounts, nearly all stemming from personal contacts made by George Power and George Mairs Jr. in the previous 40 years, and to a lesser extent, George Mairs III, as well," DeSellier said.

By 1992, the assets under management had risen to $256 million. Seven specialty plans provided a 30 percent share of this sum, two-thirds of that from the fraternal association; the two union plans accounted for another 28 percent of the total; the two mutual funds added another 16 percent; and the rest was in 120 trust and individual accounts, many of them still being managed by George Power. The five biggest accounts—the two union plans, the fraternal account, and the two mutual funds—provided 64 percent of the grand total. The Growth Fund's assets were $31.2 million; the Income Fund's $10.9 million. All, or almost all, of the business came from within Minnesota.

Because fees were the sole source of income for the firm, the sources of those fees were important. At that time, the trust and individual accounts were providing about 40 percent of the fees. Another 32 percent came from the mutual funds, 16 percent from the union plans, and 12 percent from the specialty plans.

In 1989, George Mairs III made a rare move, liquidating one of the Growth Fund's largest and most enduring holdings: IBM. The company's stock had been in the Fund from day one, in 1958, when it was the Fund's largest holding. For three straight years, 1983 through 1985, it had been the Fund's second largest holding—unusual in the 1970s and '80s for a company not based in Minnesota—and it was still its fifth largest in 1988. IBM stock had been a golden investment for millions of Americans for decades, and its large plant in Rochester had given it a notable presence in Minnesota. But serious trouble was brewing at the company. The average price of its stock, just under $28 a share in 1989, would tumble below $13 by 1993 and it wouldn't get back above its 1989 price until 1996.[7]

This 1972 aerial photo shows the size of the IBM plant on the north edge of Rochester, Minnesota, and the surrounding farmland at that time. Vincent H. Mart photo. Photo courtesy of the Minnesota Historical Society.

In his annual letter to Growth Fund shareholders In February of 1990, George III looked back on the 1980s as an historic time: Federal corporate and personal income tax rates had been sharply reduced; Paul Volcker and the Federal Reserve had tamed inflation; the fall of the Iron Curtain had opened much of the world to market-oriented policies. "Relaxation of political tension between the East and West will result in a reduction of federal defense outlays and the freeing up of people and capacity for more productive use," he predicted.

DESELLIER LEAVES

Early in 1992, on Valentine's Day, Ron DeSellier resigned. It was a Friday afternoon. He left his resignation letter on the desks of his two partners, George Mairs III and George Power. In his letter, he said he would remain at the firm until June 30, if they so requested, to help with the transition to his successor. George Power took him to lunch a few days later and asked him to stay until then, and he did. DeSellier's stake in the firm had grown to 43.1 percent by February 14, but the other two partners had control. George Mairs held a 44.4 percent stake; George Power had 11.1 percent (Kathy Kellerman held the remaining 1.4 percent).

The run-up to DeSellier's resignation was not amicable. In emails for this project, he said his concerns had been building as he paid more attention to the need for the firm to adhere more closely to the growing number of rules and regulations. He described some of this problem as perhaps common to businesspeople who had built their careers in small, private offices and were of a generation less inclined to take compliance matters as seriously as he did (George Mairs and George Power were 13 and 26 years older than he was). But despite such caveats, he came to see his partners' approach to compliance processes as not rigorous enough.

DeSellier envisioned two career paths open to him. One would have been to eventually run the firm; the other to leave with a nest-egg he had been building up for years and become a free spirit. By early 1992, with tensions mounting after several disagreements between him and his partners, he decided, in his words, "to walk away." The minutes of the firm's June 30 board meeting, attended by all three partners, said only that DeSellier had resigned, effective July 1, and that Bill Frels had been hired to succeed him as secretary and assistant treasurer, also effective July 1. We don't know George Mairs III's side of the story, or George Power's, since they left no record of their role in DeSellier's departure.[8]

Then DeSellier retired. In an email, he said he was fortunate to leave when he did, despite all the successes the firm has had since he left. His first wife died in 2004. He remarried in 2007, has homes in Oregon and Arizona, travels often, maintains many good friendships, and is financially secure. "A man is a success if when he gets up in the morning and when he gets to bed at night, in between he does whatever he wants," he said, quoting a friend from Hibbing.

THE RISE OF PERSONAL FINANCE JOURNALISM

During the 1980s, financial media outlets came to play a far greater role in the mutual fund industry and the broader investment world. Under-appreciated at the time, this shift ultimately led to much more emphasis on performance. It became a change that Mairs & Power had to learn to live with.

In 1972, Time Inc. launched *Money Magazine.* Financial journalist Joe Nocera noted that initially, the magazine had little impact. Instead of focusing on money, it functioned as a toned-down version of *Consumer Reports*, publishing annual ratings of automobiles, comparing vacation spots, and warning about defective products. The magazine had difficulty finding its niche, but as the 1980s dawned and money market funds boomed, stories about handling money began to appear more often. Many publications joined the rush into personal finance journalism, with *Money* leading the way.[9]

In 1980, Marshall Loeb took over as *Money's* editor. "When the bull market came along two and a half years into his tenure, Loeb could scarcely contain himself," Nocera wrote. "Covering a roaring bull market is a little like covering a baseball team on a winning streak; the mood becomes so infectious that even the most objective reporter is bound to get a little jazzed-up about the goings-on. The bull market meshed perfectly with Loeb's own natural optimism."

On the magazine's tenth anniversary, in October 1982, Loeb pointed out that adjusted for inflation, the Dow Jones Industrials had fallen 60 percent since 1972. It was time to buy stocks. Loeb urged Americans to

do so, particularly by investing in equity mutual funds, and they did. As he would later note, the stock market soared, quadrupling its value from August 1982 to May 1994. Nocera criticized Loeb as a relentless cheerleader for stocks who downplayed the risks of investing in them, but he conceded that Loeb had been remarkably successful in turning the magazine into a money machine for Time Inc.

Much of the increased coverage in 1980s focused on top-performing fund managers. Peter Lynch, who led Fidelity's highly successful Magellan Fund from 1977 to 1990, built perhaps the highest profile of any of these managers. Lynch won an enormous following. His two books, *One Up on Wall Street* (1989) and *Beating the Street* (1992), were best-sellers.[10]

MORNINGSTAR BECOMES A FORCE

The 1980s also saw the birth, in 1984, of Morningstar Inc., the publisher of a newsletter that grew with the fund industry to become perhaps the most widely watched independent source of information for financial journalists and investors following mutual funds. Today, the firm administers $244 billion, has diversified into a wide array of financial services, and operates in 29 countries. Morningstar started writing about the Growth Fund in 1995 and began giving it analyst ratings in 2013. It sells an app that enables investors to follow Mairs &

Power's mutual funds, as well as hundreds of others. Morningstar became famous for its concise, one-page summaries of mutual funds: their asset breakdowns, turnover, expense ratios, and other data, notably including a star system rating the funds' performance in a manner mindful of the stars awarded by restaurant or movie critics.[11] The Investment Company Institute's Matt Fink noted while Morningstar maintained that its stars were not intended to be buy and sell recommendations, many investors came to see them that way.[12]

Fink recalled that the fund industry had sought more media coverage for decades, with limited success. "By the early 1990s, the fund industry, due to its size (in 1993, $2 trillion in assets) and visibility, found itself in a totally different situation," he wrote. "There was heavy media coverage every day. The few reporters with experience covering mutual funds were suddenly outnumbered by rookies. Editors and reporters were particularly fascinated by the industry's claim that it had avoided major scandal. Each wanted to be the first to uncover and expose a critical flaw." In 1994, Fink asked veteran mutual-fund reporter Tom Petruno of the *Los Angeles Times* why news coverage of the fund industry had become so harsh and intense. "Matt, I can tell you in three words—$2 trillion dollars," Petruno replied.[13]

Thus, the media-saturated, performance-driven, growth-oriented environment that would now describe the playing field for the mutual fund industry had arrived. As Mairs & Power moved more deeply into the stages of its journey dominated by George Mairs III, he and the firm, which had always judiciously avoided the fishbowl, would soon be in it.

CHAPTER 8

From Anonymity to Celebrity

The financial universe was exploding as Mairs & Power moved into the 1990s. Globally, investors were engaging across national borders as never before celebrating the fall of the Berlin Wall, the break-up of the Soviet Union, the rise of containerized shipping across the seas, stronger global supply lines, and growing ties with China's exploding economy. In Europe, the Common Market held great promise; capital and expertise were pouring into the former Soviet Bloc countries. Many of them would soon be sharing a common currency. Financial historian John Steele Gordon estimated that by 1995, nearly 3,000 overseas phone calls were originated in the U.S. for every single call made in 1950. Computers, not human beings, were making most of these calls to other computers, instantly transferring massive amounts of data, and assets, back and forth around the world.[1]

Globalization helped Mairs & Power by benefiting the stocks of the successful, increasingly worldly Minnesota companies in its portfolios: 3M, Medtronic, Ecolab, Donaldson, and others. By the mid-1990s, 40 percent of the companies in the Growth Fund derived at least a third of their revenues from abroad. Yet in 1992, Mairs & Power was still an almost invisible dot on America's financial map—a local company with five-sixths of the $256 million it managed in separately managed accounts of Minnesota-based union pension funds, institutional specialty funds, high net-worth individuals and families, and a scattering of other institutional clients. The firm had just eight employees. Even in the financial community, it was nearly unknown beyond St. Paul.

By 1994, the Growth Fund had doubled its assets to $41.9 million from $20.6 million in 1988, but the mutual fund industry was growing even more rapidly. Over the same period, total fund assets rose

The co-inventor of Post-It Notes, 3M scientist Art Fry, stands in front of a billboard advertising the Notes near I-94 in 1989. 3M scientist Spencer Silver formulated the low-tack adhesive in 1966 used on the Notes, but until Fry came up with a use for this adhesive, 3M had a "solution in search of a problem." The national sales release of Post-it Notes occurred in April 1980 and they quickly became a best seller among office products. Rita Reed photo, copyright *Star Tribune,* 1990.

to $2.15 trillion from $809.4 billion, with the number of funds rising to 5,324 from 2,737. Earlier, insurers and securities firms had moved into the mutual fund business. Now the banks were there, too. By the early 1990s, they were managing 10 percent of all mutual fund assets.

One route into the money management business, or to expand if a firm was already in it, was to buy an enterprise already in the field. Smaller entities, such as Mairs & Power, were plentiful and often sought out. One of the potential suitors was the Resource Trust

This is the first Target store, which was in the St. Paul suburb of Roseville. Prominently displayed in this 1963 photo is Target's original logo, now long forgotten. Norton & Peel photo. Photo courtesy of the Minnesota Historical Society.

Company, owned by Conley Brooks Jr., a successful Minneapolis businessman. Over lunch with George Mairs III, Brooks explored the idea of buying Mairs & Power. Ron DeSellier described that effort and others as among the many "feelers" that came the firm's way. He identified IDS and Chicago-based Stein Roe & Farnham among the other parties interested in buying Mairs & Power. Nothing had come of any of the feelers. George III, the largest owner of Mairs & Power stock, simply didn't want to sell his firm.[2]

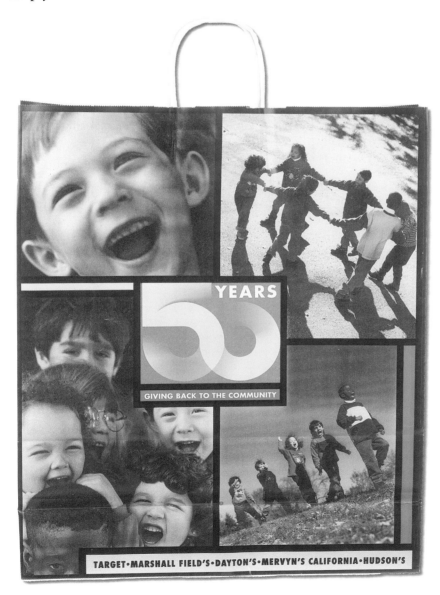

Consolidation in ownership of bricks-and-mortar department stores occurred in the 1990s. This shopping bag for Target, Marshall Field's Dayton's, Mervyn's California, and Hudson's, which were at one time all owned by the Dayton Hudson Corporation, epitomized this trend in retailing. Later Macy's bought Dayton's in 2006. Photo courtesy of the Minnesota Historical Society.

George Mairs III: Deliberate, Unpretentious

George Mairs III's first car, a vintage-1920s Chevrolet, would only turn right. A few weeks after he acquired the vehicle, most likely in 1944, he sold it for about $20 to a buyer who apparently took the car for its parts. That experience sparked a smoldering love affair with automobiles that burned on for the rest of his days. So it went with stocks, too, ever since his boyhood days when his father gave him a share of Goodyear stock. Late in 1951, when he was 23 years old, he joined the investment firm his father had founded. His initial salary was $180 a month—the same amount, he recalled years later, that trainees at the First National Bank of St. Paul were then being paid. He went on to place stock-picking at the center of his 58-year career in investing and lead the firm from obscurity into the national spotlight.[3]

He was "George" to his partners at work; "Mr. Mairs" to the rest of the staff there; and "Geordie" to immediate family members. Some said he had the magic touch— an idiosyncratic, almost mystical sense, in his most successful years, of how to assemble a package of equities that would invariably gain considerable value over long stretches. Mark Henneman, Mairs & Power's current CEO, made a priority of figuring out how he did it. Soon after he joined the firm in 2004, Henneman began closeting himself in George's cubicle—a nondescript office about the size of a standard kitchenette—to gain a better understanding of his special style of investing. Eventually, Henneman would put it into words, in a manner that could be passed on to the firm's growing number of analysts and portfolio managers.[4]

"I had the opportunity to spend hundreds of hours with him learning the recipe to that secret sauce," Henneman said. George made mistakes, as do all investment professionals, but he didn't dwell on them. He could be impatient, even prickly. One day, Henneman could see it coming and left George's office after about 30 seconds. Yet experiencing such moments seemed a small price to pay in exchange for an inspiring engagement that would run on for four years. "It was a relationship I absolutely cherish," Henneman said. "I sat at the feet of the master. When you look at the heart of what Mairs & Power does, it's really George's style."

Chip Emery, who was the CEO at MTS Systems, a stock the Growth Fund held for many years, remembers George for his ability to draw out information that mattered. "He would ask, 'What's your vision for MTS for the next five years? How are you going to grow without making big acquisitions? Why didn't you get into this or that?' They were always good business questions. He would tell me, 'Well, I don't think that's right thing to do, Chip, but you're the CEO.' Or if he felt we were doing the right thing, he'd validate it. He was probing without being a jerk. He looked for good companies that were run by people who knew what they were doing.[5]

"I wish I could remember all the stories that guy knew. He just knew everybody. He was a treasure chest of information about the movers and shakers and some who weren't moving and shaking as much as you thought they were."

Rejecting Showiness, Embracing Thrift

Stories abound about George's aversion to showy amenities and his thriftiness. He avoided first-class flights unless he got a bargain upgrade. He lived in unpretentious apartments and, for the last 28 years of his life, in a modest suburban townhouse. Once, one of his best friends, Jim Johnson, an actuary at Minnesota Mutual (now Securian Financial) in St. Paul, invited him and his wife, Dusty, to dinner at a fancy restaurant. George turned down the invitation. "He said, 'Oh Jim, that's way too expensive for me,'" Johnson recalled. George was frugal, sometimes to a fault. After secretaries took paper-clipped wads of bills to the bank for deposit, they brought the paper clips back to the office.[6]

George Ficocello, who had barber shops in downtown St. Paul for 40 years, was George's lifetime barber starting in the early 1970s. "He never tipped me once until Dusty got hold of him," Ficocello said. That didn't happen until the mid-1990s, when she asked her husband how much of a tip he was planning to give his barber at Christmas. "Nothing," he replied. She advised him to change his practices. He did,

When George Mairs III was in fourth grade in 1937, he completed this page of long division problems as part of his education in arithmetic. Photo courtesy of the Mairs family.

giving Ficocello a $100 Christmas tip that year. George was a minimalist in his tastes for apparel and furniture, preferring fewer rather than many clothes and opting for the sleek functionalism of Scandinavian tables and chairs. Ficocello said it seemed as though he always wore the same sports jacket, almost like a uniform.[7]

His deep knowledge of the history of St. Paul enabled him to discuss the lives of countless people identified on gravestones as he strolled through the city's Oakland Cemetery with Dusty and to give his children chapter and verse on historic sites as he ushered them along the sidewalks of downtown St. Paul. Yet he left only sparse records of his own achievements. He turned down a request from the Ramsey County Historical Society for an interview. He was a judicious eater, slim and trim and known in downtown business circles for his "chicken soup lunches" where that was all he had for lunch. There was a reason for that. He had a digestive condition that led his doctor to recommend that he limit his dietary choices.

George had a very high regard for his father, George Jr. He called him almost every evening after his mother, Louise, died in 1981, until his dad passed on two years later. During this period, George and Dusty took his father out to dinner once a week. George once told Mark Henneman that "my dad created the company out of nothing. I could never have done that." But there were differences. His father was a golfing devotee, a regular at the Somerset Country Club in Mendota Heights. His son never touched a golf club. Instead, he played tennis, and never joined Somerset even though he and Dusty lived just five blocks from the club. "Why join?" he would say, "The dues are expensive, and I don't golf." George Jr. played bridge; his son didn't. George Jr. spent the early years of his career specializing in bonds. His son was unshakably committed to stocks for his entire career. Still, they shared much more, most of all an uninterrupted, lasting devotion to their firm and families, deep commitments to Macalester College, and their incurable passions for cars.

The children of the blended Mairs family in about 1943, left to right, back row, George III, Nancy, Bobby, and front row, Teedie, Angus, and Jean. Photo courtesy of the Mairs family.

Straight Talker

While many remember George for his kind and gentlemanly manner, he could be firm if he felt the situation called for such an approach. Jim Johnson recalls the time when the head of a sizable non-profit (a major beneficiary of George's largesse) was skeptical about the advice he had been getting from a well-paid consultant. He invited George to a meeting to evaluate the consultant's work. Point by point, George discredited his work. "George absolutely demolished the consultant," Johnson said. "I've never seen anything quite like it." Soon after the meeting, the consultant was let go.

George sometimes acted on firmly held beliefs, such as his disdain for excessively well-paid CEOs. UnitedHealth Group's culture of consistently granting huge paydays to its top executives led George to keep that company's promising stock out of the Growth Fund. After he died, the Fund added UnitedHealth. "He told me many stories about companies he would not invest in because the CEO was too generous to himself and not to other people in the company," Johnson said.

George was an insatiable reader, known for his command of a wide range of topics, his witticisms, and his quick, wry sense of humor. His Saturday afternoon walks with longtime friend Neal Sedgwick became a neighborhood legend in Mendota Heights. Sedgwick would sometimes bring a paper bag stuffed with news clippings that they would then hash over, within earshot of nearby residents, as they strolled along Dodd Road. In later years, George's son, Todd, would join them. "That's how I learned about business and investing," Todd said.

George saved newspapers and magazines. When he and Dusty moved to their Mendota Heights townhouse shortly after they were married, he made several trips back to his apartment in St. Paul to

transport them to his new residence. In 2008, shortly before Thanksgiving, when the stock market was close to its bottom during the financial crisis, Mairs & Power marked the 50th anniversary of the Growth Fund with a glitzy celebration at St. Paul's Town & Country Club. George asked not to speak, but he was introduced as he sat on a ledge near the fireplace of the club's main banquet room. "I'm over here on the ledge, but I'm not jumping off," he quipped. The audience, packed with Growth Fund shareholders, advisory clients, and friends of the firm, exploded with laughter.[8]

Why So Much on This George?

George Mairs III gets particular attention in this history partly because he passed on in 2010, 27 years after his father's death and 15 years after George Power died. More people are around today who remember him. Also, the era when he was in his prime at Mairs & Power—in his view from 1984 to 2004, when he led the Growth Fund through a period of immense growth—was neatly sliced in half in 1994 by the revelation of George's successful record in running the Fund. It was like B.C. and A.D. The first 10 years of this period were the silent decade, when the firm was a small, almost anonymous entity. The Georges preferred privacy then, and before, and that's what they got. The only news coverage Mairs & Power received before 1994 came in the form of "fillers," a few sentences squirreled away next to the stock market tables at the back end of the local dailies' business sections.

The high school graduation photo of George Mairs III. Photo courtesy of the Mairs family.

Much was starting to change at Mairs & Power as George gradually opened up to the media and hired trusted professionals less inclined toward privacy than either he or the other two Georges had been. George did not solicit the attention of media outlets to start reporting, late in 1994, about the success of the Growth Fund. They discovered him and the Fund. He instinctively preferred to hold onto elements of the privacy that had been so much a part of him, preserving little about himself or Mairs & Power except for the reports the firm was required to file with regulatory agencies. But once financial journalists began calling, he obliged, giving them many interviews. They responded, sometimes with splashy coverage.

George became the go-to source to explain the rise of Mairs & Power. His stock-picking savvy was providing good copy with newsworthy twists: his buy-and-hold style, a focus on Minnesota stocks, low fees, and the firm's culture of frugality. Dusty Mairs saved these stories in a scrapbook that grew to become two inches thick. The Growth Fund's assets would soar to $2.06 billion at the end of 2004 from $17.3 million in 1984. Speaking invitations rolled in from a parade of Twin Cities organizations—the Chartered Financial Analysts, the Executive Women International, the American Association of Individual Investors, the Yale Alumni Association, the Minnesota Club. George could address many topics: the history of St. Paul and its leaders, the stock market, the economic outlook, and of course, automobiles (particularly classic cars), and, if need be, how to change a tire.

He never missed the annual auto show in Minneapolis, but mostly he went to look at cars rather than buy them. Sometime around the early 1980s, he cooled on Buicks, donating his trove of brochures about them to the Buick Club of America, and settled in to buy a new Honda every two years. He gave the old one to a family member. Eventually, as many as half a dozen or more Hondas could be seen parked near family gatherings. This may have seemed odd since he could easily

George Mairs III kept his pocket calendars with his appointments for nearly every year between 1969 and 2009. Photo courtesy of the Mairs family.

afford more expensive cars, but Hondas apparently suited George because they were modest, utilitarian cars built to last. Meanwhile, back at the firm, it was George who took on the primary responsibility of building the firm to last. He enabled Mairs & Power to make the transition from family ownership to a steadily widening roster of professionals and administrators at the firm by working with others there to craft a plan to gradually sell Mairs & Power stock to insiders for a notably lower price than he could have fetched by selling out to outsiders—a move that would have spelled the end of independence for the firm.

Growing Up

George Mairs III arrived on the planet on June 15, 1928. He was the second-born of the four children from his father's first marriage to Jean McLeod. In May 1938, 18 months after Jean died, his father remarried. His second wife, Louise Ritchie Power, had two children, one older and one younger than George. She had lost her first husband, also due to an early death. Shortly after the two households merged, George showed his entrepreneurial bent, at age 10. He won a spiffy new bicycle, smartly outfitted with balloon tires and shiny silver fenders, by selling subscriptions to the *St. Paul Daily News*. He developed his passion for cars by memorizing all the makes and models, from his perches on a couch in the family living room or from his third-floor bedroom window, as motorists passed by on St. Paul's Summit Avenue. Years later, at a St. Paul

YMCA camp, he gave his rowing mate, Don Mains, a lesson in seamanship when they scrambled into their canoe. George quickly settled into the stern of the canoe. "I didn't realize that you worked harder in the bow, where you had to paddle all the time," Mains said. "George was smart enough to get in the stern. I was in the bow." About 15 years later, Tradehome Shoes, the Mains family company, became one of Mairs & Power's earliest institutional clients.[9]

In 1946, George graduated from St. Paul Academy, where he had formed lifelong friendships with some of his fellow students. He had been the business editor of "Now and Then," a student publication at SPA. Then it was off to Yale University for college, but soon he transferred to Macalester, where he graduated in 1950 with a Bachelor of Arts degree. Soon after the Korean War broke out, the army drafted him. After serving at Fort Leonard Wood in Missouri, he was discharged in the fall of 1951. Late that year, he joined his father's firm. Two years later, he was named a partner and given a 15 percent stake in the firm, soon to grow to 33 percent. A few years later, as mutual funds were starting to pop up around the country, he was among those who persuaded his father to launch the Growth Fund.[10]

In 1961, George got married. He and his wife, Nancy, had two children, Todd and Ann. Their marriage ended with a divorce in 1965. He continued to be a loving, supportive, and generous father and today, his children are part of an extended Mairs family that has grown to

Dusty, left, and George Mairs III in the 1980s. Photo courtesy of the Mairs family.

more than 50 children, grandchildren, great-grandchildren, nieces and nephews, brothers-in-law, and sisters-in-law. George taught finance courses for many years as an adjunct faculty member at the University of Minnesota. In 1980, he was named president at Mairs & Power. Two years later, he and Dusty, who had known one another for years through her church, St. John the Evangelist Episcopal in St. Paul, were married. At first, they rotated their places to worship, going to her church one Sunday and his, House of Hope Presbyterian, the next. Eventually, George decided to switch to St. John's, breaking from a long-standing Mairs family tradition of being members at House of Hope.

Recasting Firm, Giving Away Wealth

During his long tenure at the helm of the firm, Mairs & Power reshaped itself. Over that stretch, its two mutual funds' share of the overall assets managed by the firm rose from about 20 percent to 57 percent. The Growth Fund's surge drove this shift. The increase in the firm's separately managed accounts also grew, just not nearly as rapidly as the mutual funds' assets. By 2004, seven partners had stakes in Mairs & Power, up from three in 1984. By mid-2021, the

ownership had spread to 16 employees. Long before he died, George gave away much of his personal wealth, largely to institutions in St. Paul. His two largest beneficiaries were Macalester and the Wilder Foundation.

At Macalester, the Mairs Concert Hall, one the most striking of such venues in the Twin Cities, was named in honor of George, Dusty, and George's parents. At Wilder, George became the leading benefactor in a major fund drive that enabled it to sustain and move forward on a sweeping makeover that included sales of many properties, spinoffs, consolidations, construction of a modern headquarters, and a shift from government grants, which were declining, to significant new funding from private donors. George remained in the background as a silent benefactor, even declining to go on Wilder's board. Tom Kingston, who was Wilder's CEO from 1990 to 2010, said he first got to know George in about 2004. At an early meeting, George startled him with his knowledge of Wilder's century-old history—he knew more about that than Kingston did. (Shortly before he died, George asked Kingston to deliver one of the two eulogies at his funeral service; Jon Theobald, who later would become the firm's CEO, was the other eulogist.)[11]

George gave annually to the United Theological Seminary of the Twin Cities and received its Joshua Society Award for cumulative giving. Other beneficiaries of his giving included the St. Paul Chamber Orchestra (he was the orchestra's third president, and a connoisseur of classical music), St. John the Evangelist Episcopal and House of Hope churches, Presbyterian Homes, the Union Gospel Mission, the St. Paul Area Council of Churches, the Indian Head Council of the Boy Scouts, the Como Park Zoo, the Ramsey County Historical Society, the Minnesota Medical Association, and Planned Parenthood. In 2002, the Boy Scouts honored him with their Community Builder Award, which typically goes to governors, mayors, and other high-profile leaders.

George Mairs III in the 1990s. Photo courtesy of Mairs & Power.

In 2004, Dusty and George endowed the Mairs Family Chair at the University of Minnesota. The chair supports the Musculoskeletal Bone and Soft Tissue Tumor Center in the University's Department of Orthopedic Surgery. Dr. Edward Cheng, who was George's specialist, has held the chair since it was established. Cheng said that for some time after George became his patient, around 2000, "I had no idea who he was." They had never discussed financial matters. He only learned about George's career after coming across an article about him in a financial magazine. "He was as humble as any individual I've ever known," Cheng said. Eventually, George mentioned that he wanted to contribute to Cheng's research. Cheng referred George's proposal to officials at the school's foundation. Following established policies, the officials asked Cheng to meet with George to discuss a gift. He was uneasy about the suggestion but raised the matter over lunch with George. "I was nervous," he said. The foundation, working with George, took it from there.[12]

In 2010, George died at home, 18 days before his 82nd birthday. After he passed on, the condolences stressed his generosity and stewardship, his love of history, his humility and unpretentious manner, his commitment to family, his frugality, and his intellect and wit. One commentator said she didn't know of anyone else who could capture the attention of a three-year-old grandson by reading the *Wall Street Journal* to him. Many recalled his lifelong passion for automobiles.

One of the most moving tributes came from his doctor. "As a physician, I was accustomed to being the caregiver yet George, in his own unique way, completely turned this around," Dr. Cheng wrote. "I became impressed that someone would take such an active interest in caring about me. He was fortunate to have a powerful intellect and as an articulate speaker, it was evident that he used it widely. I sensed that his diligence played a role in developing his strong character, organizational skills, and work ethic. What I ardently admired was the fact that despite these qualities, he remained a patient, caring, and humble person who was loath to draw attention to himself."[13]

Mairs & Powers investment professionals and outside, independent mutual fund trustees paused one of their meetings for this photo that was probably taken in the fall of 1994. The back row, left to right, is Bill Frels, Don Garretson, George Mairs III, and Peter Robb. In the front row are George C. Power Jr., Litton Field, and Tom Simonet. The outside trustees at that time were Garretson, Field, and Simonet. Photo courtesy of Mairs & Power.

Immediately after Ron DeSellier left in mid-1992, George III began working with his successor, Bill Frels. Here was a long-familiar face in the Twin Cities investment community. Frels began his career at the First National Bank of Minneapolis in 1962 and worked at First Trust Company in St. Paul for nearly two decades. He took over the Balanced Fund (formerly the Income Fund, which was renamed in 1997), over-saw administrative work, and started building a stake in the firm.

In April 1994, Frels recruited Peter Robb, who had worked with him at First Trust, in large part to take over the separately managed accounts that George Power had handled for decades. It had been a months-long courtship. Robb wanted to stay at First Trust long enough to get his bonus and he was uneasy about leaving the security of a large, established organization for the uncertainties of tiny Mairs & Power, but in the end, he concluded that it was a risk worth taking. "When Bill hired me, he said we have a diamond in the rough that needs some polishing," Robb said.

LAGS IN APPLYING TECHNOLOGY

Robb was surprised by his new employer's slow embrace of technology. Back-office workers were still using an adding machine for various data tabulation tasks then, including to record securities trades and then to post the data manually in ledgers. "I felt I had gone back to the '50s," Robb said. "I just couldn't believe it." Then again, he noted that "there weren't a lot of trades," given the firm's unusual preference for holding securities over long periods. And both George Mairs III and George Power were older, and thus came from a less tech-savvy generation than Robb and his contemporaries. More up-to-date equipment would soon replace the adding machines at Mairs & Power.

Robb's heavy engagement in dealing with the separately managed accounts led him to advocate for centralizing the arrangements for designating custodians for these accounts. As many as 20 outside firms were acting as custodians—brokerage firms or banks that held clients' securities for safekeeping to prevent them from been stolen or lost—for these accounts. Often, the custodians were Wall Street brokerage firms that provided free securities research to Mairs & Power in return for getting its custodian and brokerage business. George III valued that research, but Robb felt the brokerage firms were charging too much in trading commissions and that it would be better to have just one custodian as opposed to many.[14]

Enter Charles Schwab and Company. Schwab was a leading discount brokerage firm that had benefited immensely from the federal government's move in 1975 to force Wall Street to abandon its 183-year-old practice of charging fixed commissions for securities trades (today, Schwab is the third largest asset manager in the world). Robb pushed to consolidate much of the custodian business with Schwab. Frels supported Robb. Eventually, most the firm's separately managed accounts had Schwab as custodian.

As all of this was playing out, the performance of the Growth Fund was laying the groundwork for sweeping changes at Mairs & Power. By the end of 1995, the Fund's assets would reach $70.5 million, twice what they had been just three years earlier. The Fund would soon reap rewards from the soaring values of the Minnesota stocks that dominated its portfolio. In his annual letter reviewing the Fund's performance for 1994, George III reported that CDA/Wiesenberger, which tracked mutual funds' performance, had ranked the Growth Fund as the 21st best among 289 long-term growth funds for the previous five years. George also noted in his letter that *Forbes* and *Kiplinger's Personal Finance* magazines had both featured the Fund's

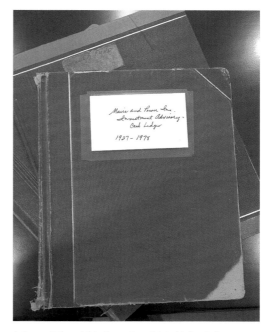

A few of the old ledgers in which Mairs & Power recorded by hand its financial transactions are still part of the firm's archives. Photo courtesy of Mairs & Power.

Peter Robb, one of the investment professionals at Mairs & Power. He is now retired. Photo courtesy of Peter Robb.

Born in 1937, Charles R. Schwab is the founder and chairman of the Charles Schwab Corporation. Schwab began his career in financial services as a traditional stockbroker, but in 1975 his firm introduced discount sales of equity securities. Also credited with emphasizing the use of technology, particularly computers, to replace handwritten financial records and execute trades, the Schwab Corporation became a registered member of the New York Stock Exchange in 1981. Bettmann photo, Getty Images.

strong performance, modest expense ratio, and low portfolio turnover in articles published just weeks earlier.

MEDIA DELUGE BEGINS

George himself had not sought out such attention. Seeking publicity was not in his DNA. But by now, following mutual funds had grown from just another niche of financial journalism to a cottage industry. Whenever a well-performing fund popped up out of nowhere, particularly one with such unusual characteristics as the Growth Fund, financial journalists would rush to cover it, often with splashy stories. Jason Zweig, then a journalist at *Forbes Magazine*, discovered the Fund's strong performance results in regulatory filings, sensed a good story, and came to St. Paul to interview George. The result was a story below a headline that described George's investing style as "Zen stock picking."

"George Mairs, 66, does things differently," Zweig told *Forbes* readers in the magazine's December 19, 1994, issue. "Mairs & Power Inc., founded by Mairs' father in 1931, has nine employees and runs a total of $300 million out of the old First National Bank Building in St. Paul, Minn. Nearly all that money is in separate accounts" [meaning accounts apart from the firm's two mutual funds].

Zweig explained that the Growth Fund owned just 28 companies, three-fourths of them within 20 miles of the Fund's office. "Mairs & Power Growth has a 4 percent portfolio turnover rate, meaning that it holds on to its average stock for an astonishing quarter of a century," he wrote. Then he quoted George: "It's a fluid portfolio. We sold IBM in 1989, and we've sold another two or three stocks since. Why, we even sold one earlier this year, Network Systems (a Twin Cities manufacturer of computer peripherals that had been in the Fund since 1986). Higher turnover just makes no sense to me. I don't know of anyone who would want to pay current taxes instead of deferred taxes." Zweig went on to note that the net asset value of a share of the Growth Fund had climbed to $39.94 from $21.52 per share over the past decade.

"At most high-turnover funds, even some with excellent results, the net asset value has barely budged because profits are dumped out on shareholders, who must pay capital gains taxes on them," Zweig

The November 2004 cover of *Barron's Mutual Funds* featuring George Mairs III in his office overlooking the Mississippi River in St. Paul. Steve Niedorf photo.

wrote. By holding instead of selling, he explained, George Mairs allows his gains to compound without the drag of taxation. Thinly staffed Mairs & Power is managed like a tortoise but runs like a hare, Zweig concluded.[15]

Fortune had weighed in, two months before the *Forbes* piece ran, with a shorter article that featured a chart based on data it had asked Morningstar to provide. The chart showed how "seven ships for calm and stormy seas" had fared during two "tough years" (1990 and 1994) and three "easy times" years (1991 through 1993). Mairs & Power was one of seven mutual funds in the chart. In the tough years, it had overall returns of 5.92 percent in 1990 and 3.55 percent in 1994 vs. 3.87 percent and -3.12 percent for the S&P 500. In the easy years, it had an overall return of 20.0 percent vs. 15.6 percent for the S&P.[16]

The *Fortune* story and the *Kiplinger's* piece came shortly before the *Forbes article,* but all three—notably Zweig's story—marked the first significant attention Mairs & Power had ever received from national financial news outlets. Soon the firm would be deluged with coverage from the armada of other publications now tracking mutual funds. Suddenly, Mairs & Power was being flooded with calls from potential customers across the country who had seen the stories about its performance. The firm was not staffed well enough to handle the heavy volume of calls. "It just kind of happened," said Peter Robb. His wife and relatives of other staffers came into the office for a mail-stuffing party to send prospectuses out to callers. "The phone was ringing off the hook," said staff member Michelle Lindenfelser. "Everything was still manual. There was so much to do. Half the calls we got, we had to say 'No, sorry we can't help you.'"[17]

That was because so many of the callers were from states where the Fund was not registered. The staffers and their friends took down the names of these callers and their states, so the firm could decide later whether to register its funds in those states. The Growth Fund was registered in just five states then—Minnesota, Wisconsin, Pennsylvania, New York, and California. Jason Zweig reported that George felt registering in every state would be too expensive and time-consuming.

The official scorecard for 1995 came early in 1996, in George's annual letter to Growth Fund shareholders. The Fund's total return for 1995 was 49.3 percent vs. 37.5 percent for the S&P and 36.9 percent for the Dow Industrials. A *Wall Street Journal* survey of fund performance for the year ranked the Growth Fund fifth out of 558 long-term growth funds. Wiesenberger had the Fund in 24th place among 312 long-term growth funds for the last five years and 19th out of 186 similar funds for the last ten years. *U.S. News & World Report* surveyed 692 long-term growth funds and found the Growth Fund in second place based on an overall performance index combining the past one-, three-, five-, and ten-year periods.

GEORGE POWER DIES

Both Mairs & Power mutual funds' reports for 1995 also noted the passing, in July of that year, of George Power. A eulogy below a half-page portrait of him recalled that his investment career spanned 62 years, from his summer job at the Northwestern National Bank in Minneapolis in 1933 to his death. "While he received many accolades along the way, he will best be remembered for his uncommon concern for all the people he knew and served during his long and fruitful career," the reports noted.

George Center Power Jr. in about 1970. Photo courtesy of the Power family.

In his summary of the Growth Fund's showing in 1996, George III described another blowout. The Fund's total return of 26.4 percent topped the S&P's 23.0 percent and for the prior three years, the Fund's average annual total return of 25.9 percent outdid the average long-term growth fund's 15.3 percent return. *The Wall Street Journal* and *Business Week* ranked the Fund as a top-tier stock fund performer over the last ten years and five years, respectively. *Kiplinger's Personal Finance Magazine* cited the Growth Fund as the only diversified stock fund to outperform the S&P in each of the past seven years. During 1996, the Fund's assets more than doubled, to $150.2 million.

George, who didn't particularly want to be bothered by the financial press—and he wasn't—before Jason Zweig and a few other journalists discovered him, was frequently fielding calls from them now. About the time he reported the Fund's 1996 numbers to its shareholders, he told *Smart Money* magazine that he had never bought an initial public offering for the Fund, but he conceded that he bought Twin Cities-based Deluxe, the check printer, just nine months after it went public in 1966. "But we had been familiar with the company for years from acquaintances we had in the company," he explained. The magazine went on to suggest that the Fund's only downside was that it was still registered in only 11 states. George countered that getting into more states wasn't worth the expense and regulatory hassle.[18]

The blistering pace of expansion at the Growth Fund continued in 1997 as its successes kept attracting more customers. That year, its assets rose to $412.6 million from $150.2 million, far outstripping the industry-wide gain. George reported that the Fund's total return that year was 28.7 percent, better than the 24.4 percent for the average diversified stock fund but below the S&P's 33.4 percent. In times of such fast-paced growth, deploying the new assets well and sustaining top performance can become problems, but a string of long-term comparisons continued to show superior performances by the Fund.

As the 1990s wound down, a muscular new source of business for Mairs & Power would surface outside of the funds, in the separately managed accounts. Clients of Minneapolis-based Dorsey & Whitney, Minnesota's largest law firm, felt they weren't being treated well enough by the big bank trust companies that were managing their money. This led the law firm to set up its own trust company, based in Sioux Falls, S.D. Some South Dakota banks opposed the move, but they lost a legal battle to block Dorsey from going ahead. Then Dorsey had to decide who would manage the money for trust clients who did not have an investment manager of their own choosing.

"I said, 'Let's try Mairs & Power,'" said Bob Struyk, a long-time partner at Dorsey, now retired, who headed the law firm's trust/estate business at the time. Mairs & Power won the business. Today, the Dorsey & Whitney Trust Company, an institutional client of Mairs & Power that represents the assets of many of the trust company's individual clients, is the largest of all of Mairs & Power's separately managed accounts. "We had no idea it would turn out to be so successful," Struyk said.[19]

MORE LEGENDARY MINNESOTA STOCKS

While some of the Growth Fund's standout Minnesota stocks first appeared in the Fund in the late 1960s, the 1990s saw George move into a trio of state-based companies—St. Jude Medical, Hormel, and Valspar—that would also generate significant gains for the Fund (see Table 1 in chapter 12). St. Jude, a pioneer in the development of artificial heart valves, ultimately became the most successful of the enterprises that were part of the innovative cluster of medical device companies founded by former Medtronic employees. Hormel, a pure commodity producer passed up by investors for decades, adroitly transitioned into a producer of branded, value-added food products sold to consumers in 80 countries.[20]

Valspar, founded in 1806 as a paint dealership in Boston, became a Minnesota company in 1970 when it merged with the Wurtele family's Minnesota Paints and moved its headquarters from Massachusetts to Minneapolis. Then a small family firm, Valspar grew to become the world's sixth largest paint company with sales of $4.4 billion in 2016. St. Jude and Valspar were both sold in 2017. Abbott Laboratories bought St. Jude for $25 billion; Sherwin-Williams acquired Valspar for $11 billion.[21]

Entrepreneur Manny Villafaña, who had been a sales representative for Medtronic in Argentina, founded St. Jude in May 1976 and took it public nine months later. After he left Medtronic, he won widespread acclaim for his success at Twin Cities-based Cardiac Pacemakers Inc. (CPI). Villafaña founded CPI in 1972 and took it public a few months later. In 1978, Eli Lilly and Co. acquired CPI for $127 million.

For years, St. Jude had been unable to win approval from the Food and Drug Administration to market its heart valves in the U.S. It had widespread regulatory approvals to sell the valves abroad—enough to capture a 24 percent share of international heart valve sales by 1982. In July 1983, Piper Jaffray analyst Elizabeth Elder noted that St. Jude had finally won FDA approval for commercialization. Based largely on that development, she predicted that St. Jude would capture a 20 percent share of the U.S. valve market by the end of 1983.

For various reasons, though, the stock had a rough year; George passed on buying it. By the end of 1990, the company's market value had climbed to $2.4 billion; it had become the ninth most valuable

The Valspar manufacturing plant in downtown Minneapolis in 1975. Steven W. Plattner photo. Photo courtesy of the Minnesota Historical Society.

With a model of a human heart in the foreground, medical device pioneer Manny Villanafaña displays an artificial heart valve engineered by St. Jude Medical, a Minnesota company he founded in 1976. Tom Sweeney photo, *Star Tribune*, 1994.

company based in Minnesota. George took a pass again. By the end of 1992, shortly after the Growth Fund added St. Jude, the company's value had fallen off to $1.4 billion. Then, the Fund, following its "buy and hold" strategy, bought more of the stock and kept building up its holding. And the stock kept on rising.

George began accumulating Hormel stock in 1995, a move widely seen at least initially as contrarian. Even then, some still knew the company best for its Spam, a pork product often served to GIs during World War II. Spam was lampooned by satirist Monty Python and the name has taken an omnipresence now as the word used to describe unwanted e-mails.

Hormel, headquartered in rural Austin, Minnesota had been relegated to obscurity by large parts of the investment community, partly because almost half of its stock was (and still is) in hands of a foundation established many years ago by Hormel. Yet Hormel went on to make the Growth Fund's annual list of its top 10 holdings five times

Famous for its 12-ounce tin with rounded corners, blue label, and yellow lettering, the SPAM can in this photo is actually a coin bank that was produced in 1982 when the Geo. A. Hormel Company celebrated the opening of a new plant in Austin, Minn. Photo courtesy of the Minnesota Historical Society.

since 1995. The Fund still owned 2.29 million shares of Hormel stock worth $106.7 million at the end of 2020. In 1983, the market valued Hormel at $269 million; in 1992, $1.7 billon; in 2021, $25.6 billion.[22]

The Fund first bought Valspar stock in 1999, and steadily increased its stake in the company to the point where it became the Fund's largest holding in 2012. Valspar had 25 factories on four continents when Sherwin-Williams acquired it. Angus Wurtele, who died in 2017, began working at Minnesota Paints in 1961 and was Valspar's CEO from 1973 until 1998. Wurtele was widely known for his philanthropy, most notably his support of the Walker Art Center and the Guthrie Theater.

Born in Minneapolis, C. Angus Wurtele (1934–2017) spent his entire business career at Valspar. He began working there in 1961, became president and CEO in 1965, and retired as chairman of the board in 2000. Regene Radniecki photo, *Star Tribune*, 1984.

WORKING THROUGH THE DOT-COM BUBBLE

The stock market of the late 1990s became known for the dot-coms—companies that did most of their business on the Internet, typically through the World Wide Web. Technology stocks saw mind-boggling run-ups. From 1995 to early 2000, the Nasdaq composite index, heavily weighted with technology stocks, rose 400 percent to 5,049. Many of the dot-coms pursued rapid sales gains while never becoming profitable. They attracted rampant speculation—until they didn't. The bubble burst after March 10, 2000, when the Nasdaq Composite peaked. By October 2002, in the wake of the dot-com crash, the Nasdaq index had fallen to 1,114. Novelist Gertrude Stein's famous quote, "There is no there there," aptly seemed to apply to many of the dot-coms, as did the wry observation of legendary investor Warren Buffett: "When the tide goes out, you see who has been swimming naked."[23]

George shunned these stocks, explaining that he didn't want to buy companies he couldn't understand. Instead, he stressed his preference for companies, such as Target, that were benefiting from applications of Internet-related technologies. But for a time, the rush of investors into the dot-coms left the Growth Fund lagging behind the major indexes. In 1998, the Fund reported a total return of 9.4 percent while the S&P's comparable return was 28.7 percent. The gap grew in 1999, with the Growth Fund's return slipping to 7.2 percent vs. 21.0 percent for the S&P. Bloomberg reported that the Fund's 1999 return was worse than 94 percent of similar funds. Critics jabbed at Mairs & Power, saying it was missing out on the dot-coms and the "New Economy" they represented.

Bill Frels in 2003. Photo courtesy of Mairs & Power.

Bill Frels had been named co-manager of the Growth Fund late in 1999. George was working much more closely with Frels now. In 2000, a bear market took hold as the dot-coms and other technology stocks crashed. That year, the Fund's return rebounded to 26.5 percent, far outdoing the S&P's negative return of -9.1 percent. The collapse of the tech stocks helped the Fund, which stood out because it had stayed away from those issues while many funds had embraced them. Four of the Fund's Minnesota companies were sold for cash in 2000, boosting the Fund's return. This was an unusually volatile year for the Fund, which had a turnover rate of 15 percent. That was still stunningly low by the standards of the fund industry, but it marked the first time since 1981 that this measure had topped 6 percent.

As the dot-coms reeled, the Fund's gains continued through 2001 and 2002. It easily outperformed the S&P in both years. Investors reacted by pouring more money into the Fund. In 2003, its assets rose from $850 million to $1.31 billion; in 2004, they shot up to $2.1 billion. Financial journalists from *Bloomberg News*, *The Wall Street Journal*, *The New York Times*, *Barron's*, *Forbes*, *Fortune*, *Money*, *CBS MarketWatch*, *Smart Money* and a bevy of mutual fund publications queued up to seek out George's thoughts about what was happening in the stock market.[24]

GETTING PAST 9/11

This period will be remembered forever for the terrorist attacks on Tuesday, September 11, 2001, on the World Trade Center and the Pentagon. Bill Frels recalled that the trustees for the Mairs & Power mutual funds were meeting when news of the attacks broke. They continued their meeting, and the firm remained open that day and for the rest of the week.

The New York Stock Exchange, all of Wall Street and many financial institutions across the world closed immediately and reopened the following Monday. It was only the third time the Exchange shut down for a prolonged period, the other two being at the start of World War I and during the bank holiday in 1933. Fear rippled across America. If terrorists could bring down the twin towers of the World Trade Center, what would they do next?

The offices of the nation's leading government bond trader, Cantor Fitzgerald, were blown to bits and the bond market itself closed.

When the markets reopened, travel, insurance, and entertainment stocks plummeted; communications, pharmaceuticals, and military-defense stocks rose. The impact of the attacks sheared half a percentage point from the gross domestic product for 2001.[25]

"The tragic events of September 11th cast a pall over security markets as well as the U.S. economy and have rendered obsolete all previous forecasts," George Mairs told Growth Fund shareholders in his third quarter report, dated November 9, 2001. He noted that the Federal Reserve, in efforts to keep the markets functioning, had slashed short-term interest rates to 2 percent, their lowest level in nearly 40 years. "We maintain our abiding faith in this country's democratic processes as well as the resiliency of its people, its institutions and its economy," he wrote.

He went on to reassure shareholders that all was well at Mairs & Power. The Growth Fund had a return of -4.6 percent for the nine months ended September 30 vs. a -20.3 return for the S&P. He cited a string of other favorable comparisons, including one from Time Inc.'s *Mutual Funds* magazine that reviewed 2,000 diversified U.S. stock funds and found the Growth Fund in the top 12.

In the separately managed accounts, Mairs & Power picked up seven more union employee benefit plans over the 1992-2004 period and it has added seven more since 2004 to bring the total number of such accounts to 16. Frels attributed the sign-up of the additional plans largely to Mairs & Power's reputation for managing the existing union accounts well and to support from a firm, based in St. Paul, that advises pension fund trustees on money management issues.

In 2003, the mutual fund business was hit with what historian and retired trade association leader Matt Fink has described as its worst scandal ever. It began when New York Attorney General Eliot Spitzer filed a complaint charging Canary Capital, a New Jersey-based hedge fund, with illegal late trading and market timing practices. Soon, the Securities & Exchange Commission launched its own probe.

Ultimately, nearly 20 mutual fund companies were entangled in the investigations, including funds advised by the Bank of America, Janus, Bank One, and Strong Capital Management. One of the most prominent of the fallen stars was Richard Strong, who had founded his namesake company, built a sprawling headquarters campus near Milwaukee, and oversaw $39 billion in assets. Strong agreed to pay

$60 million in restitution to investors. He was banned for life from the securities business.[26] Wells Fargo picked up his company's tattered remains.[27]

Though bruised, the industry shook off the Canary Capital scandal and moved on. By 2004, there were 8,039 mutual funds managing $8.1 trillion dollars, up from 3,823 funds managing $1.6 trillion in 1992. George Mairs III would soon turn the management of the Growth Fund, and the leadership of Mairs & Power, over to Bill Frels. The sun was setting on the years of the Georges, and Mairs & Power was bulking up for a new and more complicated age.

Part IV

MAIRS & POWER TODAY

CHAPTER 9

Up, Down, and Up Again

Mairs & Power was facing a new and increasingly complicated environment in 2004, when Bill Frels took the helm at the firm. Frels was the first investment veteran to lead the enterprise who was not a member of either the Mairs or Power families. He would carry forward the theories and investing style pursued by his predecessor, George Mairs III. The Growth Fund posted strong results at the beginning and end of his time, book-ending a scary and at times frightening interlude—the financial crisis—in the middle.

From the moment he walked in the door, Frels inherited Ron De-Sellier's roles as the firm's "bond guy" and as manager of the Income Fund (renamed as the Balanced Fund in 1997). There was no one else to deal with bonds until fixed-income specialist Ron Kaliebe arrived late in 2001. During the early years of the twenty-first century, the firm was confronting the challenges that came with growth: recruiting portfolio managers, analysts, other specialists, and administrators; coping with stepped-up regulation; extending the two mutual funds' geographical reach to cover the entire country; starting a third fund; and spreading employee ownership more broadly.

Frels, a native of Superior, Wisconsin, got his MBA from the University of Wisconsin in Madison and became a Chartered Financial Analyst early in his career. He had nearly 30 years of experience managing securities investments before joining Mairs & Power in 1992. Frels was a lot like George III: dedicated to following the principles of fundamental securities analysis; a history buff; a man so mindful of controlling expenses that even the ever-frugal George overruled his decision not to install a water cooler in the office. Frels was the lead manager of both the Growth and Balanced Funds until 2013; he retired at the end of 2015. George stated on more than one occasion to colleagues that had he not found Frels, he might have had to sell the firm.

Ron Kaliebe joined Mairs & Power in 2001. He was co-manager of the Balanced Fund for many years before taking over as its manager in 2013 and serving in that role until 2018. Kaliebe also was the Fund's director of Fixed Income until his retirement in 2019. Photo courtesy of Mairs & Power.

When George stepped down from his long run as the Growth Fund's manager in 2004, the Fund was experiencing another of its vintage years. It wrapped up the year posting an 18 percent total return vs. 10.9 percent for the S&P 500. This performance followed a string of strong showings in preceding years and accelerated a new surge in assets, which rose 57 percent to $2.06 billion during 2004. Again, investors were eager to get into the Fund. But this time, unlike in 1995, Mairs & Power was prepared to handle the rush. The firm, which needed more capacity to handle the new business, had been staffing up.

George Mairs III, left, and Bill Frels in 2003. Photo courtesy of Mairs & Power.

STAFF EXPANSION PICKS UP STEAM

The staff build-up, which would continue for years, put in place the framework for the Mairs & Power of today: investment professionals, managers, providers of client services, investor relations specialists, and traders. The hiring began in 1999 when money manager John Butler moved to Mairs & Power; grew late in 2001 with the arrival of Jon Theobald and Kaliebe; intensified from 2004 to 2012; and continued under the CEOs who succeeded Frels, first Jon Theobald and then Mark Henneman.

Henneman came in 2004, Andrea Stimmel in 2005, and Andy Adams in 2006. Today, Henneman, Stimmel (chief operating officer) and Adams (lead manager of the Growth Fund) plus Rob Mairs (president, who came in 2015) make up the four-person cabinet that leads the firm. The other hires who came during 2004–2012 and now hold key positions were Melissa Gilbertson, who today oversees trading and information technology; Pete Johnson, now co-manager of the Growth Fund; Glenn Johnson, now director of institutional asset management; Scott Howard, now manager of investor relations; and Beth VanHeel, now manager of mutual fund services.

Two of those hired between 1999 and 2012 replaced existing staffers; the other recruits all took new jobs created by the need for greater capacity to handle the burgeoning volume of business. Combined, the new staffers added from 1999 to 2012 brought with them more than 150

Melissa Gilbertson brought her experience in managing information technology to Mairs & Power in 2007, at a time when her skills were much needed. Today she also oversees the Trading Operations departments. Photo courtesy of Mairs & Power.

years of experience in their respective fields. They had worked at large, well-established Twin Cities companies including U.S. Bancorp, Wells Fargo, First Trust Company of St. Paul, Piper Jaffray, Ameriprise Financial, Target, Ernst & Young, The St. Paul Companies, and Securian.

Two key personnel decisions in 2004 helped the firm steer through a maze of regulations. Theobald became the chief compliance officer, and Jim Alt, a long-time partner at the Dorsey & Whitney law firm in Minneapolis, became the Mutual Fund Board's legal counsel. That year, extensive new rules promulgated by the Securities and Exchange Commission took effect. The rules were spurred by the market timing improprieties exposed at a number of mutual funds in the wake of the Canary Capital scandal and by the rapid growth in the numbers of mutual funds and investment advisers.[1]

Attorney James Alt has served Mairs & Power in multiple ways over the years. Photo courtesy of Mairs & Power.

The Board, an entity that governs the funds and is legally distinct from the firm itself, had an outside corporate lawyer as the funds' legal counsel but wanted someone more schooled in mutual fund law. Jim Alt practiced in a niche of a niche: securities attorneys known as "40 Act lawyers," who are well-versed in the provisions of the 1940 Investment Company Act. That federal legislation had laid the groundwork for the modern-day mutual fund industry. Alt, Theobald, and eventually Andrea Stimmel, who succeeded Theobald as chief compliance officer in 2012, worked as a trio to deal with mutual fund compliance issues.

When Alt retired from Dorsey in 2012 (and from serving as the legal counsel for the Mairs & Power funds), there were just a few practicing 40 Act lawyers in the Twin Cities. None offered the hands-on service, Midwestern sensibility, and reasonable fee scale that Alt had provided. The Board interviewed 40 Act lawyers in Milwaukee, Chicago, and Cincinnati, then chose Ellen Drought at the Godfrey & Kahn law firm in Milwaukee to succeed Alt. In 2015, Alt returned to the Mairs & Power Fund Board as an independent trustee.

STEERING THROUGH LEGAL THICKETS

Theobald credits Alt with leading Mairs & Power through a complex and important mutual fund reorganization in 2011. The firm's two existing funds had been incorporated in Minnesota half a century earlier, but most mutual funds started since then were incorporated in Delaware because the law was more flexible there.

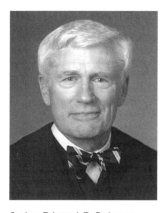

Judge Edward C. Stringer is a St. Paul native who brought to the Mairs & Power Mutual Fund Board (served 2002–2010) experience in the corporate world and federal and state governments. He was an associate justice on the Minnesota Supreme Court from 1992 to 2002, when he retired. Photo courtesy of Minnesota Supreme Court.

Retired 3M chief legal officer, Charlton H. (Chuck) Dietz, served on Mairs & Power's Mutual Fund Board between 1997 and 2006. His undergraduate degree is from Macalester College and law degree is from William Mitchell College of Law (now Mitchell Hamline College of Law), where he serves as a trustee emeritus. Photo courtesy of Chuck Dietz.

Alt explained that the funds' board could respond more promptly and effectively, and at less expense, to changing circumstances because, unlike Minnesota law, Delaware law does not require shareholder votes to make various changes. Also, Delaware law has a body of judicial precedents governing mutual funds that is considerably more developed than the counterpart body of precedents in Minnesota. Thus, a Delaware incorporation would provide greater certainty when legal questions arise. And given the number of lawyers familiar with Delaware law, incorporation there would expand the pool of qualified lawyers and law firms available for the Mairs & Power mutual board to choose from.

The firm, which was planning to launch its Small Cap Fund, wanted to consolidate all three funds as a family under a Delaware incorporation. Under Minnesota law, this process was so labyrinthine that it required 15 separate votes from the two funds' shareholders at their annual meetings in December 2011. Since then, all three funds have issued a single consolidated annual report instead of separate reports for each of the funds.

Separately, the Mutual Fund Board was changing to respond to ramped-up regulation. Over the years prior to 2004, the five-member Board had a sprinkling of independent members, including former Minnesota Supreme Court Justice Ed Stringer (from 2002 to 2010). Still, the Board had always been led by George III or his father. In 2004, the chair became an outsider: Chuck Dietz, the retired attorney who had been 3M's legal counsel for 17 years. By then, the SEC, more concerned about ethical lapses and conflicts of interest, had guidelines recommending that fund boards be led by independents and that at least 75 percent of their board members also be independent.

Subsequently, outsiders prominent in the Twin Cities business community have chaired the Board and taken most of its seats. Norb Conzemius, who rose to top positions at First Bank System during a 27-year career there, succeeded Dietz in 2006 and remained chair until 2014. Former legislator Bert McKasy, who had headed the Minnesota Department of Commerce, and practiced law with the Minneapolis law firm of Lindquist & Vennum (now Ballard Spahr), succeeded Conzemius. Mary Schmid Daugherty took over from McKasy in 2018 and remains as chair today. She began her career as an equity analyst, is a past president of the Chartered Financial

Analysts Society of Minnesota, and now teaches finance at the University of St. Thomas.[2]

In addition to Daugherty, three of the Board's other four members today are outsiders: Susan Knight, chair of medical device maker Surmodics and a former CFO at MTS Systems Corporation; Patrick Thiele, a retired CEO of reinsurer Partner Re who earlier held top posts at The St. Paul Companies; and Jim Alt.

By the beginning of 2004, the number of owners had risen to six, all at the firm: George III, Bill Frels, Peter Robb, John Butler, Jon Theobald, and Ron Kaliebe. Robb's stake would reach 25 percent in 2004. More would get stakes soon, as George III worked with others to sell his stock and spread the ownership more broadly.[3]

Toward the end of 2004, Mairs & Power had amassed enough talent to establish a well-staffed investment committee. As far back as the early 1980s, the firm had such a committee but never one with the resources it was now able to harness. Today, the committee, led by Andy Adams, discusses at length and then collaborates on which stocks should be on its recommended and holdings watchlists. These are the companies that look the most or least attractive based on the firm's valuation framework, and on an analysis of whether their competitive positions are improving or deteriorating. The information gathered for these lists drives most of the trading in the firm's portfolios. The committee also maintains regional and national watchlists, which identify companies not in its portfolios that could be promising prospects for future purchase. The committee, which meets twice a month, is made up of all the investment professionals and a representative from the compliance unit at Mairs & Power.[4]

In 2005, the Growth Fund enjoyed another strong year; its assets climbed 22 percent to $2.52 billion, giving it yet more capacity to increase its equity holdings. By then, Mark Henneman was working closely with George III to better understand his investing style so it could be passed to his successors. Little did the people at Mairs & Power, or throughout the investment world for that matter, imagine the turbulence looming just over the horizon: the financial crisis.

THE FINANCIAL CRISIS METASTASIZES

Much debate continues about how much weight to assign to the many causes of the crisis. At the risk of oversimplification, though, virtually all serious chroniclers of this saga would agree that the housing bubble that burst in 2007 was a major source of the turmoil. An intense push to expand home ownership had led to lax lending standards that became pervasive in the booming subprime mortgage market, where borrowers had limited or poor credit.[5]

These developments, combined with rampant speculation in housing markets, resulted in the industry being unusually vulnerable to a sharp decline in housing prices. In 2007, the decline deepened, battering the subprime market. Many subprime borrowers defaulted on their mortgage payments and often lost their homes. One of the most visible signs of trouble came in April 2007, when New Century Financial Corporation, the country's second largest subprime lender, filed for Chapter 11 bankruptcy. Subsequently, New Century collapsed. Trouble also surfaced at the nation's largest subprime lender, Countrywide Financial. In 2008, Countrywide nearly collapsed, and was acquired by Bank of America.

In mid-2007, the 85-year-old Bear Stearns investment firm bailed out two of its hedge funds. They had $20 billion of exposure to collateralized debt obligations including subprime mortgages. Bear Stearns claimed it had contained the problem, but by March 2008, the firm—far too entangled in the subprime lending market and highly leveraged—faced bankruptcy. The Federal Reserve Bank of New York feared that a collapse of the firm would trigger domino-like failures

In March 2008, a demonstrator holds a sign outside the headquarters of Bears Stearns in New York City questioning the U.S. government-backed sale of Bears Stearns Companies to JP Morgan Chase & Company. Jin Lee photo. Getty Images.

of other investment firms. The New York Fed ended up providing a contentious emergency bridge loan that helped JPMorgan Chase buy Bear Stearns in a highly visible government-assisted bailout.

Six months later, on September 15, Lehman Brothers declared a Chapter 11 bankruptcy. This time, the Fed did not come to the rescue. Lehman, 158 years old, was the nation's fourth largest investment bank; its bankruptcy was the largest in U.S. history. Lehman, too, was highly leveraged and deeply enmeshed in the subprime lending market. Many other companies would eventually fail, get government bailouts, or be forced to sell out.

The largest of them included longtime industry leader Merrill Lynch, which was bought by Bank of America. Fannie Mae and Freddie Mac, the giant public government-sponsored enterprises, were placed into conservatorship by the U.S. government. Insurer American International Group was bailed out by the U.S. government. Washington Mutual and IndyMac Bank both failed and were seized by the Federal Deposit Insurance Corporation. General Motors and Chrysler both filed Chapter 11 bankruptcies and were bailed out by the U.S. government. Northern Rock in the United Kingdom and many other, smaller financial companies also failed.[6]

Globally, a financial earthquake was shaking the investment community. Lehman's collapse, and assorted other troubles arising from

A ticker sign in New York City reports on September 10, 2008, that Lehman Brothers had suffered severe financial losses and was seeking to sell a majority stake in the company as it attempted to stay in business. Less than a week later, after attempts to rescue the storied financial firm failed, Lehman Brothers filed for Chapter 11 bankruptcy. Chris Hondros photo. Getty Images.

the financial crisis, sent the already-torpid stock market into a tailspin. The Dow Jones Industrials had been falling for months from their high of 14,165 on October 9, 2007. The Industrials closed the week of the Lehman bankruptcy at 11,398, ended 2008 at 8,776 and sank to a low of 6,594 on March 5, 2009. The index didn't get back to its October 2007 high until September 24, 2012. The National Bureau of Economic Research, scorekeeper for the business cycle, eventually declared that the country had been in a recession from December 2007 until June 2009—"The Great Recession."[7]

NO HARBOR FROM THE STORM

There was no way, of course, for Mairs & Power to seal itself off from the turmoil. During 2008, the assets of the Growth Fund fell 35 percent to $1.68 billion from $2.61 billion and the net asset value of a share of stock in the Fund skidded to $52.51 from $76.30. Over the course of that year, the market values of seven of the Fund's top ten holdings plunged more than 30 percent while the number of shares of them it owned changed minimally. Some of the Fund's value declines: Honeywell, -47 percent; Emerson Electric, -39 percent; Medtronic, -38 percent; Toro, -36 percent; Ecolab, -35 percent.

In their February 12, 2009, annual letter to Growth Fund share-holders, Bill Frels and Mark Henneman summed up the damage: "Responding to the bankruptcy of Lehman Bros., and the mounting loan losses being recognized by the nation's largest banks, confidence collapsed, and the economy fell into a tailspin during the fourth quarter." But they predicted the stock market would eventually rebound. It did, but full recovery ended up taking years, not months.

The Growth Fund's return for 2008 was -28.5 percent. Bad as that was, the S&P's return was worse, -37.0 percent. George Mairs III had stepped down from full-time stock-picking by 2008, but newly hired analysts were starting to carry forward his style of investing. The Balanced Fund held up modestly better, with a return of -21.1 percent, because a large portion of its assets were in better-performing fixed-income and money market fund securities. Over the next three years, both funds' returns rebounded into positive territory.

ASCENT OF THE FINANCIAL PLANNERS

In the wake of the financial crisis, Mairs & Power became more aware of the rise of financial planners. Their ranks had been growing since the late 1960s, as millions of Americans sought more help in making financial choices. Jon Theobald said that traditionally, the firm's representatives seldom talked about performance in their meetings with clients. "The exception was with larger institutional clients and their consultants, who regularly required more focus on performance as part of client meetings."[8]

Theobald recalled that in the years immediately after the financial crisis, planners began stressing performance more in meetings with their clients, an emphasis that continues today. Mairs & Power responded by changing its approach. The firm's money managers began discussing their performance routinely, particularly over the long-term, when they met with clients.

The rise of the financial planners did raise the odds that in some cases, Mairs & Power clients or prospective clients would accept planners' recommendations to take their business to other firms. Overall, though, the greater role of the planners helped the firm by changing the way most investors buy its funds. Before Mairs & Power tapped into the planners, almost all of its funds' shareholders bought the funds directly from the firm; now most of the shareholders buy the funds through financial planners.

That became possible largely because Mairs & Power established a national presence during the 2004-2012 period. Once again, Charles Schwab & Company came into the picture. Many years earlier, Schwab came up with what financial journalist Joe Nocera called one of his best ideas: a "mutual fund marketplace" or platform where investors could pick and choose among scores of no-load funds (such as the Mairs & Power funds) paying only a small transaction fee or none at all.[9]

As recently as 2004, Mairs & Power's funds had been registered in just 15 states. By 2010, the firm had registered them in the remaining 35 states. George, who had long been skeptical of the need to be in more states, eventually came around to accept the idea. Being registered in every state qualified the funds to go on the Schwab platform and other large brokerage firm platforms. Financial planners across the country could now recommend the Mairs & Power funds. Many did, and the funds' shareholder counts soared.

In late spring of 2010, George Mairs III died. Like the firm itself, he had gone from anonymity to celebrity after Mairs & Power achieved national prominence in 1995. "George used to joke about how he owed all of his success to nepotism," Theobald said. "He was very low-key, self-deprecating. You'd never get the idea that George was an important guy in town from the unassuming way he conducted himself."

In the *Star Tribune*'s obituary, business columnist Neal St. Anthony called him a "humble dean of the Minnesota investment community"

George Mairs III in 2009. Photo courtesy of Mairs & Power.

who gave money a good name." Theobald told the Minneapolis paper that George took pride in sustaining a private, employee-owned firm. "The fact that he has been a major philanthropic force really came home in recent years. As we were buying back his stock over the last several years since his retirement, we were never buying stock directly from George. It was from the nonprofits to whom he had donated the stock."[10]

By 2011, it had been 50 years since Mairs & Power launched a mutual fund. That year, after extensive legal work, it opened its third fund, the Small Cap Fund.

INCORPORATED UNDER THE LAWS OF THE STATE OF
Delaware

NUMBER
1

SHARES
10,000

MAIRS AND POWER SMALL CAP FUND

AUTHORIZED CAPITAL ___Unlimited___ SHARES $0.01 ___ PAR VALUE

This Certifies That ___William B. Frels___ is the owner of

Ten thousand (10,000)------------------------------- full paid and non-assessable

SHARES OF THE CAPITAL STOCK OF Mairs and Power Small Cap Fund

transferable on the books of the Corporation in person or by duly authorized Attorney upon surrender of this Certificate properly endorsed. In Witness Whereof, the said Corporation has caused this Certificate to be signed by its duly authorized officers and sealed with the Seal of the Corporation. this ___Eleventh___ day of ___August___ A.D. 2011

Jon A. Theobald
SECRETARY

William B. Frels
PRESIDENT

DWIGHT & M. H. JACKSON
205 W. RANDOLPH STREET

CORPORATION SUPPLY CO.
CHICAGO, ILLINOIS 60606

Mairs & Power incorporated its Small Cap Fund in the state of Delaware in August 2011. This is a photo of the Fund's first share of stock that was issued. Photo courtesy of Mairs & Power.

The Frels regime closed at the end of 2012, when Theobald succeeded him as CEO. As the leadership changed hands, Morningstar named Frels and Mark Henneman, who worked closely together in managing the Growth Fund, as domestic stock managers of the year. They beat out finalists from three much larger fund families—Fidelity, American Funds, and Oakmark—for the honor. It was an accolade guaranteed to draw still more investors to Mairs & Power's flagship fund in 2013.[11]

Mark Henneman, left, and Bill Frels were the co-managers of the Mairs & Power Growth Fund in 2012. Morningstar honored them as the 2012 Fund Manager of the Year for Domestic Stock based on the Growth Fund's superior performance.

CHAPTER 10

Tying the Strands Together

Mairs & Power was riding high when Jon Theobald became its CEO in January 2013. The transition at the top was no surprise. It had been telegraphed to the world beyond the firm well in advance of the actual handover, much as the plan for Bill Frels to succeed George Mairs III had been. Theobald, a lawyer who specialized in estate planning and trust administration, had been gathering experiences suitable for the job for years.[1]

When he joined Mairs & Power early in 2002, Jon Theobald had worked for more than three decades at St. Paul trust companies, including oversight of buying and selling securities owned by high-net worth individuals. Many of his clients at the trust companies eventually followed him to Mairs & Power. Soon after Theobald came to the firm, the playing field for mutual funds grew much more complicated and laced with legal minefields, mostly due to fallout from the Enron scandal and heated controversy over other questionable corporate financial practices. One measure of the increased regulatory burden placed on Mairs & Power and other financial services firms was the growing size of the annual reports for the Growth Fund and the Balanced Fund. Combined they took up 59 pages in 2011, up from just 26 pages 15 years earlier. Greater compliance and disclosure requirements, along with the growth of the firm, had ushered in a complex new era almost unimaginable during the days of the Three Georges. The time seemed right to put a seasoned lawyer in the driver's seat.

After George Mairs III named Theobald president and chief operating officer in 2007, he became responsible for coordinating the firm's expanding web of specialized functions. This meant signing off on all the hiring decisions for all of the investment professionals; serving as the primary intermediary between the firm and its funds

Hired in 2001, Jon Theobald succeeded Bill Frels as CEO of Mairs & Power in 2013. He retired from the firm in 2017, following 16 years of service. Photo courtesy of Mairs & Power.

On January 27, 2013, Mairs & Power proudly announced in the daily newspapers of St. Paul and Minneapolis that Morningstar had honored Bill Frels and Mark Henneman, co-managers, with its award as Fund Manager of the Year for Domestic Stock based on the Growth Fund's excellent performance in 2012. Photo courtesy of the Mairs & Power.

MAIRS & POWER FUNDS
Investing for the long-term

2012 MORNINGSTAR U.S. DOMESTIC-STOCK FUND MANAGER OF THE YEAR:

Bill Frels and Mark Henneman
MAIRS & POWER GROWTH FUND

63% of Growth Fund investments are in
Minnesota Companies:

3M CO.	PATTERSON COS. INC.
U.S. BANCORP	GRACO INC.
MEDTRONIC INC.	TORO CO.
TARGET CORP.	TECHNE CORP.
GENERAL MILLS INC.	TCF FINANCIAL CORP.
ECOLAB INC.	STRATASYS LTD.
FASTENAL CO.	H.B. FULLER CO.
ST. JUDE MEDICAL INC.	MTS SYSTEMS CORP.
PENTAIR LTD.	G & K SERVICES INC.
C.H. ROBINSON WORLDWIDE INC.	SURMODICS INC.
HORMEL FOODS CORP.	MEDTOX
VALSPAR CORP.	NVE CORP.
DONALDSON CO. INC.	

Mark Henneman   Bill Frels

Awards 2012

Morningstar Awards 2012©. Morningstar, Inc. All Rights Reserved. Awarded to Bill Frels and Mark Henneman as 2012 Morningstar Domestic-Stock Fund Manager of the Year for Mairs & Power Growth Fund, USA.

board; making all the compensation decisions relating to personnel; having the final say on compliance issues; acting as the lead salesman on most of the new business the firm landed; representing the firm to various constituencies; and overseeing how well the firm was adjusting to ever larger and always changing markets.

The numbers were in for 2012; the Growth Fund, paced by robust run-ups in five of its stocks—Minnesota-based Valspar, Pentair, H.B. Fuller and Toro plus Baxter International in Chicago—had experienced a very good year. So good that Morningstar had pronounced the Fund's managers, Frels and Mark Henneman, as the best domestic stock fund managers of the year.

This prestigious designation gave Mairs & Power a lot to talk about. Traditionally, the firm had avoided advertising, other than sponsorships on Minnesota Public Radio. Now came an occasion that called for a departure from tradition. The firm took half-page color ads in the St. Paul and Minneapolis dailies and in the regional edition of the *Wall Street Journal* to let more investors in the Upper Midwest know about the Morningstar honor. New business flowed in, for both the

Shortly after noon on January 3, 2013, when CNBC announced on TV that the Growth Fund at Mairs & Power had won the Morningstar Award for Domestic Stock performance in 2012, everyone at the firm enjoyed watching the broadcast and a festive lunch to celebrate, including a chance to honor this accomplishment with a toast. Photo courtesy of Mairs & Power.

mutual funds and the separately managed accounts. A few months later, the firm hired Kevin Earley to help absorb the increased volume of business. Earley brought 27 years of experience as an analyst and portfolio manager with him.

Talking up the Growth Fund's successes a bit more than in the past fit neatly into the prevailing mood in the stock market. The bulls were roaring again. By June, the Dow Jones Industrials were about 7 percent above their pre-financial crisis high. They finished the year at 16,576—16 percent above their pre-crisis peak—and would keep rising for the next four years. At Mairs & Power, the five-year stretch that had begun in 2013 would see stepped-up efforts to distribute the funds more widely, additional hiring, greater attention to securities research, more strategic planning, improved team-building, and increased outreach to the community.

The stage had been set for expanding the reach of the funds now that they were available across the country. Still, if the plan was to market them more aggressively, the firm needed to comply with the rules established by the Financial Industry Regulatory Authority (FINRA). FINRA, an independent nongovernment organization, required Mairs & Power to retain a fund distributor to oversee an employee licensed to market the funds. The firm hired ALPS, a Denver-based distributor. Scott Howard, who acquired the necessary licenses, was moved from his job as mutual funds services manager to a new role marketing the funds and overseeing investor relations. Until then,

As a vice president and investment manager as well as the lead manager of the Balanced Fund, Kevin Earley also serves on the Mairs & Power Investment Committee. He joined the firm in 2013. Photo courtesy of Mairs & Power.

Pentair, which was founded in 1966 and has its headquarters in Minneapolis, partnered with the Minnesota Twins baseball team to install an innovative rainwater recycling system at Target Field when it opened in 2010. This system reduces reliance on municipal water for irrigating the playing field, which yields an average annual savings of about 2 million gallons of water. Frank Romeo photo. Shutterstock.

the firm could only respond to inquiries about the funds. Now Howard could actively promote them directly to financial planners. This helped, particularly in the Twin Cities, where Mairs & Power could capitalize on its positive name recognition.

An unexpected staff change occurred in the summer of 2013, when John Butler—one of the firm's owners—resigned to take over the management of his family's private foundation. Allen Steinkopf, who had been an asset manager at U.S. Bancorp, replaced Butler.

The larger staff and other rising expenses significantly increased Mairs & Power's cost of doing business. On April 1, 2014, the firm raised the fees it charged clients with separately managed accounts for the first time in more than 30 years. The minimum size of these accounts rose to $2 million from $1 million and the fees per amount of assets rose on a sliding scale that declined as the size of the account grew. These increases affected only clients who opened accounts after April 1. Existing clients remained on the old fee schedule.[2]

STRATEGIC PLANNING TAKES HOLD

Strategic planning came of age during this period. In 2007, the firm's management had initiated half-day planning sessions with a Saturday meeting in the office. Ten employee-owners and those employees who were expected to become owners soon participated. Four similar sessions were held, every 18 months or so, over the next five years.

Attendees discussed how big the firm should be, what kinds of business it wanted to attract, marketing ideas, operational improvements, and changes in fee structures. In the summer of 2014, an outside consultant, the Prouty Project, was called in to help plan and facilitate a more extensive gathering, a two-day getaway at the Sugar Lake Lodge in Grand Rapids, Minnesota.

Decisions made after they were hashed out at the earlier planning sessions had included the moves to hire ALPS and to launch the Small Cap Fund. At the meeting in Grand Rapids, Jon Theobald confirmed his plan to retire at the end of 2017. He had led the firm through many thorny legal situations, among them moving its corporate status to an S- Corp from a C-Corp.—a sensitive shift that made more sense for the firm from a tax perspective. It also helped to broaden the firm's employee ownership plan.

News of Theobald's planned retirement led to concerns, openly voiced in advance of the Grand Rapids meeting, about how his many roles would be parceled out and when that process would begin. Theobald had been thinking more about that in the months before

In mid-August 2014, senior Mairs & Power leaders held a strategic planning meeting in an outdoors setting at Sugar Lake Lodge in northern Minnesota. Photo courtesy of Mairs & Power.

the meeting. By then, it had become a foregone conclusion that Mark Henneman would become the CEO. He had been at Mairs & Power for a decade, became co-manager of its flagship Growth Fund in 2006, and was named as the Fund's lead manager in 2013. Still, it seemed as though Henneman would need more horsepower at his side. Because of all his responsibilities as the senior investment officer in the firm (Growth Fund manager, chief investment officer, and portfolio manager for many of the firm's largest separately managed accounts), adding the CEO duties appeared to make the job too big of a lift for him to carry alone.

WEE-HOURS EPIPHANY

In the middle of the night, a few weeks before the 2014 getaway in Grand Rapids, Theobald woke up with what felt like more than just a bright idea. What about bringing in Rob Mairs? Theobald and Mairs had known one another for 15 years. Like Theobald, Mairs was a trusts and estates attorney who advised high-net worth clients on estate planning and charitable-giving practices. The morning after he came up with his idea, Theobald called Mairs to set up a breakfast meeting. Then and at another meeting a week before the Grand Rapids getaway, they explored the idea more seriously.

The president, chief compliance officer, and general counsel of Mairs & Power is Robert W. (Rob) Mairs. He joined the firm in 2015 and is a graduate of Dartmouth College and has his law degree for William Mitchell College of Law (now Mitchell Hamline College of Law). Photo courtesy of Mairs & Power.

Mairs had earned an undergraduate degree from Dartmouth College and a law degree from William Mitchell College of Law. He began his career as an assistant bank and trust officer at Norwest Bank in St. Paul. He was climbing up the ladder as a 16-year veteran and partner at the Minneapolis law firm of Gray Plant Mooty when he got the call from Theobald.

Rob Mairs was both a Mairs and a Power. His father, Bob Mairs, was the son of Louise Power, who married George Mairs Jr. in 1938, after his first wife and Louise's first husband had passed on so prematurely. As one of the six children in the blended family raised by George Jr. and Louise, Bob took on the last name of Mairs and so, of course, would his son Rob.

Theobald told the attendees at the 2014 meeting in Grand Rapids that he intended to retire at the end of 2017. He suggested that the firm consider bringing in Mairs, not to replace him as CEO but to take over some of the tasks Theobald had been handling that Henneman would not have time to do. Unlike Theobald, Henneman would also have the firm's heaviest investment responsibilities in addition to the CEO role. The group reacted favorably. Negotiations with Mairs then began. Early in 2015, Rob Mairs agreed to join the firm later that year as general counsel and assistant to the chairman. In 2017, Mairs was named chief compliance officer and in 2018, president.

At the Grand Rapids meeting, the group also decided that the firm needed another full-time equity research analyst. Justin Miller, who had 15 years of experience as an equity researcher and portfolio manager, filled that spot early in 2015. A new flurry of hiring followed. With the retirement of Bill Frels looming at the end of 2015, a spot opened for a fixed-income specialist. Robert Thompson, who had 20 years of experience as a bond analyst and portfolio manager, got that job. Earlier in 2014, Heidi Lynch, with 14 years of experience, had joined the firm as a fixed-income and institutional trader. Soon, two more full-time equity analysts would arrive: Michelle Warren (the first woman to be an investment professional at the firm) in 2016 and Chris Strom in 2017.

Mairs & Power convened another two-day strategic planning session, at Madden's on Gull Lake near Brainerd, Minn., with Prouty as planner and facilitator, in the summer of 2017. This time, 15 owners and key employees attended. A new approach to the way the firm dealt with the separately managed accounts emerged from the discussions. The old model of having investment professionals do both securities research and portfolio management continued, but a new model of having a professional manage portfolios without research responsibilities would also be employed. This would enable a portfolio manager working under the new model to handle more accounts. Pat Farley, hired in 2018, was the firm's first investment professional to operate in this manner.

Out of the 2017 huddle at Madden's came a stronger commitment to charitable giving: annual donations of at least 2 percent of pretax profits, primarily to recipients in St. Paul and the East Metro region. The firm's giving, just $5,000 in 2004, had risen to $150,000 by 2017. Bringing it up to the 2 percent level would more than double the donations, to over $400,000. At the session, those attending decided to continue George Mairs III's practice of giving that took the form of supporting community organizations by sponsoring their fund-raising events. They also decided to establish a formal charitable

Heidi Lynch, who joined Mairs & Power in 2014, is on the investment team for the firm's Minnesota Municipal Bond ETF. She is also a fixed-income trader and an assistant portfolio manager. Photo courtesy of Mairs & Power.

As an investment professional, Michelle Warren serves as an assistant vice president and equity analyst at Mairs & Power. She is also a member of the firm's Investment Committee. Photo courtesy of Mairs & Power.

As Senior Vice President and Director of Institutional Asset Management, Glenn Johnson has been at Mairs & Power since 2010. Among his many duties, he serves on the firm's Investment Committee. Photo courtesy of Mairs & Power.

Bob Thompson is another member of the Mairs & Power Investment Committee. As a vice president and director of fixed income, he's the co-manager for the firm's new Minnesota Municipal Bond ETF. Photo courtesy of Mairs & Power.

giving program and an employee-matching gift program. Both new directives were implemented in 2018.

The 2 percent policy marked a shift from the days of the Three Georges. In the past, most beneficiaries of their personal donations saw the Georges' quiet philanthropy as coming from the firm, since the Mairs and Power names were familiar to insiders in the St. Paul charitable-giving community. But those earlier donations weren't coming from Mairs & Power. Instead, they were coming directly from the Georges, whose personal wealth had been generated by their firm's success.

Increasingly, the firm's outreach to the community took the form of volunteerism on the part of its growing staff. This was led by Theobald, who had been encouraged by George Mairs III to consider community activities as "part of the job." Theobald's activities leading up to and in most cases continuing during his tenure at Mairs & Power included being a board member at the Saint Paul Foundation, the St. Paul Riverfront Corporation, the Tozer Foundation, Visitation Convent School, and Saint John's University; and board member and president (or chair) for the Northern Star Council of the Boy Scouts of America, the F.R. Bigelow Foundation, the Hardenbergh Foundation, the Ramsey County Bar Association, and the Minnesota Club.

Over time, Mark Henneman became a board member of the Ordway Center for the Performing Arts and also chair of the investment committee for the Saint Paul and Minnesota Foundations; Andy Adams joined the board of the Northern Star Council/Boy Scouts; Glenn Johnson became a trustee and chair of the investment committee at the F. R. Bigelow Foundation; Kevin Earley joined the Wilder Foundation's board; Andrea Stimmel joined the board of Public Art St. Paul; Rob Mairs became a board member and officer of the Ramsey County Historical Society and board member of the St. Paul Chamber Orchestra; Bob Thompson joined the board of the YMCA of Greater Twin Cities and became the chair of the downtown St. Paul YMCA; and Melissa Gilbertson became a trustee of the Episcopal Homes of Minnesota.

The firm's rapid growth during this time led to a need for more physical space. The firm remodeled its office, which occupied all of the 15th floor at the First National Bank Building in downtown St. Paul, and then occupied half of the 14th floor. This project, completed in 2015, expanded the office space by 50 percent.

How Tumult in the Trust Business
Spelled Opportunity for Mairs & Power

A problem arose, back in the early 1970s, when a potential client offered Jon Theobald the opportunity to land a new account as part of Theobald's job of administering trusts at First Trust Company of St. Paul. The proposed new account was less than $100,000. That was below the minimum account size the trust company would accept. "Why don't you send him upstairs to Mairs & Power," a senior officer at First Trust suggested. "What's Mairs & Power?" Theobald replied. After he received an explanation, he referred the client there, as he later would several others with accounts below First Trust's minimum. At the time, Mairs & Power, still a bare-bones operation with only four or five employees, was little-known, even in St. Paul.[3]

Theobald stayed at First Trust until 1990, when he moved on to head American National Bank's trust department. When American National was sold in 1996, he left to start a St. Paul office for Minneapolis-based Resource Trust Company. In 2001, he joined Mairs & Power; a decade later, he was tapped to become the firm's chief executive officer. Over the years, other First Trust officers, money managers, and analysts also found their way to Mairs & Power. First Trust in effect served as a training ground for them. As word spread about the successful long-term performance of Mairs & Power's investments, some First Trust clients began moving their money upstairs

to Mairs & Power, a short elevator ride away in St. Paul's First National Bank Building. Eventually, many more investors would turn to Mairs & Power instead of First Trust or other competing money managers.

For decades, First Trust sat at the gravitational center of the city's business and financial community. It was closely aligned with the First National Bank of St. Paul, basically acting as First National's trust department. In the twentieth century, First National grew to become a far more dominant force on the city's banking scene than were the leading banks in other cities of comparable size. Parker Paine founded the bank, which eventually became known as First National Bank of St. Paul, soon after he arrived in the city by steamship in 1853. Minnesota, still a territory, became a state in 1858. Five years later, Congress passed the National Banking Act that established national charters for banks. Paine had retired by then, but his partners, brothers Horace and James E. Thompson, obtained the first national charter for a bank in Minnesota and began running Paine's enterprise as the First National Bank of St. Paul.[4]

Bank's Rise Tied to Railroads
James J. Hill, head of the Great Northern Railroad, bought the bank in 1912, consolidated it with the city's Second National Bank, and concentrated his far-flung business accounts—the source of much

of the city's wealth—at the First National. A few years later, Hill's massive Railroad and Bank Building in downtown St. Paul opened as the headquarters for his railroad, the Northern Pacific Railroad, and First National. Fast forward 15 years, to 1931. First National built a 31-story skyscraper and moved its headquarters there. The tower and the bright red "1st" sign that capped it, visible from much of the city, promptly took command of the downtown skyline, much as the bank prevailed in the city's financial community.[5]

In 1973, Ron DeSellier, the first investment professional not from the Mairs or Power families to join the firm, came from First Trust. Six years earlier, DeSellier, armed with an economics degree from the University of Minnesota, sought an investment job. "I tried a Minneapolis employment agency to see if there were investment positions available in the Twin Cities," he recalled. "They sent me to First Trust in St. Paul, about a non-investment opening. I said, 'No thanks.' They said, 'Wait a few days.' I heard they had a deep conversation with a research analyst they had hired quite recently and voilà, there was the opening I had hoped for. My stay at First Trust lasted five years, and while the excitement level was low, I still have many close friends from my time there."[6]

Peter Robb, employee No. 8 at Mairs & Power, was first an equity analyst and then a portfolio manager at First Trust. His move was not an easy decision. Robb was coming from the security and prestige of

the city's leading financial institution to a small, little-known firm. "It was a real gamble," he said. In 1994, Mairs & Power hired him in part to take over the accounts that had been closely overseen for years by George Power, who was then nearing retirement. Robb also dealt with a steady stream of clients referred to Mairs & Power by Roger Katzenmaier, a longtime principal at the Wilkerson Guthmann accounting firm in St. Paul. Such firms had many clients with significant wealth who sought advice about how to invest it well. Robb retired in 2020 after handling the accounts of scores of individuals for 26 years.[7]

Peter Robb had wide experience in financial services when he was hired by Mairs & Power in 1994. Initially he worked closely with George C. Power Jr. This photo is from 2019. Robb retired from the firm in 2020. Photo courtesy of Mairs & Power.

Bill Frels, who hired Robb in 1994, had been at First Trust from 1971 through 1990. Frels then went to American National with Theobald but left that bank in 1992 to join Mairs & Power. "When Bill hired me, he said we have a diamond in the rough that needs some polishing," Robb said. Frels and George Mairs III worked well together; in 2007, Frels succeeded George III as CEO. He held that position until 2012.

Others from Mairs & Power who had earlier been at First Trust include Glenn Johnson and Ron Kaliebe. Johnson is director of portfolio management at the firm. He was an analyst and later a portfolio manager at First Trust. Kaliebe, who was the lead manager of the Balanced Fund from 2013 to 2018, came to Mairs & Power in 2001 after several years as the chief investment officer at MSI Insurance Company. Before that, he had been a fixed-income specialist for many years at First Trust; he retired in 2019. Mary Schmid Daugherty, chair of the Mairs & Power mutual fund board, got her start in the investment field as an equity analyst at First Trust. Over the years, the fund board has also included several trustees with First Trust backgrounds: Norb Conzemius, who was the board's chair from 2006 to 2014; Tom Simonet; and Bert McKasy.

George Power, one of the "Three Georges" who led Mairs & Power for 75 years, could be considered a partial alum of First Trust. He worked for First Service Corporation from 1937 to 1942, before military service, and joined Mairs & Power in 1946. First Service, like First Trust, was part of the First Bank Stock Corporation holding company. At First Service, Power's job was to do securities analysis that likely was a significant source of information for First Trust's money managers.

Theobald recruited Lynn Hayek and Cathy Brandes, who had been at First Trust, to key administrative positions at Mairs & Power. Hayek had worked at First Trust, primarily as Bill Frels's administrative assistant, from 1974 to 1990. Then she joined Frels and Theobald at the trust division of St. Paul's American National Bank. In 1996, after American was sold to Firstar of Milwaukee, Theobald hired her at Resource Trust. In 2007, she joined Mairs & Power as an administrative assistant and later she became a customer service specialist. She retired in the summer of 2021. Cathy Brandes worked at First Trust, primarily as a receptionist, from 1974 until 2000 and again from 2011 to 2014 after that firm was reorganized. In 2014, she joined Mairs & Power as a receptionist, a position she has held since then.

Disruption Spurs New Competition

According to Jon Theobald, in the early 1970s, First Trust managed roughly 90 percent of the personal and employee-benefit trust assets in the city. In the 1960s, '70s, and well into the '80s, First Trust—part of the Minneapolis-based bank holding company that also had a trust operation in Minneapolis—managed close to twice the personal and employee-benefit assets that its Minneapolis trust counterpart had under management, Theobald added.

By the late 1980s, however, First Trust's grip on the market had weakened significantly. Rivals from the Twin Cities (including American National's trust department run by Theobald) came in to challenge what they saw as First Trust's clubby, cozy franchise. The creators and beneficiaries of fresh fortunes in the Twin Cities area found

Although the setting, year, numbers, and faces might change over time, this 1950 photo of the members of the Board of the First National Bank of Minneapolis typified the make-up of local financial services boards for many years.

new caretakers to manage their wealth. And First Trust faced internal turmoil as new leadership at its parent holding company, First Bank System, sought company-wide efficiencies by consolidating First Trust's operations with those of the system's Minneapolis affiliate. First Trust's top officers and staffers felt the consolidation effort was disrupting the long-standing, deep ties between them and their clients.[8]

The disruption led to an exodus of talent and clients from First Trust, including the loss of business from 3M, its largest corporate client. Richard Slade, great-grandson of James J. Hill and a former president of the Northwestern National Bank of St. Paul, recounted the troubles in his 2005 book, *Banking in the Great Northern Territory*. Slade wrote that the CEO at First Bank System had recruited an outsider to combine the trust operations in both cities. This newcomer hired employees who "would now also conduct fiduciary services under contract for the

trust department of the Minneapolis bank; certain First Trust officers doing business from Minneapolis offices, would thus be officers of both First Trust *and* First Bank/ Minneapolis."[9]

By the early 1990s, different versions of this scenario were playing out in other cities as new trust companies, law firms, financial planners, and accounting firms emerged as rivals competing with established bank trust departments. By then, new trust documents—wills and living trust arrangements, typically drawn up for trust beneficiaries by an estates/trusts lawyer specializing in estate planning—almost always included language enabling the beneficiaries to move their assets from a corporate trustee, such as First Trust, to another corporate trustee, such as Wells Fargo. Theobald said such language was rarely seen when he got into the field in 1970.

Later in the 1990s, the Dorsey & Whitney law firm in Minneapolis entered the trust field by establishing its own trust company. Eventually, Dorsey Trust assets became Mairs & Power's largest separately managed account (see Chapter 8).

In the end, the splintering of the trust business in the Twin Cities was mindful of the "creative destruction" that occurred in the region when the breakup of Control Data led to the birth of new firms. As so often happens in such situations, much of the talent and many of the clients of the trust companies going through uncertainty scattered to the winds. Some of the breezes sprinkled gold dust onto Mairs & Power.

THE SAGA OF MTS SYSTEMS

In 2016 Mairs & Power decided to liquidate one of its longest-held and more successful investments in the Growth Fund: the common stock of MTS Systems, whose headquarters and principal operations were in the Minneapolis suburb of Eden Prairie. In 1966, MTS had become a free-standing, publicly held company when it was spun out of Research Inc. That company, in turn, had been formed in 1951; its stock was among the earliest securities to be traded in the Twin Cities over-the-counter market that became so frenzied in the late 1950s.

Mairs & Power was for many years one of MTS's largest shareholders. George III had picked the stock for the Growth Fund in 1981, buying 4,000 shares for $64,500. It broke into the Fund's top 10 holdings just once, in 1991, and its value in the Fund never topped $1.5 million until 1996. But then the stock took off, zig-zagging its way up to become, by 2013, a Growth Fund holding worth $85.5 million. In 2016, MTS, on the hunt for acquisitions, decided to buy PCB Group, an upstate New York producer of sensor equipment.

Mark Henneman and Andy Adams, then co-managing the Fund, and Justin Miller, the analyst responsible for researching MTS Systems, scrutinized the PCB deal. When they completed their analysis, they had significant reservations about the agreement. Mairs & Power hosted a meeting with the MTS board's executive committee to discuss the problems they had discerned. The board dismissed their concerns, and thus Mairs & Power began a systematic liquidation of its MTS stock over a period of months in order to avoid jolting the stock. "In addition to our concerns about execution of the current business, we did not believe the strategy behind the acquisition was sound," Henneman and Adams would later explain to Growth Fund's shareholders. "It added to the company's existing sensor business, where the company does not enjoy a strong competitive advantage, it diluted MTS' durable competitive advantage in its core test business and added substantial leverage to the balance sheet."

By some measures, MTS had been a classic Growth Fund stock. It was a Minnesota manufacturer that had been ignored for years by investors beyond the region. For much of its life, no securities analysts followed it. Chip Emery, who became the CEO at MTS in 1998, recalled that analysts picked up coverage in the 1990s but dropped it by 1999 when the dot-com frenzy took hold. "All the analysts decamped for greener pastures," Emery said. Yet in the Twin Cities high-tech community, and at Mairs & Power, MTS Systems continued to be held in high regard.

MTS, which had constantly expanded its suburban compound, makes test equipment for some of the world's best-known corporations. For years, the company has been packed with engineers who had come up with sophisticated equipment that simulates earthquakes for the Japanese government and electronic systems designed to make amusement park rides more exciting. They produced the motion and control electronics for Disneyland's "Indiana Jones" ride. Chip Emery and Susan Knight, MTS's chief financial officer, drove over to St. Paul annually to meet with George and others at Mairs & Power's offices.[10]

MTS stock, hit hard by the economic downturn resulting from the COVID pandemic, fell to its lowest level in 17 years shortly after the virus spread across the U.S. in the spring of 2020. The stock had climbed halfway back to pre-pandemic levels when Connecticut-based Amphenol announced that it intended to bid for the company. At the end of the year, however, MTS reported the fourth biggest loss ($276 million) for any of Minnesota's 50 largest companies in 2020. In January 2021, Amphenol disclosed a second transaction, to sell MTS's test and simulation business to Illinois Tool Works, a 109-year-old enterprise that *Fortune* magazine ranked as one of the country's 200 largest companies.

Chip Emery, seen here in the foreground of a photo from 2003, was the CEO of MTS Systems Corporation at that time. Behind him is a road simulator that MTS was then building for Audi at the MTS plant in a Minneapolis suburb. Glen Stubbe photo. Photo copyright 2003 by the *Star Tribune*.

The future could turn out well for MTS in Minnesota given that Illinois Tool Works is a highly regarded company, but the MTS story has already ended favorably for Mairs & Power. In 2016, the Growth Fund recognized a gain of $59.9 million from its investment after liquidating its MTS stock. Two years later, at Theobald's suggestion to the Mairs & Power Mutual Funds Board, Susan Knight was elected to the Board as an independent trustee. The firm's decision to get out of this stock—like its decision years earlier to sell off its long-held position in IBM stock—stands as a reminder that Mairs & Power's "buy and hold" practice of hanging onto stocks doesn't mean "hold forever."[11]

Insofar as the stock market was concerned, the wind had been at Theobald's back. Over the five years that ended on December 31, 2017, when he stepped down from his CEO post and retired:

- The Dow rose 85 percent, to 24,719 from 13,104.
- The S&P 500 Index climbed 88 percent, to 2,674 from 1,426.
- The assets of the Growth Fund rose 89 percent, to $4.7 billion from $2.5 billion. Adding in the firm's other two funds and the separately managed accounts, assets under management at Mairs & Power now topped $10 billion.

Norb Conzemius, the St. Paul banker who chaired the fund board for much of Theobald's time as CEO, praised him, particularly for his work in compliance procedures and for tightening up the management at Mairs & Power. On January 1, 2018, Mark Henneman took over as chairman and CEO. Like Theobald, he had been preparing to take on his new responsibilities for years. The shift, widely expected, was another seamless transition.[12]

CHAPTER 11

Amid Uncertainty, Preparing Mairs & Power for a New Century

A more unsettled environment awaited Mark Henneman, who became the CEO at Mairs & Power at the start of 2018. The next three-and-a-half years would be marked by wild gyrations in the stock market, the growing dominance of a handful of Big Tech stocks, and the COVID-19 pandemic. This turned out to be a time for cool heads, flexible leadership, and new ideas. The firm was able to make more key hires and engineer smooth transitions among fund managers. It carried out a modest rebalancing of the Growth Fund's portfolio, worked through a dip and then a rebound in the Fund's relative performance, developed an exchange-traded fund (ETF), studied other non-traditional initiatives, and shaped an increasing commitment to diversity as Minnesota and the nation struggled with divisive cultural, gender, and racial controversies.

Henneman had already seen plenty of turbulence in the securities markets. Before he came to Mairs & Power in 2004, he had spent 13 years analyzing securities and managing money at three of the Twin Cities' largest asset management firms. After getting an MBA from the University of Minnesota's Carlson School of Management in 1991, he began his investment career as an analyst at the St. Paul Companies (now Travelers Companies). He went on to become a portfolio manager at Advantus Capital Management, an arm of St. Paul based-Securian Financial Group. Then he moved to U.S. Bancorp Asset Management (now Nuveen Asset Management) as a managing director and process leader.

Mark Henneman has been the CEO of Mairs & Power since the beginning of 2018. Photo courtesy of Mairs & Power.

The biggest uncertainty Mairs & Power faced during these years was the onset and spread of the worst pandemic since the "Spanish

Andrea Stimmel is the chief operating officer at Mairs & Power. Photo courtesy of Mairs & Power.

Flu" contagion swept across the world in 1918. Suddenly, in March 2020, employers everywhere had to shut down their workplaces and send their workers off to do their jobs entirely online, from offices in their homes. Andrea Stimmel, the firm's chief operating officer, drew on her experience with technology to help the firm prepare and carry out a disaster recovery plan to keep operating if its staffers would no longer be able to work at the office.

Under Stimmel, Mairs & Power had made significant investments in technology. Her undergraduate degree from Lafayette College, the alma mater of the firm's founder, was in international affairs. She went on to earn an accounting degree at the University of Wisconsin-Eau Claire. Stimmel joined Mairs & Power at the start of 2005, but she had been auditing the firm's mutual fund books from 1996 to 2002, when she was at the Ernst & Young accounting firm. She knew many of the people at Mairs & Power long before she joined the firm.[1]

DRESS REHEARSAL FOR THE COVID-19 PANDEMIC

"Andrea convinced me that it would be a good idea to plan a work-from-home day to see if all the new systems really worked," Henneman said. "So, on a beautiful, warm summer day [August 8, 2019], the entire staff stayed home and attempted to work remotely. There were lots of issues that came up that day, but the vast majority of them were resolved immediately and we were proud to say that Mairs & Power could indeed continue to operate, even if we couldn't get into our downtown St. Paul office."[2]

By late February 2020, as the virus was spreading around the world and beginning to adversely affect securities markets, the leaders of the firm—Henneman, Stimmel, and Rob Mairs—implemented a partial disaster recovery plan. Anyone who chose to work from home could do so; several staff members did. On March 13, with the public health emergency worsening rapidly, the committee fully executed its disaster recovery plan. All staffers were expected to work from home, effective Monday, March 16—11 days before Minnesota's governor issued a stay-at-home order.

Henneman said the preparation plus staff members' adaptability, focus, and flexibility were the keys to avoiding the disruption the pandemic might have caused. "Our staff quickly learned how to use the new tools that contributed to their productivity in the new working reality," he said. Management worked out arrangements with staffers who needed to adjust their schedules to care for their children or their parents. There were no unexpected departures from the company. Instead, Mairs & Power hired new employees in its investor relations and private capital management departments. The staff focused on making sure its clients' investments were not a source of concern for them, in part by accelerating the issuance of the firm's quarterly letter. And, as Henneman noted, investment managers were taking advantage of the crash in the market to aggressively buy stocks at very attractive prices.

It was a bruising if not chilling time. The cascading Dow Jones Industrials and S&P 500 both hit their 2020 lows on March 23—the Dow at 18,916, down from 28,538 at the start of the year; the S&P at 2,237, down from 3,320 over the same period. The National Bureau of Economic Research declared in June what everybody knew by then: that the economy had fallen into a recession in February. Yet in the end, the disruption caused by the pandemic turned out to be largely just another day at the office—in this case, many offices in employees' homes—for Mairs & Power.

The funds' quarterly letter to shareholders, sent in April 2020, sought to reassure them. Fund managers Andy Adams, Henneman, and Pete Johnson wrote that they were greatly comforted by two factors: the Federal Reserve's aggressive moves to support the U.S. financial system and the strength of the banking system, which was in much better shape than it had been going into the financial crisis of 2008–2009. The market hammered the Growth Fund's first quarter return, -18.8 percent; the S&P fared worse, -19.6 percent.

The funds' managers began their letter with sobering words that described the shock waves the pandemic had set off in the stock market. "On Feb. 19, the S&P

In 2018 Andy Adams became the chief investment officer at Mairs & Power. The following year he became the firm's lead manager of the Growth Fund. Photo courtesy of Mairs & Power.

Pete Johnson was named the co-manager of the Growth Fund in 2019. Photo courtesy of Mairs & Power.

James Alt is an independent trustee on the Mutual Fund Board at Mairs & Power. Photo courtesy of Mairs & Power.

Mary Schmid Daugherty is an independent trustee on the Mutual Fund Board at Mairs & Power. Photo courtesy of Mairs & Power.

Susan Knight is an independent trustee on the Mutual Fund Board at Mairs & Power. Photo courtesy of Mairs & Power.

Patrick Thiele is an independent trustee the Mutual Fund Board at Mairs & Power. Photo courtesy of Mairs & Power.

500 closed at an all-time high of 3,386," they wrote in their April letter. "Not many days before, the Dow Jones Industrial Average set a new closing record of 29,551. Then the astounding 11-year bull market came to a screeching halt. We are all too familiar with the reasons. The novel coronavirus and COVID-19 illness it caused was the trigger, as the entire world came face-to-face with a pandemic whose length and breadth remain uncertain. The social distancing, shelter-in-place orders, closing of retailers and restaurants, and massive layoffs are wreaking havoc on the domestic and global economies."

In April, the Mairs & Power Mutual Fund Board changed its schedule from quarterly face-to-face meetings to weekly virtual meetings and written updates from the company. In June, the board shifted to monthly meetings. In September, it went back to quarterly meetings.

By the summer, Mairs & Power had partially reopened its office to staff members. All employees will want the option of at least occasionally working remotely once the pandemic has passed, Henneman said later. "We will accommodate that. Our approach to getting people back together again will be to use a magnet, not a mandate." The pandemic forced Mairs & Power to cancel another offsite strategic planning session that had been scheduled for mid-2020. Instead, participants met for three half-day sessions on Zoom.

HEADWINDS SHIFT TO TAILWINDS

The firm's flagship Growth Fund, the principal yardstick for its overall performance, encountered headwinds in 2019 and 2020. The S&P 500 outperformed the Growth Fund by one to three percentage points in each of those years. In 2020, the market turbulence led the Growth Fund to post a 14.5 percent turnover rate (the share of a portfolio's holdings replaced in a given year). This rate, still extremely low for the industry, nonetheless was the highest for the Fund since 2000.

Figure 2
Turnover Data for the Mairs & Power Growth Fund, 1975-2020

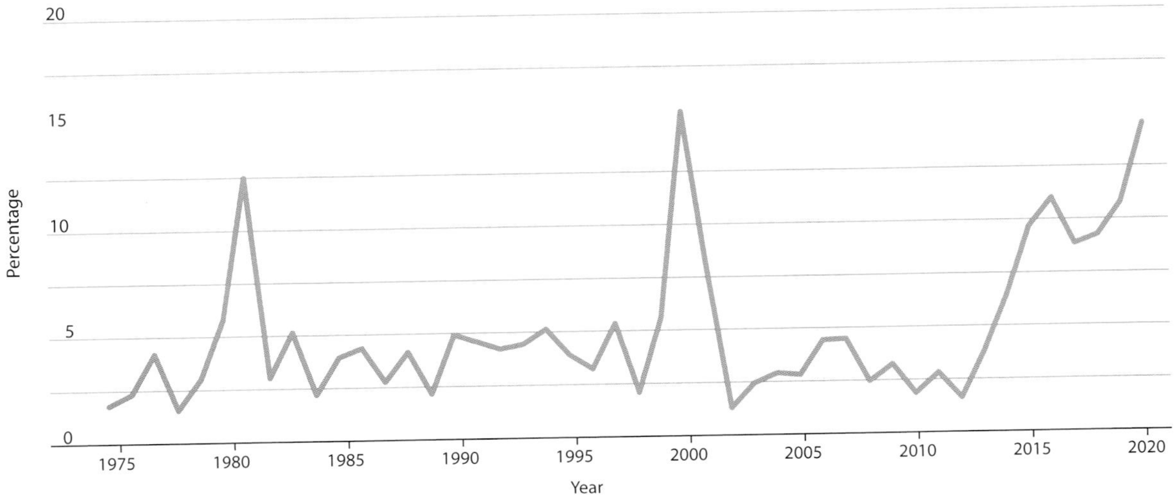

But in the year ended June 30, 2021, the Fund, while still lagging over five- and ten-year periods, moved ahead in the one-year comparison by posting a 43 percent return vs. the S&P's 40.8 percent. These mid-year performance numbers reflected a stunning rebound for the overall market, which had still not climbed back to its pre-pandemic high by mid-2020. On June 30, 2021, the Dow closed at 34,502 and the S&P at 4,298, far above their pre-pandemic highs.

The firm's total assets under management, which had reached $9.7 billion at the end of 2017, didn't return to that level until closing out 2020 at $10.5 billion. Then they rose to a record $11.7 billion at mid-2021, with roughly half of the increase coming from the Growth Fund.

The annual turnover rate for stocks in the Mairs & Power Growth Fund as seen in Figure 2 has been remarkably and consistently far below the average turnover rate for similar funds, reflecting the carefully researched "buy and hold" style of investing followed by the Fund's managers. Since 1975, turnover rates have topped 10 percent just five times. In most years, this rate has been below 5 percent.

Most of all, the tailwinds had been whipped up by Big Tech, notably the "FAAMG" stocks—Facebook, Apple, Amazon, Microsoft, and Google (Alphabet)—which had sometimes almost single-handedly been fueling the bull market in recent years. By early 2021, just these five stocks had accounted for 29 percent of the rise in all 500 of the S&P stocks over the past five years. The pandemic acted as a rocket booster for them. Millions of Americans, who had suddenly turned their homes into their offices, became more dependent on Big Tech's goods and services.[3]

As the manager of the Growth Fund, George Mairs III bought stocks if he understood their business model and could see a defendable and sustainable path of profitability. In the 1990s, most technology stocks came up short on one or both of these counts. George saw Twin Cities-based ADC Telecom as an exception. It met both of those criteria and differed from many of the rest of the stocks in the dot-com and tele-com bubbles. ADC actually made things of lasting value: fiberoptic cable and other telecommunications equipment that the big phone companies needed to build out the infrastructure for the burgeoning Internet. But in the late 1990s, the stock got swept up in the fervor for tech stocks. The Fund benefited from the run-up in ADC stock. In 1997 and again in 1999, it was the Fund's largest holding. Mark Henneman looked back on that time. "In 1999, when the

In this photo from 1998, workers at the ADC Communications plant in Hopkins, Minn., are assembling circuit boards for installation in the company's products. This photograph was part of a project on telecommunications workers sponsored by the Minnesota Historical Society. Stephen M. Dahl photo, copyright 1998 by Stephen M. Dahl.

pressure was greatest on George Mairs III to join the party and buy high-flying technology stocks, he not only resisted the temptation but showed unwavering conviction in his investment discipline by selling a quarter of the Growth Fund's shares in ADC because he viewed the stock as wildly overvalued," Henneman said.

While George had almost totally steered clear of technology companies up to and during the dot-com craze in the late 1990s, the 2018–2021 period was a time when "tech stocks" took on a new meaning—Big Tech. Andy Adams, the Growth Fund's lead manager, conceded in a July 2021 call that "we were a little late" to realize the strength of today's Big Tech companies. Perhaps inevitably, though, the FAAMGs had by then gained a significant presence in the Fund. It got into Alphabet in 2016, Microsoft in 2018, and Amazon in the last half of 2020. By the end of 2020, Alphabet and Microsoft had become the Fund's first and second largest holdings, respectively. By mid-2021, Amazon had become the Fund's fourth largest holding, behind Microsoft, first; Alphabet, second; and UnitedHealth Group, third. Another Big Tech giant, NVIDIA, was fifth.

How could the Fund's current managers square their newfound commitment to technology stocks with George Mairs III's aversion to such stocks? The answer was that the firm's analysts found that Alphabet, Microsoft, and Amazon had gained enduring competitive advantages like those that George had discerned for the stocks he picked. The Big Tech companies bore no resemblance to the dot-coms (though it should be noted that Amazon got its start as a dot-com). They were highly profitable, scaled up to mammoth sizes, operated globally, and held commanding positions in their markets. While in earlier times, larger tech companies could be disrupted by upstarts barely out of the founder's garage, the FAAMGs seemed immune to such threats because of their immense market power and deep pockets.

Although the Growth Fund had notably bulked up its holdings in Big Tech, it had not gone overboard in acquiring these powerful companies; instead, it maintained its tilts toward value investing and holding stocks from companies in Minnesota and nearby states. That proved helpful in the first half of 2021. Piper Sandler's index of Minnesota companies, a rough measure of how well their stocks are performing, was up 7.3 percent through the first six months of the 2021; it had fallen 11.6 percent in 2020. Minnesota stocks' share of the Growth Fund, measured by the number of stocks and by their market value, did not change significantly during the first six months of 2021.

In 2019, Morningstar singled out the Growth Fund as one of 10 equity funds with high "wide moat" rankings, meaning that these funds concentrate their investments in companies with competitive advantages strong enough to fight off challengers. Morningstar analyst Tony Thomas noted that while the Growth Fund's managers favor companies headquartered near their office in St. Paul, their preference for regional stocks "does not keep them from investing elsewhere given the right opportunities."[4]

The name "Growth Fund" is shorthand for a more nuanced package of stocks. Morningstar classifies it as a "large blend" fund, which suggests a combination of both growth and value large capitalization stocks. While the Fund focuses on large-cap stocks, it also includes a sprinkling of mid-cap and small-cap stocks. And above all, it focuses on stocks best suited for long-term investors.

Thomas has given the Growth Fund a "silver" ranking, Morningstar analysts' second highest ranking, for four years. His March 29, 2021, report on the Growth Fund gave it above-average ratings for its approach to investing, the quality of its managers and investment professionals, its low charges to investors, and its ability to adapt to a new era by launching a new fund in 2021. He noted that the Fund's performance had slipped in recent years due to its relatively light tech holdings and modest showings by its financial picks. But by early 2021, Thomas had noticed a "headwinds to tailwinds" shift at the Growth Fund. Soon, the shift became more pronounced. For 2021 through August 23, Thomas found that the Fund was performing in the top 11 percent of all the funds in its category.

"I'd just say that the improved performance is typical for the Growth Fund's long history, and it shows the value of being patient— both as a portfolio manager and as a fundholder," Thomas said. "Two of the Fund's worst performers in 2020 were banks, U.S. Bank and Wells Fargo. A short-term investor might have sold both stocks on such weak performances, but Mairs & Power—which has owned both for at least three decades (perhaps even longer) in the Growth Fund— stuck with them. Both stocks are among the Fund's top performers in

2021. The patience of Mairs & Power's managers paid off—and similarly, fundholders who stuck around through 2020s middling performance have fared pretty well in 2021."

Thomas likened Mairs & Power to Dodge & Cox, a much larger mutual fund firm in San Francisco. Both firms are unusual in that they have endured for so long. Dodge & Cox was founded in 1930, a year before Mairs & Power got started. Both are employee-owned, focus on long-term investing, and have similarly structured investment committees.

EDGING INTO ETF TERRITORY

In March 2021, Mairs & Power surprised many fund-watchers by introducing an exchange-traded fund (ETF) designed for fixed-income investors: the Minnesota Municipal Bond ETF. The firm had been quietly exploring the idea for several years. By limiting its portfolio to Minnesota-only securities—the bonds of highly-rated issuers such as the State of Minnesota, the Metropolitan Airports Commission, and certain counties, cities, school districts, and special agencies—the new fund was sticking with and putting a new twist on the firm's traditional Minnesota/regional focus. Brent Miller, a Minnesota native and the current president of the Minnesota Society of Municipal Analysts, was named as the lead manager of the new fund.

In early 2021, Mairs & Power established its Minnesota Municipal Bond exchange-traded fund (ETF) and named Brent Miller its lead manager. Photo courtesy of Mairs & Power.

The new fund, the first Minnesota-only municipal ETF bond fund, was also designed to tap into the popularity of ETFs. Most of the money pouring into these funds had gone into index-based ETFs that hold a basket of stocks representing the entire market, such as the S&P 500 Index. "Passive investors"—content to let the index funds "buy the market" instead of delegating the decisions to fund managers—had become more prevalent in recent years. Index-based ETFs can charge investors less because they don't need to retain research staffs. According to the Investment Company Institute, the assets of index-based ETFs accounted for 7 percent of all mutual fund assets at the end of 2010;[5] by the end of 2020, their share had risen to 22 percent.[6]

Unlike mutual funds, ETFs can be traded on an exchange at any time during the trading day just as stocks are (the Mairs & Power ETF trades on the Chicago Board of Options Exchange). While the firm's

ETF leaves the decisions on what bonds to buy to Mairs & Power, it offers a diverse selection of bonds, charges low fees, and pays Minnesota investors dividends that are exempt from federal and state taxes.

Mark Henneman saw the firm's move to establish an ETF as offering a twofold advantage for Mairs & Power and its clients. First, the new fund gave its shareholders trading flexibility and lower transaction costs while at the same time not distributing capital gains to them. Second, creating the fund gave the firm the opportunity to gain expertise in the management and administration of ETFs. "There is an emerging trend to move more actively managed mutual funds to ETFs," Henneman said. "While there are a number of hurdles still to clear, I predict that Mairs & Power will be an early participant in actively managed ETFs, similar to the way we were early participants in mutual funds."[7]

DEFINING A BROADER VISION

One of the country's most jarring mood swings in recent times came in 2020. That was the year of the death of George Floyd, which ultimately led to the conviction of Minneapolis police officer Derek Chauvin on two counts of murder and one of manslaughter. Floyd was an African American. His death led to widespread protests around the world and heightened concerns about racial inequities. This was also a time of many high-profile controversies about gender inequities. Leaders at many corporations and other institutions began to think harder about diversity issues.

Henneman had established an Inclusion & Diversity Committee in 2019, before the Floyd death and subsequent unrest in the Twin Cities. The Committee stepped up its activity after those developments, proposing new initiatives on recruiting, training, creating goals, and measuring progress in meeting them.[8]

The Winds of Change: Inclusion and Diversity

Among the initiatives that came out of Mairs & Power's strategic planning process in 2017 was one that has taken on a higher priority since then: diversifying its staff and supporting inclusion and diversity in other ways. A mounting number of studies in recent years have strengthened the arguments for embracing this concept.

One came from the Chartered Financial Analysts Research Foundation, which said this: "With the complex problems faced in investment situations, groups can get stuck if they have limited diversity where everyone thinks in the same way. Such difficulties are far less likely if the diversity is deep and derived from wider sources of knowledge, perspective, experience, values, and ways of thinking."[9] Another, from the Credit Suisse Research Institute, found that companies with higher female participation at the board level or in top management exhibit higher returns, higher valuations, and higher payout ratios.[10] The McKinsey & Company consulting firm has followed this topic in articles and research for years. "The business case for gender equality, diversity, and inclusion is strong and growing stronger," McKinsey said in 2021.[11]

In 2019, Mark Henneman established an Inclusion and Diversity Committee at Mairs & Power to strengthen the firm's commitment to diversity. The six-person committee, chaired by human resources manager Tammy Osman, seeks to assist the leadership of the firm "in maintaining a climate of broad inclusion and to help managers and employees professionally thrive in a diverse environment." The firm created the Committee to help it avoid "group thinking" that suppresses innovation. The Committee's guiding principle is to assist in implementing diversity of thought in the workplace "because that will lead to better collaboration, problem-solving solutions, and overall success." The four-person management team that leads Mairs & Power strongly supports the Committee's role.[12]

A Widening Perspective

After the death of George Floyd in Minneapolis in the spring of 2020, Committee members began talking about racial inequities and social justice issues. Melissa Gilbertson, an Inclusion & Diversity Committee member and the firm's information technology and trading manager, said this marked the first time the group discussed such matters openly. The discussions led the Committee to shape a broader view of diversity—for example, asking whether the firm should give this concern more attention in its charitable giving and volunteer activities.[13]

One result: a donation to the Hazelden Betty Ford Foundation in Center City, Minnesota, for a continuing education program designed to help attorneys and law enforcement officials deal with the unique challenges facing those with substance abuse disorders and legal issues. These problems disproportionately affect African American communities. Other recent donations have gone to the International Institute of Minnesota, one of the state's principal refugee resettlement agencies, and to Ujamaa Place, a St. Paul nonprofit that works with a wide array of community partnerships to help young black men in the Twin Cities area raise their odds for success. Veteran portfolio manager Glenn Johnson has been volunteering at Ujamaa Place since 2010. Staff members continued to help Habitat for Humanity build homes for families needing affordable housing, an outreach effort they began in 2015, but they also got engaged in new efforts designed to help minorities. Gilbertson and Mary Schmid Daugherty, who chairs the firm's mutual fund board, began working with the Academy of Finance, a program at Como Senior High School in St. Paul that introduces students—many of them women and minorities—to business and finance.[14]

Mairs & Power, like many firms in the financial sector, did not put a priority on diversity until recently. The leadership of the industry, particularly on Wall Street, has long been dominated by older, white men. That began to change at Mairs & Power when Andrea Stimmel joined the firm at the start of 2005 as its accounting manager. The firm's accounting systems, manageable when it was smaller, had become inadequate as it had grown. It had

a capable and committed operations staff but lacked the expertise that Stimmel had. She was a certified public accountant with experience not just at the Ernst & Young accounting firm but also with several retailers including Target and Banana Republic. "Over the next several years, Andrea gradually established herself as treasurer and chief operational officer much before she actually was given those titles," Jon Theobald said. (She was named chief operating officer in 2018).

Reconciliations for some of the firm's accounts were being done only once a quarter. Stimmel upgraded the accounting system so reconciliations could be done daily. She became the primary liaison with the Charles Schwab Corporation on both the separately managed accounts and the mutual funds; advocated for adding staff in human resources, finance, information technology, and operations; and was the principal driver of moves to outsource functions such as financial reporting, performance measurement, and expense management. She introduced annual budgets and performance reviews, worked closely with Theobald on compliance issues, and succeeded him as chief compliance officer in 2012. After an SEC exam in 2008, Mairs & Power agreed to engage an outside consultant, Vista 360, to do a thorough audit of all the firm's compliance activities. Stimmel worked closely with Vista 360's year-long audit, and led the effort to implement its recommendations, a huge undertaking that took another two years.

Women had been given low single-digit stakes in the firm over the years, but Stimmel, who initially purchased stock in the firm in 2007, became the first woman to own a significant stake—one comparable to the portions owned by the men at the top of the firm. Gilbertson, who had a background of technology and project management experience before coming to the firm in 2007, became a shareholder in 2015. Michelle Warren came to Mairs & Power in 2016, becoming its first female investment professional. Soon she became an owner. Elizabeth VanHeel, the operations manager, who had joined the firm in 2011, became an owner in 2021. So Mairs & Power, where no woman held a significant ownership stake before 2007, had four women with important investment and management jobs among its sixteen owners by 2021.

In 2018, Mary Schmid Daugherty became the first woman to chair the firm's Mutual Fund Board. At the same time, Susan Knight, a former CFO at MTS Systems who went on to become chair of the board at Surmodics Inc., joined the fund board. Thus, two of the funds board's five members were women. The legal counsel for Mairs & Power's mutual funds is Ellen Drought, who specializes in mutual fund law for the Godfrey & Kahn law firm in Milwaukee.

In the summer of 2018, Wendy Lee came to Mairs & Power for a summer internship. Lee had attended an international school in Thailand and wanted to pursue undergraduate studies in U.S. She was drawn to the University of Wisconsin-Madison by the school's economics program and business school. Lee earned an undergraduate degree in business administration from UW-Madison and then a graduate degree in finance, with a specialty in applied securities analysis, from the school. In 2019, Mairs & Power hired her as an analyst, joining Michelle Warren as the firm's second female analyst.

CEO Mark Henneman is deeply committed to diversity. He and his wife, both graduates of Gustavus Adolphus College and significant donors there, have established an annual scholarship designed primarily to encourage women and minorities at the school to pursue careers in finance. Their daughter is a recruiter for Ameriprise in Minneapolis.[15]

Test for the Industry

The challenge of becoming more diverse is hardly limited to Mairs & Power. It's now widely seen as a special concern in the investment business vs. other major professions. In 2018, a *New York Times* reporter raised the question of why so few women run mutual funds. Working with Morningstar and Flowspring, an independent asset manager research firm, the reporter found that less than 10 percent of U.S. portfolio managers at mutual funds and exchange-traded funds were women. "We've been looking at this for years," said Laura Pavlenko, head of fund research for North America Morningstar. "Women are just stuck at that number." In 2015, Morningstar found that 37 percent of doctors, 33 percent of lawyers, and 63 percent of accountants and auditors were women.[16]

Closer to home, the Minnesota Chartered Financial Analysts Society, the principal organization for investment professionals, has been tracking the numbers for years. In 2021, six of its fifteen directors were women. Yet surveys have consistently shown that a far lower share of its members are women.[17] The Minnesota CFA's parent organization surveys its Minnesota membership annually. In 2020, its survey found that women accounted for just 13 percent of the Minnesota affiliate's 1,381 members. This share was virtually unchanged from 2014 and, according to Susanna Gibbons, hasn't changed much since the mid-1980s. Gibbons is the managing director for Carlson Funds Enterprise, the investment program run by students at the University of Minnesota's Carlson School of Management. She has watched the diversity story unfold for more than 30 years, first as an analyst at J.P. Morgan in Manhattan and later for several other firms there and in the Twin Cities.[18]

The research arm of the CFA Institute found that in 2016, women represented 57 percent of all college graduates in the U.S., 50 percent of the certified public accountants, 48 percent of medical students, and 47 percent of law students. Yet among CFA charter holders—those who have earned the gold standard for professional money managers and analysts—just 18 percent were women.[20]

In 1999, Mary Schmid Daugherty founded the Aristotle Fund, a student-run investment fund at the University of St. Thomas like the student program that Gibbons manages at the Carlson School. The gender breakdown of the students in the St. Thomas fund typically shows an overwhelmingly male tilt: just two of the fourteen students in the fall of 2020. Daugherty cannot recall a single occasion since 1987, the year she began teaching at St. Thomas, when a first-year woman student asked her about the prospects for a job in investment banking.[21]

Why haven't more women gone into finance? The answers are complicated. Part of the problem is the culture, which is hard to change. For many decades, the men who have run the investment firms routinely recruited other men, who ultimately succeeded them. The Inclusion and Diversity Committee has been trying to change that pattern by suggesting non-traditional recruiting strategies as well as focusing on creating an inclusive culture to retain all employees. Often, firms focus on attractive candidates, only to fail at supporting and retaining them. The firm identified inclusion as an important part of its efforts to diversify its employee pool.

Daugherty blames some of the difficulty in recruiting women to the hit the industry took during the financial crisis in 2008–2009. Many women, on the cusp of choosing careers, saw their parents lose jobs at investment firms. Thus, they chose to begin their work life in other fields, often less turbulent and, they felt, more likely to offer better opportunities for advancement.

Many argue that financial sector leaders compounded the problem by failing to do enough, many years ago, to open doors for women and minorities to rise from middle management jobs into top leadership positions. Gibbons said an entire generation of women concluded they couldn't move up, so "they dropped out of the pipeline." Today, she said, the men at the top of many investment firms acknowledge this and are trying to change the culture of their enterprises, but often they face resistance from men in middle management positions.

"I think a lot about this topic," said Andrea Stimmel. She cited as one factor the lack of role models at the top of investment firms.

Many say the industry's negative image, as portrayed by the media and Hollywood, has chased women away. While a number of television shows have presented lawyers favorably, Wall Street financial executives—almost always men—have been depicted less positively. Frequently mentioned in this regard is the searing portrait that director Martin Scorsese drew of Wall Street in *The Wolf of Wall Street*, a 2013 film that became the first major American movie to be released exclusively through digital distribution. Financially, the movie was a huge success, grossing more than $392 million worldwide to become Scorsese's highest-grossing film.[22]

Is the harsh image deserved? Many might look back at the long track record of Wall Street scandals and say yes. In 2012, Jack Bogle, who founded the Vanguard mutual fund group, wrote this: "When I came into this field, the standard seemed to be 'there are some things that one simply doesn't do.' Today, the standard is 'if everyone else is doing it, I can do it, too.'"

Is it different in Minnesota, far from the dog-eat-dog, transactional, anything-goes culture that continues to characterize so much of Wall Street? Yes, from the perspective of Susanna Gibbons, who sees the ethical standards and practices that prevail in the Twin Cities investment community as far higher than on Wall Street. But what about the investment community's commitment to better opportunities for women and minorities? While Gibbons credits Mairs & Power for tackling this challenge, she feels that generally, investment firms in the Twin Cities still lag behind their counterparts in Manhattan.

How does Mairs & Power stack up against its peers on efforts to foster inclusive environments for people and groups based on race, gender, age, or sexual orientation? Andrea Stimmel and Melissa Gilbertson cite significant progress on this front at the firm. "We do well," Gilbertson said. "Could we do better? Absolutely."

Skywater Technology, located in Bloomington, Minn., manufactures semiconductor chips that are used in electronics, automobiles, medical devices, aerospace, and weapons. In late 2020, the U.S. Department of Defense paid $170 million to fund the cost of constructing a third clean room at Skywater's plant. Brian Peterson photo. Photo copyright 2021 by the Star Tribune.

Starting in 2020, initial public offerings, long dormant in the Twin Cities, began showing signs of life. Mairs & Power's funds don't normally buy shares of companies when they go public, but occasionally they add them shortly afterward. Newly public companies expand the pool of stocks that the firm's funds can consider for investment. Both the Growth Fund and the Small Cap Fund took positions in Jamf Holding Corporation, a Minneapolis company that helps businesses and institutions manage Apple devices, after that firm went public in 2020. The Small Cap Fund added Skywater Technology, a Bloomington computer chipmaker, after that company went public in 2021. By summer of 2021, three more Minnesota companies had gone public, and others were considering doing so.[23]

"It's wonderful, from our standpoint," Andy Adams, lead manager of the Growth Fund, said of the uptick in Minnesota IPO activity. He noted that acquisitions of Minnesota companies and other factors had reduced the number of public companies based in the state. "At the core of our strategy is getting to know companies well and even with all of the technology we have at our disposal these days, it still is great to be able to talk with a management team in person and tour their facilities," Adams said. "Certainly, having more companies within driving range makes that easier for us to accomplish."[24]

The Web Marketing Association named the Mairs & Power website as 2020's Best Mutual Fund Website. The award was presented to Sun-Star Strategic, the marketing firm that redesigned the site.[25]

During the 2018–2021 period, Mairs & Power continued its smooth transitions in the lead management of its mutual funds, and of avoiding the potential fallout that can occur when a "star" mutual fund manager retires or leaves for some other reason. Typically, the firm handled these shifts by moving a fund's seasoned co-manager into the lead manager's role. Kevin Earley became the lead manager of the Balanced Fund and Bob Thompson its co-manager in 2018 upon the retirement of long-time fund manager Ronald Kaliebe; Thompson was also named co-manager of the new bond ETF fund in 2021. Andy Adams succeeded Henneman as chief investment officer in 2018 and became lead manager of the Growth Fund in 2019. Also in 2019, Pete Johnson was named co-manager of the Growth Fund and Allen Steinkopf became the lead manager of the Small Cap Fund. In 2021, Chris Strom joined Steinkopf as co-manager of that Fund. On the separately managed side of the business, Justin Miller and Pat Farley took over the management of the accounts that had been handled by Peter Robb, who retired at the end of 2020.

BUILDING FOR TOMORROW

Mairs & Power continued to build out its capacity through new hires during this period. In addition to Pat Farley, mentioned in the previous chapter, the firm added more analysts: in 2019, Brent Miller, who had been a fixed-income analyst at the Travelers Company and would soon be

In 2019 Allen Steinkopf became the lead manager of the Small Cap Fund at Mairs & Power. Photo courtesy of Mairs & Power.

Chris Strom is currently the co-manager of the firm's Small Cap Fund. Photo courtesy of Mairs & Power.

Justin Miller joined Mairs & Power in 2015. Four years later, he was promoted to vice president and investment manager. Photo courtesy of Mairs & Power.

Hired in 2018, Pat Farley is also a vice president and investment manager at Mairs & Power. Photo courtesy of Mairs & Power.

As an equity analyst at Mairs & Power, Supanan (Wendy) Lee does analytical research on a wide variety of companies and investments. Photo courtesy of Mairs & Power.

tapped to lead the ETF bond fund, and Supanan (Wendy) Lee, who had interned at BNP Paribus in New York City and at Mairs & Power, as an equity analyst.

These newcomers, arriving in the wake of many others, brought the firm's staff count to 42, roughly four times the number of employees 20 years earlier. The staff included 11 analysts and portfolio managers; 7 in the management group, compliance, and human resources; 5 in operations and information technology; 5 client service support specialists; 4 in accounting and finance; 3 traders; 3 in investor relations; and 2 others in various support roles. Together, they provided the infrastructure the firm needed to oversee the $11.7 billion in assets that the firm managed as of June 30, 2021. About 59 percent of that total was in the three mutual funds and the ETF; the rest was in separately managed individual and institutional accounts.

Today, the firm estimates that the Growth Fund has more than 71,000 shareholders, nearly 44,000 of them in omnibus accounts. These accounts take the form of a single account on a brokerage platform

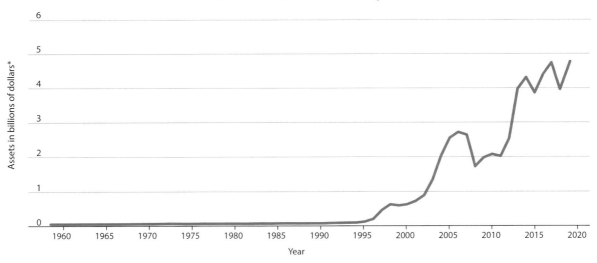

Figure 3
Mairs & Power Growth Fund Assets by Year, 1958–2020

*Assets at the end of the year

Figure 3 shows that the assets in the Mairs & Power Growth Fund slowly grew from the Fund's inception in 1958 until about 1995 when its assets increased significantly. Since 1995, the Growth Fund has returned to a slow and steady increase closing in on $5 billion at the end of 2020.

with underlying individual accounts, often with financial planners co-mingling the fund with other mutual funds and ETFs (see Figure 3).

Sixteen investment professionals and managers now hold an ownership stake in the company. They were invited to buy Mairs & Power stock after they had been at the firm for a year or more, and they will have to sell it back to their partners at the company when they retire or leave the firm. No one shareholder currently holds more than a sixth of the enterprise. This plan fulfills George Mairs III's vision that under broad, multiple-employee ownership, the firm would be far more likely to maintain its independence than under just one or two owners.

Mairs & Power, unlike almost all of its peers in America's formidable investment ecosphere, was still standing strong as an independent, employee-owned enterprise, after 90 years of doing business.

CHAPTER 12

The Benefits of Proximity

A close look back, at the geographical locations of the companies in the Mairs & Power Growth Fund since its birth in 1958, illustrates one of the firm's most significant characteristics: a commitment to investing in the region, particularly Minnesota. For decades, the Growth Fund, which accounted for 47 percent of the assets managed by the firm as of June 30, 2021, has distinguished itself by investing in Minnesota companies. It wasn't always that way. In 1958, just four of its 24 common stocks—3M, St. Paul Fire & Marine, Red Owl (then the dominant grocery retailer in the Twin Cities market), and Wood Conversion (a building materials producer)—were Minnesota companies. In only one of the Fund's first 13 years was the largest holding a Minnesota company. For four straight years, from 1967 to 1970, its largest stake was in a faraway company whose eye-grabbing signs were blitzing the country's new interstate highways: Holiday Inns, based in Memphis.

In 1966, just nine Minnesota companies accounted for 24 percent of the Fund's assets; yet new opportunities were percolating for its investors. By 1972, 19 state-based firms represented 40 percent of the assets. This rise continued for years, finally peaking in 1998, when Minnesota companies made up 80 percent of both the stocks and the assets. By mid-2021, state-based stocks had fallen to 39 percent of all stocks in the Fund and 41 percent of its assets (see Figure 4).

But the Fund's Minnesota focus, augmented today by a shift to invest more in stocks in neighboring states and by the establishment of a Small Cap Fund that follows a similar geographic strategy, still sets Mairs & Power apart from its peers. According to Russel Kinnel, who has tracked regional funds over the years for Morningstar, nearly all the regionally focused funds across the country have shut down due

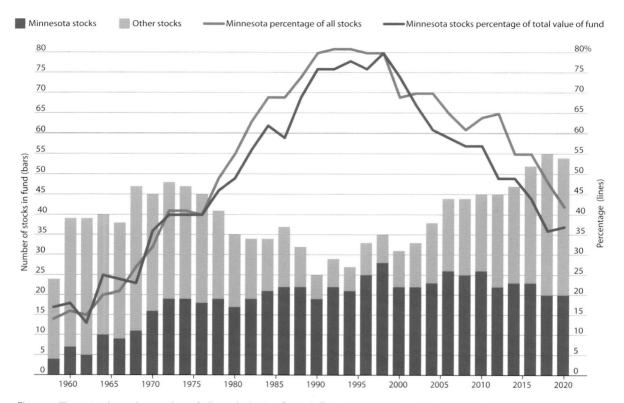

Figure 4
Minnesota Stocks Compared to All Stocks in the Mairs & Power Growth Fund, 1958–2020

■ Minnesota stocks ■ Other stocks —— Minnesota percentage of all stocks —— Minnesota stocks percentage of total value of fund

Figure 4 illustrates how the portion of all stocks in the Growth Fund that are stocks in Minnesota companies has changed since the Fund's inception in 1958. The share of the Fund represented by the number of Minnesota stocks and by their market values is down from its peak in the late 1990s, but it still looms large in the Fund. Shares of the Fund are shown in two-year intervals.

to declines in listings of public companies, fewer regional brokers, and other factors.[1]

CEO Mark Henneman continues to view regional investing as one of the three pillars of Mairs & Power (the other two are a focus on investing for the long term and offering clients the opportunity to invest in companies of all sizes). The firm's patient investing style—buying and holding stocks and trimming or boosting its stakes after meticulous research, often despite tumult in the market—contrasts with the much more frequent trading of most of its competitors.[2]

SHUNNING THE FRENZY

During its early years, the fund largely spurned a cloudburst of opportunities to invest in Minnesota companies. In 1957, the year before the Growth Fund's inception, William Norris and his associates had formed Control Data Corporation by selling stock directly to the public, without an underwriter as an intermediary, for a dollar a share. By mid-1960, the stock was trading at $46. Its runup sparked an explosion of startups that offered their stock to all comers. Minneapolis investor Don Hall chronicled the action in his 2014 book, *Generation of Wealth*. The excitement led to mind-blowing gains of stocks traded in the local over-the-counter (OTC) market—animal spirits extraordinaire.[3]

Each morning, banks, brokerage houses, and other interested investors would receive a consolidated quote sheet reporting the previous day's bid and asked prices for a list of local stocks. The daily newspapers published the list. Traders and investors tracked price changes during the day through a telephone network or by checking the latest quotes at brokerage firms in the downtowns of Minneapolis and St. Paul. In 1961, Jim Fuller left his job as a reporter for the *Electronic News* to start *The Upper Midwest Investor*, a publication he established to follow the hectic activity. A plate full of frenzy greeted him. The local quote sheets added 13 companies in the last half of 1959; another 13 in the first half of 1960; 24 in the last half of 1960; 42 more in the first half of 1961; an astonishing 54 in the last half of that year.

"Whether you realized it or not, you have recently witnessed the most fantastic period in local financial history," wrote Robert Smith, a principal in a St. Paul investment firm. "What has happened in our local securities market in the past two years, in many respects is far more unbelievable than was the 1929 stock market boom. In '29, if a stock went up 100 percent in six months, it was quite an event. Yet in our local market this year, many of our low-priced stocks went up 100 to 600 percent in six days to six weeks. And a new issue that went up only 50 percent was quite a disappointment."

The Three Georges who were partners at the firm then—George Mairs Jr., his son George Mairs III, and George C. Power Jr.—were unwilling to expose the fledgling Growth Fund to the risks of rampant speculation. Instead, in 1961 they launched the firm's second mutual fund, the Income Fund (later rebranded as the Balanced Fund). It was

a contrarian move designed to attract more sober-minded investors by offering them a mix of bonds and familiar large-capitalization stocks. The idea was that if stocks were not faring well, bonds would be. And vice versa. Generally, two-thirds or more of the Balanced Fund's stocks have been large companies based beyond Minnesota.

THE EUPHORIA'S COMPLEX LEGACY

By the end of 1961, the Growth Fund still had only half a dozen Minnesota stocks in its portfolio. Don Hall found that the Cities' two leading local brokerage firms then—Piper Jaffray & Hopwood and J.M. Dain & Co.—steered clear of the booming local stock market. "They didn't consider it intelligent investing," he noted. The stocks of most of these newly public companies soon crashed and burned. Was it wise for the Fund to pass on the local stock market boom at the time? "That's a reasonable assumption," Hall said. Andy Adams, who today is chief investment officer and lead manager of the Growth Fund, said he likely would have avoided such a market had it unfolded on his watch.[4]

Many would agree. When the Dow Jones Industrial Average plunged 26 percent in the spring of 1962, the tide went out on the local stock market. From March to June, Control Data's stock fell by half; the stocks of scores of other newly public firms plunged, or their companies simply collapsed. Later in the 1960s, the Growth Fund picked up a few of the most promising Minnesota companies. It bought Rosemount Engineering in 1963 and Tonka Toys in 1965. Both had been trading in the local market. Deluxe went public in 1965; the Fund picked it up the following year. Medtronic, which first appeared in the local quote sheets in 1960, showed up in the Fund in 1969. H.B. Fuller's initial public offering arrived in 1968; the Fund first acquired it in 1971. Dayton's (now Target) went public in 1967; the Fund added it in 1973. In 1968, the fever returned to the local stock market with 79 new listings. Again, the Growth Fund largely shunned them.

In the end, the local market provided critical early-stage financing for Control Data and later for Medtronic. These two companies became springboards for dozens of entrepreneurs. They left to launch a blizzard of startups in the computer hardware and medical technology sectors. Some of them survived for many years, as did stocks in other industries that managed to graduate from the local stock market and become well-established public companies today. A handful of them are still prominent in the Fund's current portfolio—Medtronic, Ecolab, Donaldson, Toro. Others, such as St. Jude Medical, produced significant gains for the Fund when they were acquired.

As Don Hall wrote: "Too many good things were happening. A new economy was developing that would eventually surpass lumber and mining in economic impact on the state

William Norris, seen here in 1983, was then the chairman of the Board of Control Data. He was a vocal advocate for Control Data turning social needs into business opportunities. Charles Bjorgen photo. Photo copyright 1983 by the *Star Tribune*.

Frank Werner (1922–2016), right, seen here with Vernon Heath, the company's secretary and treasurer in 1959, co-founded Rosemount Engineering in 1956 to develop temperature- and pressure-measuring sensors for jet airplanes and the U.S. space program. Rosemount later diversified into manufacturing industrial-pressure and temperature-measurement systems. Earl Seubert photo. Photo copyright 1959 by the *Star Tribune*.

Even though the consumer market for toys is highly competitive, Tonka has been able to sustain its sales success over time by manufacturing realistic-looking steel trucks and other construction equipment, as seen in this busy assembly line for front-end loaders. Duane Braley photo. Photo copyright 1984 by the *Star Tribune*.

of Minnesota." Better opportunities for picking good Minnesota stocks were growing and so were the Fund's stakes in them. In the years to come, such favorable circumstances would draw other Twin Cities investment firms to launch Minnesota-focused mutual funds. These included Perkins Capital Management, Kopp Investment Advisors, and Platt-Tschudy (its funds eventually became part of Investment Advisors Inc.). Today, those funds no longer exist.[5]

REACHING THE PEAK

Minnesota stocks have generated enormous gains for Growth Fund shareholders over the decades. At the highest point of the Growth Fund's Minnesota investing in 1998, 80 percent of the companies in the Fund's portfolio—28 of 35—and 80 percent of the value of the portfolio were Minnesota stocks. Then, the Minnesota presence in its portfolio began falling due in large part to a low-interest-rate environment that favored mergers and buyouts and to fewer companies going public. Chuck Dietz, the retired chief legal counsel for 3M who chaired the Mairs & Power mutual funds' board from 2004 to 2006, put it this way: "The local scene couldn't accommodate the growth that they were enjoying."[6]

By 2010, the market value of the Minnesota companies in the Fund had grown almost three-fold from 1998, but their share of the Fund's assets had fallen to 64 percent from 80 percent. Over that stretch, the Minnesota companies share of all companies in the Fund fell to 58 percent from 80 percent.

In 2017, a decision by the business desk at the *Star Tribune* illustrated how the falling number of public companies in Minnesota had reduced the choices available to Minnesota-only investors. The newspaper cut its annual performance roster of the state's 100 largest public

As a market leader in retailing, work at a Target store continues even after all its customers have gone home. Stephen M. Dahl photo. Copyright 1993 by Stephen M. Dahl.

Bloomington-based Donaldson Company manufactures a wide range of commercial and industrial filters, such as these engine filtration products. Sales of its filters have grown due to public health concerns about airborne germs and noxious particles resulting from the COVID pandemic, forest fires, and other harmful events. Photo courtesy of the Donaldson Company, Inc.

companies to the 50 largest. In 2000, the paper's list-makers still had 202 public companies based in the state to choose from; by 2020, that pool had fallen to around 75.[7] The decline in Minnesota mirrored the broader picture. The *Wall Street Journal* reported the number of domestic companies listed on U.S. stock exchanges dropped to 3,671 in 2017 from 7,322 in 1996.[8]

By 2020, Andy Adams was overseeing the deployment of the roughly $6 billion in the firm's three mutual funds and serving as the lead manager of the Growth Fund. He had spent the early stages of his career specializing in small-capitalization stocks for two large, diversified financial corporations in the Twin Cities. Adams loved the challenge of picking stocks, but his first employer decided to divest its equity funds. At his next stop, he became frustrated by the bureaucracy and departmental competition for resources. "Then, one day, Mairs & Power flashed up on my caller ID," he recalled. Mark Henneman, who years later would become Mairs & Power's CEO, wanted to know if Adams would consider moving to the firm. Adams was impressed by its reputation, its aversion to chasing short-term performance through heavy trading, and its employee ownership structure. In 2006, after nine months of back and forth, he accepted a job offer as a portfolio manager.

LOOKING MORE TO THE REGION AND BEYOND

A key part of Mairs & Power's response to the declining number of public companies in Minnesota was to search more broadly for opportunities in an Upper Midwest region, defined by the firm as a company located in states within a day's drive of the Twin Cities: Illinois (primarily the Chicago area), Minnesota, Wisconsin, Iowa, and the Dakotas. In 1993, the Growth Fund held the stock of just one company in the five nearby states; in 2020, only seven. In addition, the Fund began turning to stocks beyond these states. By the end of 2020, half of its 54 companies including two in Europe were based beyond the six-state region. By mid-2021, the Growth Fund's two largest holdings were Microsoft and Alphabet (Google); Amazon was the fourth largest. These "Big Tech" goliaths were among the six most valuable companies in the world. The Fund's 13th largest holding was Roche Holdings, the Swiss-based giant that includes U.S.-based Genentech and is the world's largest pharmaceutical company.

Andy Adams's Holy Grail is a stock that generates a strong return on investment and plows

Cleanliness is a very necessary condition in the assembly of medical products, such as these catheters manufactured by St. Jude Medical. Glenn Stubbe photo. Photo copyright 2003 by the *Star Tribune*.

Here workers assemble Pentair water pumps by hand in its Twin Cities plant. Bruce Bisping photo. Photo copyright 2012 by the *Star Tribune*.

its money back into the company. So much the better if it's a company based in the six-state region. Adams says he has visited roughly half of the 445 public companies in the region since coming to Mairs & Power. The overwhelming majority of them are Illinois (260), Minnesota (94), and Wisconsin (58). Another 33 are in Iowa, North Dakota, and South Dakota. In addition, the Growth Fund tracks return on invested capital and price-earnings ratios for companies based in three other interior states—Colorado (142 companies), Ohio (129), and Michigan (85).

MAPPING THE SECRET SAUCE

As the Growth Fund has become less "Minnesota-centric," the Fund's managers have changed the way they monitor existing stocks and choose new ones (see Table 1). George Mairs III relied heavily on intuition and familiarity with the top executives of the Fund's companies to make investment decisions. Much of his successful modus operandi was in his head, as opposed to a written process that could be passed on to portfolio managers and analysts. In 2004, when George III stepped down from managing the Growth Fund, Mark Henneman took on the task of capturing and preserving his style. "I had the opportunity to spend hundreds of hours with him learning the recipe to that secret sauce," Henneman said.[9]

Table 1. Cumulative Total Returns for Six of the Growth Fund's Most Successful Stocks, 1969–Present

NYSE Symbol	Company Name	Initial Purchase Date	M&P Cumulative Total Return (%)	S&P 500 Cumulative Total Return (%)
ECL	Ecolab	3/28/1969	41,210	19,538
MDT	Medtronic	4/30/1969	131,410	19,358
GGG	Graco	7/16/1970	52,779	18,696
STJ	St. Jude	10/15/1992	1,389	787
HRL	Hormel	7/17/1995	1,604	985
VAL	Valspar	5/11/1999	605	135

Table 1 shows how the cumulative total returns for six of the Growth Fund's most successful Minnesota stocks over the years compare with returns for the S&P 500 as of December 31, 2020. Currently, Ecolab, Medtronic, Graco, and Hormel are still in the Fund. St. Jude and Valspar securities were sold when those firms were acquired by other companies.

At Graco, this robot never gets tired assembling air hose needle valves for use by building contractors and paint stores serving the residential market. Glenn Stubbe photo. Photo copyright 2020 by the *Star Tribune*.

Michael Porter is a professor at the Harvard Business School who has written extensively about business strategy and competition. One of his best-known books is *Competitive Strategy: Techniques for Analyzing Industries and Competitors* (1980). Bloomberg photo. Getty Images.

Henneman's effort eventually led the firm to develop a framework for evaluating companies based on how much of a competitive advantage they have over their rivals. This structure builds on the work of Michael Porter, a business strategy expert at the Harvard Business School. In 1979, Porter identified five principal forces that a company operating in a competitive environment must deal with: the number and strength of the company's competitors; the power of its suppliers to charge higher prices; the likelihood that customers can find substitutes for the company's goods or services; the power of its customers to dictate prices; and the threat of new rivals entering the company's markets.[10]

The strongest and most enduring companies turn out to be those with "durable competitive advantages" over their rivals. Microsoft, the world's largest software company, is frequently cited for having such an advantage because of its ability to change swiftly. Many other professional investors who emphasize investing for the long haul have used durable competitive advantage analysis successfully for years. George III, who died in 2010, endorsed this process as an accurate representation of how he chose the enterprises in which he invested. He became a master of stock picking, thanks in large part to his intimate familiarity with nearby companies and their leaders. Today, analytical tools that weren't available then can help his successors to repeat his achievements. By 2020, 11 portfolio managers and analysts at Mairs & Power were doing durable competitive advantage studies of roughly 50 companies per year. The more straightforward of these studies might take only 50 hours of work; the most complex can require as much as 200 hours.

RETAINING COMMITMENT TO STATE, REGION

Even as the Minnesota presence in the Growth Fund has declined relative to the overall make-up of the fund, Mairs & Power retains its commitment to investing in the state's companies. Part of this allegiance is based on the conclusions of research such as the durable competitive analyses. But in a November 2019 address to the University of Minnesota's Carlson School of Management's "First Tuesday" gathering, Henneman also attributed the firm's still-large stake in Minnesota companies to the state's specialness: the diversity of its economy, a low unemployment rate, the quality of its work force, its high per capita gross domestic product, a large contingent of Fortune 500 companies, and strong commitments to the arts, charitable giving, and volunteerism. Despite the rising presence of Big Tech companies in the Fund, 6 of its 10 largest holdings were still Minnesota companies: UnitedHealth Group, Ecolab, U.S. Bancorp, Medtronic, Bio-Techne, and Graco. Seven more companies in the five neighboring states accounted for another 13 percent of the stocks and 11 percent of the value of the Fund.

Soon after Adams joined Mairs & Power in 2006, he was laying the groundwork for the Small Cap Fund. He launched it in 2011 and

Bio-Techne manufactures biotech research supplies, such as tissue-culture reagents, as well as instruments and clinical diagnostic products used in genomics research. Anthony Souffle photo. Photo copyright 2017 by the *Star Tribune*.

served as its lead manager until 2019. The fund was founded on the belief that "small acorns can grow to mighty oaks." The Small Cap Fund helped Mairs & Power build a greater geographical reach in the nearby region. From its beginning and since, most of this Fund's companies have been based in Minnesota and the rest of the region: 35 of 44 in 2012; 41 of 49 at mid-2021. Its largest holding in 2012 was MDU Resources Group, a diversified energy company headquartered in Bismarck, North Dakota. Its largest at mid-2021 was Wintrust Financial, a Chicago area company that grew by acquiring a string of suburban community banks in the wake of the financial crisis. At mid-2021, the 21 stocks in the region beyond Minnesota accounted for 50 percent of the value of the Small Cap Fund and the 20 in Minnesota had a 35 percent share.

Adams set up the Small Cap Fund to act much like an off-stage Broadway production can serve as a proving ground for casts and producers to graduate to the bright lights of Broadway. For example, Twin Cities-based Proto Labs, which provides rapid prototyping and related services for manufacturers, went public in 2011. The Small Cap Fund acquired it a few months later and valued this holding at $776,000 by the end of that year. In 2015, Proto Labs graduated to the Growth Fund and by mid-2021, the larger fund's stake in this company had risen to $11.5 million.

The future of the firm's commitment to Minnesota and nearby states will depend on whether the opportunities continue to be as fruitful as they have been. But for now, a regional approach to choosing companies to invest in, with a concentration on Minnesota stocks, has endured—now extended to the Small Cap Fund. Investment managers have known the companies in their neighborhood well, taken sizable stakes in the best of them, and spread their investments to companies of all sizes and industries. As Andy Adams put it: "I'm still a believer that this region is an awfully good pool to fish in."

Vicki Holt, who recently retired after seven years as CEO of Proto Labs, is seen here explaining how Proto developed an innovative process for using injection liquid silicone rubber as a substitute for glass in a variety of manufactured products. Proto Labs is an online and technology-enabled manufacturer of quick-turn computer numerical control machined and custom-molded parts for prototyping and short-run production. Bruce Bisping photo. Photo copyright 2015 by the *Star Tribune.*

Epilogue

Over its first 90 years, Mairs & Power had always invested in publicly traded stocks and bonds. In contrast, 2021 saw the birth of an entirely new line of business: private funds. The firm would continue to invest in large, mid-sized, and small-capitalization public companies on behalf of its mutual fund shareholders and the separately managed accounts of its clients, but now it would add financing venture-stage companies in Minnesota and five nearby states. In January, the firm established Mairs & Power Private Capital Management LLC, a wholly owned subsidiary. This move marked a seminal shift for the firm.

At the same time, other changes were also reshaping the structure and the culture of the company. For several years, Mairs & Power had been looking into the growing ESG movement—directing investments to companies that adhered to certain environmental, social, and governance standards. Generally, the firm's professionals had already been applying similar criteria in making their decisions on investments. But in 2021, Andy Adams, who heads the Mairs & Power Investment Committee, rolled out a plan to formally incorporate ESG standards into the firm's investment process.[1]

Another innovation: early in 2021, Mairs & Power became part of the rapidly growing move to Exchange-Traded Funds by establishing its Minnesota Municipal Bond ETF, which invests entirely in fixed-income securities sold by Minnesota governments. The firm is looking closely at the prospects for moving more deeply into ETFs.

And as discussed earlier, this was also a time of growing controversy over racial and gender inequities. In the wake of the death of George Floyd in Minneapolis, members of the firm's Inclusion & Diversity Committee stepped up their efforts to find ways—through non-traditional recruiting efforts, charitable donations, and volunteering—to engage more directly in dealing with these concerns. Other components essential to the future of the firm—strategic planning, team building, enhanced compliance processes, modern office technology, and updated administration—were now firmly in place.

Simply put, this isn't the Mairs & Power of the Three Georges anymore. Many other changes from their days are hard to miss: the firm's staff size and skill sets, its number of investment and management professionals, the scale and scope of its assets under management, and its capacity to deal with whatever comes its way as the world beyond grappled with the often-tempestuous times of the early 2020s.

Nonetheless, Mairs & Power was sticking with the menu that had made it so successful over the years under George Mairs Jr., his son George III, and George Power. Mark Henneman had a succinct, confident description for the process that was unfolding: "Preparing Mairs & Power for the next century."

The biggest takeaway from working through this saga in its totality is that after nine decades, Mairs & Power has endured as an independent firm—strong, prospering, and growing now under multiple employee-owners. Conversely, just about all other investment firms of one species or another that were doing business in the 1930s and '40s and for that matter much later, are long gone. They collapsed in one way or another, or were swallowed up by stronger firms, which in turn were often rolled up, spun out, split up, or turned on their heads.

Documenting this vanishing act would require a separate book, or perhaps several. Think about just the companies alluded to in this book: the original White, Weld, where Ron DeSellier worked before coming to Mairs & Power, and the rest of the wire houses that pre-dated modern times; Lehman Brothers, Bear Stearns, and even mighty Merrill Lynch, which was folded into the Bank of America; and the subprime mortgage firms that did so much to lead us into the financial crisis of 2008–2009. In Wisconsin, Strong Capital Management (born, 1974, died 2004) is gone. In St. Paul, once-dominant First Trust Company splintered. In the Twin Cities area, virtually none of the investment firms that were around 90 years ago remained as free-standing independents throughout this stretch.

A CAST WITH MANY PLAYERS

How much was the survival of Mairs & Power due to the Three Georges? For sure, not all of it. They didn't do much on their own to take their business beyond Minnesota and a few other states. They introduced two mutual funds early on, in 1958 and 1961, but came up with little in the way of new investment products or services after that. They did relatively little to introduce new technology to back-office operations. The firm was still posting data in hand-written ledgers long past the time when its counterparts had abandoned them. Ron DeSellier helped out.

There is ample reason to believe that had Mairs & Power gone on like this much longer, it would have disappeared due to the relentlessly competitive pressures and market volatility that came to characterize much of the early twenty-first century. But George III, the last of the Three Georges to lead the firm, did come around to see the need for registering the firm's mutual funds in all 50 states, for launching the Small Cap Fund, and for other moves necessary to bring Mairs & Power into the modern era. And under the Three Georges, the firm gained much institutional business—from foundations, nonprofits, unions, and profit-sharing plans.

Combined, the Georges came up with a formidable and very special menu: investing for the long-term; analyzing, buying, and holding stocks; seeking the best-performing companies in Minnesota and the region for their clients' portfolios; developing and sustaining trusted relationships with their clients; and building up multiple employee ownership to make the firm's lasting independence far more likely.

While Mairs & Power grew briskly at times during the long realm of the Three Georges, they were not asset gatherers who sought rapid growth in order to juice up fee income. Instead, they were asset managers, focusing on enduring investment opportunities, eschewing flashy marketing and promotion gimmicks, and preferring to let business come their way based on steady performance and constant attention to the needs of their clients. Their aversion to empire-building probably protected them and their enterprise from the hubris that led to the downfall of countless other financial firms.

George Mairs Jr., backed by the resources of his family, meticulously prepared to start his business. He earned a seat at the table of the

St. Paul's financial elite at an early age and studied investment practices under the guidance of a leading economist at the University of Minnesota. George Power drew on the banking traditions of his family to build lasting ties with his clients. George III became the quintessential stock picker. In 1995, he was responsive when financial journalists suddenly sought him out for interviews; yet his newfound celebrity status did little to change his unpretentious, plain-spoken manner.

Perhaps most importantly, the Georges and their successors hired well, turning the leadership of their firm over to professional, effective managers who had perspectives more suitable for a new time and the experience essential to doing business in a more competitive, complicated, and occasionally almost chaotic environment.

Their ancestors came from New England and upstate New York and brought with them the entrepreneurial culture that laid the groundwork for the rise of Mairs & Power. The Mairs and Power families grew up in St. Paul and their patriarchs aligned themselves with the leadership of the community and its financial establishment as the city prospered, having attracted immigrant workers, and established innovative businesses such the Emporium Department Store and the Dyer Music Store in the city's downtown. St. Paul emerged as a great railroad center, and the fixed-income securities that had been so important to financing the railroads became a key element in George Jr.'s original investing strategy.

THE GROWTH FUND AND MINNESOTA ROSE TOGETHER

The flagship of Mairs & Power and its most successful creation, the Growth Fund, turned out to be a remarkable reflection of the economic changes that remade the economy in the Twin Cities and Minnesota. In the mid-1930s, when George Mairs Jr. was establishing his firm in the investment business in St. Paul, *Fortune* magazine portrayed the Twin Cities as a snake pit of mob activity, miserable labor relations, boundless corruption, and profound anti-business sentiment. Business leaders in St. Paul fought back with fierce rebuttals, but there was little doubt that the region's business climate left much to be desired.

The Growth Fund receives much attention in this history, in part for a reason better dealt with here than in the chronological narrative of the book. The Fund's rise paralleled the ascent of the Twin Cities—some might say up from the ashes of the 1930s—to become one of the nation's leading regional business centers. By the 1970s, Minnesota's economy, driven significantly by the corporate successes in the Twin Cities, had done a flipflop from the 1930s. *Fortune*, which was part of the twentieth-century media empire built by Henry Luce, recognized the change. By the 1970s, Minnesota-based companies' representation on *Fortune*'s annual list of the country's largest publicly held corporations stood out. Even today, 18 of the 500 companies on the list are headquartered in Minnesota—more than twice the state's share of the country's population. Many of these Minnesota companies rose to become standout performers in the Growth Fund.

Luce's flagship publication, *Time* magazine, put Minnesota on its cover in 1973, hailing the state as the best of all 50 states in providing the good life for its citizenry. The state was a place where, for the most part, we all got along. While much of this story was an accurate portrayal, it was also a Panglossian view—too rosy. Minnesota's population then was much less diverse in the 1970s than it is today, and thus the state faced less of a challenge in achieving harmony among its citizenry than did, say, states with larger and more diverse metropolitan areas such as Illinois and Michigan. Now Minnesotans too are struggling to create a more inclusive and harmonious society for all of the state's citizens, perhaps a bit later than some of her peers. So has turned the world Mairs & Power operates in today.[2]

That said, by many measures, Minnesota had become a better place by the 1970s, and today, than it had been in the 1930s. A primary reason for that was the improvement in the state's economy, which had been underperforming that of the nation. By the 1970s, that had changed. Louis Johnston, an economist at St. John's University in Collegeville, Minnesota, has studied this change by looking at shifts in per capita income in the state vs. the nation.

Johnston found that by this measure, the state lagged behind the nation from 1920 to the 1970s. Then Minnesota caught up and since 1980, has fared better than the country (see Figures 5 and 6).

Johnston cites improvements in the state's human capital including better educated workers and more women in the work force, a better physical infrastructure (schools, roads, water, and sewer systems), an economy that became much more diverse, and the robust growth of Minnesota's corporate sector. But Johnston's view is also that continued success for the state's largest companies on the scale of their past advances is not inevitable. "We can't be complacent. We could lose all of this pretty fast if we're not careful."[3]

Figure 5

Per Capita Income for Minnesota
Relative to the National Average for the U. S., 1880–2020

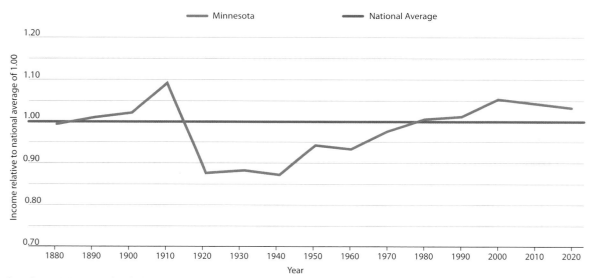

Source: For 1880,1890,1900,1910: Alexander Klein, "New State-Level Estimates of Personal Income in The United States, 1880-1910," Research in Economic History, 29 (2013): 191-255; for 1920: Richard A. Easterlin, "State Income Estimates," in Simon Kuznets and Dorothy S. Thomas, Population Redistribution and Economic Growth, United States, 1870-1950, vol. 1 (Philadelphia: American Philosophical Society, 1957); and for 1929-2020: Bureau of Economic Analysis, United States Department of Commerce: https://www.bea.gov/regional/index.htm

Figure 5 defines just how Minnesota's per capita income has fared between 1880 and the present. The railroad boom of the late nineteenth century boosted the incomes of Minnesotans. The Great Depression began for citizens of the state in the 1920s when agricultural prices fell sharply following World War I. Then Minnesota incomes gradually improved until they surpassed the national average in the late 1970s.

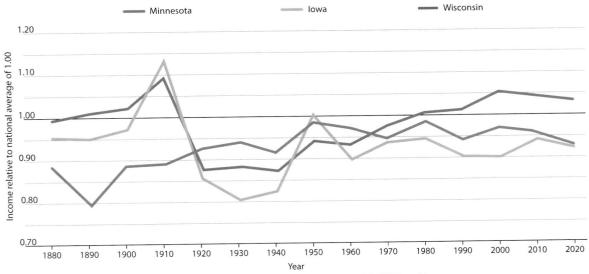

Figure 6

**Per Capita Income for Minnesota, Iowa, and Wisconsin
Relative to the National Average for the U. S., 1880–2020**

Source: For 1880,1890,1900,1910: Alexander Klein, "New State-Level Estimates of Personal Income in The United States, 1880-1910," Research in Economic History, 29 (2013): 191-255; for 1920: Richard A. Easterlin, "State Income Estimates," in Simon Kuznets and Dorothy S. Thomas, Population Redistribution and Economic Growth, United States, 1870-1950, vol. 1 (Philadelphia: American Philosophical Society, 1957); and for 1929-2020: Bureau

Figure 6 puts the per capita income for Minnesota in perspective relative to its neighboring states of Iowa and Wisconsin between 1880 and 2020. Although the graph lines follow generally similar trends up to about 1980, Minnesota has done better than its neighbors over the last 40 years.

The rise of the Growth Fund occurred almost in lockstep with the ascent of the state's economy. Today, as this history has shown, Minnesota stocks are not as dominant in the Fund as they were in the late 1990s. Yet even as virtually all other regional stock funds have disappeared, that characteristic of the Growth Fund endures and seems likely to remain for the foreseeable future—assuming today's strong contingent of Minnesota companies endures and fares well. If not, it is probably safe to assume that the Growth Fund will naturally gravitate to greener pastures. The Fund hasn't focused on Minnesota stocks to cheerlead for the state. As the illustrations in this book suggest, these companies have done well for their investors because they have been innovative and visionary in developing, producing, and selling products that meet the needs of their customers.

A STAGE FOR VIEWING
THE MARKET'S RESILIENCE

Tracking the long journey of Mairs & Power has been an enriching experience because it offered a front-porch view of the growth of the mutual fund industry, the dramatic twists and turns in the stock market, and the market's resilience (see Figure 7). In the mid-1950s, middle-income Americans finally pivoted to stocks from the stick-your-money-under-the-mattress mentality that took hold during the Depression. A few years later, Mairs & Power wisely remained on the sidelines as the Twin Cities saw the birth of a local over-the-counter market that became a cauldron of frenzied ups and downs in the stock price of scores of local companies.

Figure 7

U.S. Markets Have Displayed Resilience Despite Turbulent Events

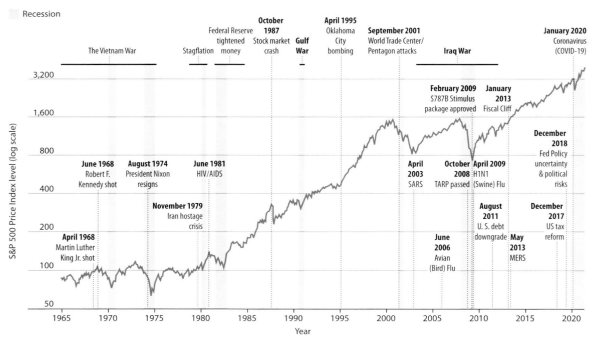

Source: Wells Fargo Investments, Bloomberg, and Ned Davis Research, as of December 31, 2019. The S&P 500 Index is a market-capitalization weighted index considered representative of the U.S. stock market. An index is unmanaged and not available for direct investment. Note, the S&P 500 Price Index is a logarithmic scale.

Figure 7 shows just how resilient the U.S. stock market has been over the last 55 years despite unexpected crises and significant national economic downturns.

In the 1970s, the stock market fell into a coma-like state. Then, after pundits had declared the equities market all but dead, it suddenly awakened from its big sleep and charged ahead into a long-running bull market. Well, not quite. We had a few hiccups: the crash of 1987; the dot-com bubble's euphoric rise and fall; the 9/11 terrorist attacks; the financial crisis of 2008–2009; the COVID 19 pandemic.

Through it all, the stock market was the place to be, if you somehow managed to stick around for the long haul. That's what the Growth Fund did. Remember, as the prologue noted, that if your father, grandfather, mother, or grandmother bought $1,000 worth of Growth Fund shares in 1958 and you kept those shares in the family, you would have about $1 million today. You wouldn't need an inflation calculator to conclude that this would be a pretty good situation insofar as your personal finances were concerned.

While a company history is almost all about the past, it also provides an occasion to look ahead. To that end, Mairs & Power's move into financing venture-stage companies merits particular attention. To carry out this new mission, the firm plans to match its growing capacity to analyze public companies with the expertise of a seasoned investor in private companies: John Bergstrom, who had 25 years of experience in the venture capital business. Early in 2021, Mairs & Power hired Bergstrom, who became chief investment officer of Mairs & Power Private Capital Management. A few months later, the firm hired Elizabeth Caven to join him. Bergstrom and Caven established a second Mairs & Power office a few blocks from its headquarters in downtown St. Paul. Caven, who had launched two startups, worked for a fintech startup accelerator program sponsored by two large Twin Cities insurers (Securian Financial and Allianz Life).[4]

The idea of launching early-stage venture funds has been percolating for several years. In 2017, Mark Henneman met with Bergstrom who, like Mairs & Power, had deep roots in St. Paul, the city where he grew up, and had long championed as a good place for business. Bergstrom had worked for Cherry Tree Ventures, a suburban Minneapolis venture firm, from 1985 until 1995, and since then at RiverPoint Investments, where he served on the boards of more than 20 venture and growth-stage companies.

RiverPoint also specialized in angel investing, where individual financial backers join with families of the founder and friends to put money into startups at their earliest stages. In 2019, Henneman became an angel investor. He quickly learned that while many entrepreneurs have solid ideas, they frequently lack the capital needed to build up their companies. "That caught my attention," Henneman said. "I thought maybe there's a business opportunity here." (Henneman noted that venture-stage investing is fundamentally buy-and-hold investing, a natural extension of the firm's traditional investing style.) Indeed, Mairs & Power's financial statements suggested as much. For 90 years, all its revenue had come from fees generated by its mutual fund shareholders and the clients whose accounts it managed. Now there would soon be a new stream of revenue: fees and gains realized from its private fund investments.

More change seems likely at Mairs & Power, but the characteristics that have made it special are embedded in its history and appear unlikely to change anytime soon. Today, twelve of the thirteen investment professionals at Mairs & Power hold the Chartered Financial Analyst designation and the thirteenth will soon. CFA Charter status, achieved only after rigorous testing, is generally seen as the highest standard for professionals in the industry. Fred Speece, who founded the Minneapolis investment firm of Speece-Thorson, twice chaired the international CFA Institute, which administers the tests and sets voluntary ethical standards for the investment industry. According to Speece, it is exceptional for a firm to have all its investment professionals hold CFA Charter status. His firm, like Mairs & Power, follows the principles of fundamental investing for the long-term. Speece views both firms as part of "a rare but not dying breed" that scrutinizes companies' managements and cultures and considers their prospects over many years to come. In contrast, he said, most contemporary investing is done by algorithmic formulas and machines with short-term horizons.[5]

It has been a privilege to assemble this narrative and put it into the form of a physical object—a book with a permanence that is unmistakable. Only a handful of histories have been written about Minnesota financial firms. Why not more? Perhaps because so few companies in this stormy industry have been around for as long as Mairs & Power. George Mairs Jr., George Mairs III, and George Power, by their nature and their upbringing, valued their privacy. They might never have wanted this book written, but their day was a different time. Today, an uneasy world saturated with confusing messages needs to learn more about institutions that have endured and how they have done it.[6] As the saying goes, don't hide your light under a bushel. If you have a rich history and a bright future, a good story to tell, well then, tell it.

THE PEOPLE AT MAIRS & POWER

Andrew R. Adams, CFA, CIC

Executive Vice President &
 Chief Investment Officer
Growth Fund Lead Manager
Small Cap Fund Co-Manager
Joined the firm in 2006
Industry experience since 1996

Michael J. Alden

Assistant Portfolio Manager &
 Equity Trader
Joined the firm in 2017
Industry experience since 2006

Debra J. Beltrand

Client Support Specialist
Joined the firm in 2013
Industry experience since 1987

John C. Bergstrom

Private Fund Manager
Joined the firm in 2021
Industry experience since 1985

Jeff R. Bogaard

IT Generalist
Joined the firm in 2012
Industry experience since 2012

Cathy A. Brandes

Receptionist/Administrative
 Assistant
Joined the firm in 2014
Industry experience since 1974

Elizabeth A. Caven

Private Fund Manager
Joined the firm in 2021
Industry experience since 2003

Kevin V. Earley, CFA, CIC

Vice President & Investment
 Manager
Balanced Fund Lead Manager
Joined the firm in 2013
Industry experience since 1986

Patrick J. Farley, CFA, CIC, CFP®

Vice President & Investment
  Manager
Joined the firm in 2018
Industry experience since 1992

Marissa E. Gehling

Senior Mutual Fund Analyst
Joined the firm in 2017
Industry experience since 2017

Melissa M. Gilbertson

Assistant Vice President &
  IT and Trading Manager
Joined the firm in 2007
Industry experience since 2002

Elizabeth M. Hemauer

Marketing Coordinator &
  Digital Analyst
Joined the firm in 2020
Industry experience since 2020

Mark L. Henneman, CFA, CIC

Chairman & Chief Executive
  Officer
Joined the firm in 2004
Industry experience since 1991

Scott D. Howard

Vice President & Investor
  Relations Manager
Joined the firm in 2011
Industry experience since 1983

Glenn E. Johnson, CFA, CIC

Senior Vice President &
  Director of Institutional
  Asset Management
Joined the firm in 2010
Industry experience since 1985

Pete J. Johnson, CFA, CIC

Vice President & Investment
  Manager
Growth Fund Co-Manager
Joined the firm in 2010
Industry experience since 2003

Lea M. Kammerer

Office Administrator
Joined the firm in 2017
Industry experience since 2017

Annette R. Lance

Investor Relations Assistant
Manager
Joined the firm in 2014
Industry experience since 2014

Kristen A. Larsen

Portfolio Administrator
Joined the firm in 2011
Industry experience since 1992

Janice L. Ledman

Client Support Specialist
Joined the firm in 1998
Industry experience since 1998

Supanan (Wendy) Lee

Equity Analyst
Joined the firm in 2019
Industry experience since 2019

Michelle L. Lindenfelser

Portfolio Administrator
Joined the firm in 1990
Industry experience since 1988

Heidi J. Lynch

Assistant Portfolio Manager &
Fixed Income Trader
Joined the firm in 2014
Industry experience since 2001

Robert W. Mairs

President, Chief Compliance
Officer & General Counsel
Joined the firm in 2015
Industry experience since 1997

Tiffany L. Marx

Trading Settlement Specialist
Joined the firm in 2016
Industry experience since 2008

Brent S. Miller, CFA

Assistant Vice President &
    Fixed Income Assistant
    Portfolio Manager
Minnesota Municipal Bond ETF
    Lead Manager
Joined the firm in 2019
Industry experience since 2011

Justin M. Miller, CFA, CIC

Vice President & Investment
    Manager
Joined the firm in 2015
Industry experience since 2000

Connie M. O'Brien

IT Business Analyst
Joined the firm in 2012
Industry experience since 2012

Luke A. Odegaard

Accounting & Finance
    Manager
Joined the firm in 2016
Industry experience since 2016

Jeff L. Olson

IT Project Manager
Joined the firm in 2019
Industry experience since 1995

Tammy L. Osman

Human Resources &
    Administration Manager
Joined the firm in 2012
Industry experience since 1994

Deborah A. Resch

Shareholder Servicing
    Representative
Joined the firm in 2008
Industry experience since 1982

Jane M. Rossini

Investor Relations Associate
Joined the firm in 1999
Industry experience since 1999

Allen D. Steinkopf, CFA, CIC

Vice President & Investment
  Manager
Small Cap Fund Lead Manager
Joined the firm in 2013
Industry experience since 1993

Andrea C. Stimmel, CPA (inactive)

Chief Operating Officer
Joined the firm in 2004
Industry experience since 1997

Christopher D. Strom, CFA

Vice President & Investment
  Manager
Small Cap Fund Co-Manager
Joined the firm in 2017
Industry experience since 2005

Robert W. Thompson, CFA, CIC

Vice President & Director of
  Fixed Income
Co-Manager, Balanced Fund
Co-Manager, Minnesota
  Municipal Bond ETF
Joined the firm in 2016
Industry experience since 1994

Kelly E. Trevenna

Assistant Portfolio Manager &
  Equity Trader
Joined the firm in 2011
Industry experience since 2007

Chelsea L. Tvedt

Client Support Specialist
Joined the firm in 2015
Industry experience since 2015

Amy S. Vanderhoff

Client Service Manager
Joined the firm in 2017
Industry experience since 1999

Elizabeth M. VanHeel

Operations Manager
Joined the firm in 2011
Industry experience since 2007

Michelle A. Warren, CFA

Assistant Vice President &
    Equity Analyst
Joined the firm in 2016
Industry experience since 2001

Brent M. Williams

Compliance Manager
Joined the firm in 2018
Industry experience since 2015

Mairs & Power would also like to acknowledge and thank
these retired employees who have not otherwise been mentioned
in the book but who all contributed to the success of Mairs & Power:

Loreen (Larry) Blood

Manana Bro

Beverly (Bev) & Daryl Coulthart

Sue Crawford

Lisa Hartzell

Virginia (Ginny) Hughes

Collyn Iblings

Rosemary Schultz

Connie Spreigl

Linda Trandahl

APPENDIX OF GRAPHS

Figure 8

Mairs & Power's Assets in Mutual Funds Compared to Its
Assets Under Management, 2004-2020 (in billions $) *

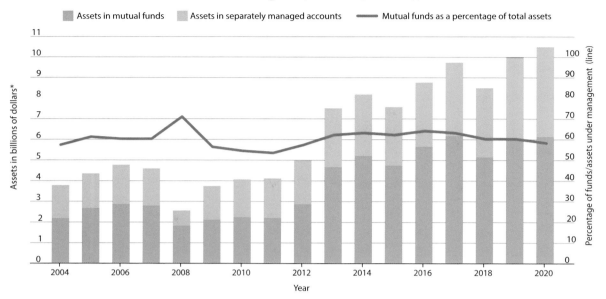

*Assets at the end of the year

The assets Mairs & Power manages fall into two overall categories: mutual funds and separately managed accounts. Until the mid-1990s, most of the assets were in the separately managed accounts. Since then, the mutual funds have held the larger share. This graph shows that the mutual funds' share has ranged from 50 percent to 70 percent since 2004.

Figure 9

Mairs & Power Balanced Fund Assets by Year, 1961-2020 (in millions $)*

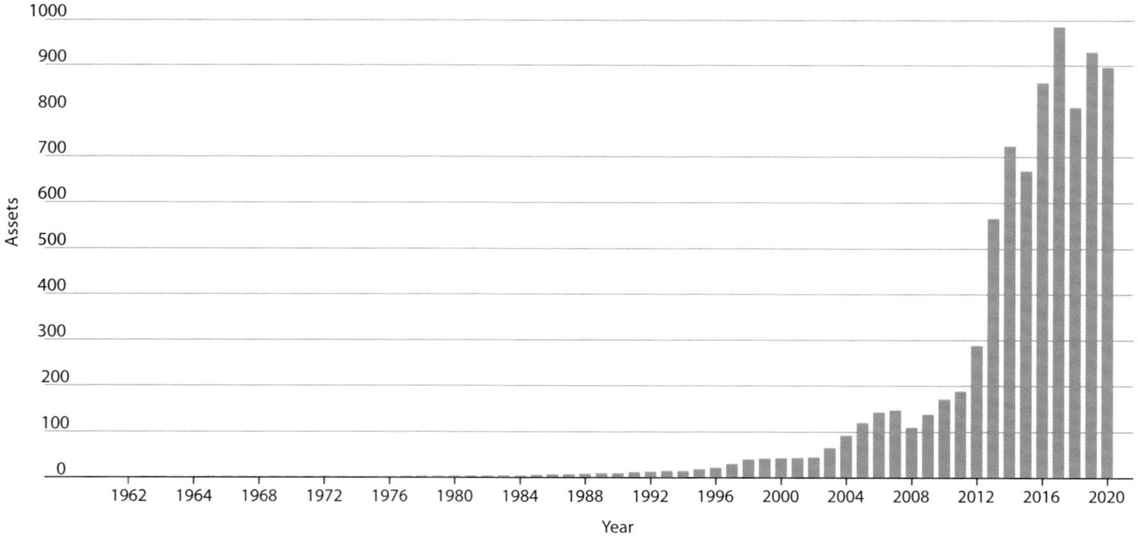

*Assets at the end of the year

This bar chart shows the assets in the Mairs & Power Balanced Fund since its inception in 1961.

Figure 10
Mairs & Power Small Cap Fund Assets by Year, 2012-2020 (in millions $)*

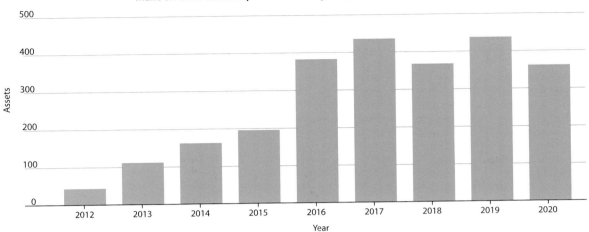

*Assets at the end of the year

This bar chart shows the assets in the Mairs & Power Small Cap Fund since its inception in 2011.

Figure 11
Assets Held by U.S. Mutual Funds, 1955-2020 (in trillions $)*

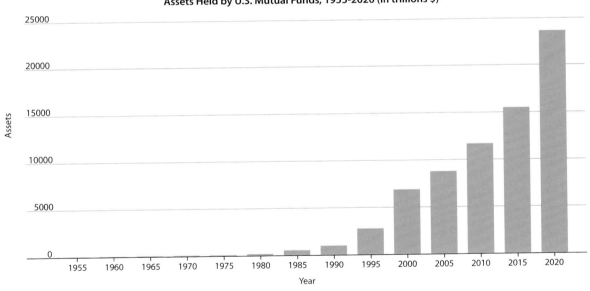

*Data at the end of the year
Source: 2021 Investment Company Institute Fact Book

This bar chart shows the growth of assets in all U.S. mutual funds at five-year intervals since 1955.

Notes

PROLOGUE

1. "Revolt in the Northwest," *Fortune* (April 1936): 113–197.
2. Email to the author from Mairs & Power, July 6, 2021.
3. Interview with Mark Henneman by the author, October 14, 2020.
4. Jason Zweig, "Yes, Mutual Funds Can Stand Out from the Herd," December 14, 2016, https://jasonzweig.com/yes-mutual-funds-can-stand-out-from-the-herd/ accessed June 27, 2021.
5. "The Good Life in Minnesota," *Time*, August 13, 1973, 24–35.

CHAPTER 1. THE ENTREPRENEURIAL CULTURE OF THE FOREBEARS

1. Thomas G. and Marjorie P. Mairs, *Samuel Mairs: Ancestors and* Descendants (St. Paul: privately printed, 1998). Samuel Mairs (1879–1955) was a great-grandson of Rev. George Mairs Sr. Samuel Mairs, who rose to become the chairman at Archer-Daniels-Midland Company, was Thomas Mairs's father. George Mairs Jr. and Thomas Mairs were cousins. The 123-page Mairs family genealogy was materially helpful in writing portions of this Chapter.
2. Will of Amelia Dyer Mairs, Ramsey County Probate Court, St. Paul, May 27, 1910; 1880 U.S. Census, as reported by Ancestry.com.
3. "House of W.J. Dyer & Bro. More Than 50 Years Old," *St. Paul Pioneer Press*, March 4, 1923; "Pioneer Music Firm Here Established 61 years ago," *St. Paul Pioneer Press*, April 19, 1931; Email from Rich Arpi, Ramsey County Historical Society, November 18, 2020.
4. "George A. Mairs Dies Here at 71," *St. Paul Pioneer Press*, May 2, 1944.
5. Email from Rich Arpi, November 12, 2020.
6. "W.J. Dyer's Estate Valued at $115,000," *St. Paul Pioneer Press*, June 25, 1925; Will of Amelia Dyer Mairs.
7. Email from Diane Power, January 15, 2021.
8. The discussion of the Power genealogy that follows is based on various emails from Diane and George C. Power III including a research project, *Helendale Farm and the James B. Power Family* (St. Paul: Warren Research and Publishing Co., 1998) and provided to the author by George C. Power III.
9. "William J. Dyer," *Northwestern Bulletin-Appeal*, June 17, 1925.
10. "Angus McLeod" extract from *Minneapolis Tribune*, July 23, 1899; "St. Paul's Big New Store," *Minneapolis Journal*, March 30, 1901.
11. John G. Rice, "The Old-Stock Americans," in June Drenning Holmquist, ed., *They Chose Minnesota: A Survey of the State's Ethnic Groups* (St. Paul: Minnesota Historical Society, 1981.
12. Colin Woodard, *American Nations: A History of the Eleven Rival Regional Cultures of North America* (New York: Viking Press, 2011); Joel Garreau, *The Nine Nations of North America* (Boston: Houghton Mifflin, 1981). Both books argue that the United States (and adjacent parts of North America) can be better understood by mapping and describing its regions, each of which exhibit the distinct cultures and values of their original settlers, as opposed to its 50 states.

Woodard identified as "Yankeedom" a region that stretches from Canada's eastern-most provinces, New England, and upstate New York to portions of northern Ohio, Michigan, northern Illinois, and Wisconsin to the Twin Cities. He wrote that the Yankee settlers came as families and were generally middle-class, well-educated, roughly equal in material wealth, and supporters of government, anti-slavery views, and the public interest more than the people of other regions. Many of today's leading corporations and some prominent churches in the Twin Cities trace their roots to entrepreneurial settlers from the cradle of Yankeedom in the Northeast. Garreau's regions and descriptions of them were similar, but the region that corresponded to Yankeedom did not include part of the Midwest.

13. "Guitar Purchased from W.J. Dyer & Bros., St. Paul," *Collections Up Close: Podcast and Blog* by Matt Anderson, May 7, 2010, http://discussions.mnhs.org/collections/2010/05/guitar -purchase, accessed November 17, 2020.

14. "W.J. Dyer, head of Music House Since 1871, Dies," and commentary about him, *Northwestern Bulletin-Appeal*, June 27, 1925.

15. Kristal Leebrick, *Thank You for Shopping: The Golden Age of Minnesota's Department Stores* (St. Paul: Minnesota Historical Society Press, 2018); "The Emporium: Grand Opening," *St. Paul Globe*, March 1, 1902; St. Paul's Big New Store.

16. "Angus M'Leod, Emporium Chief, Dies in St. Paul," *St. Paul Pioneer Press*, February 2, 1924.

17. Walter Heyler, *Steamboat Traffic on the Upper Mississippi River* (typescript, 1919); Lucille M. Kane, *The Falls of St. Anthony: The Waterfall that Built Minneapolis* (St. Paul: Minnesota Historical Society Press, 1987).

18. Warren Upham and Rose Barteau Dunlop, compilers, *Minnesota Biographies, 1655–1912* (St. Paul: Minnesota Historical Society, 1912), 41.

19. Ralph W. Hidy, Muriel E. Hidy, Roy V. Scott, and Don L. Hofsommer, *The Great Northern Railway: A History* (Minneapolis: University of Minnesota Press, 1988).

20. U.S. Census population for St. Paul by decades, 1880–1920.

CHAPTER 2. ST. PAUL SLOGS THROUGH THE DEPRESSION

1. "Barker-Karpis Gang," MNOPEDIA: Minnesota's Encyclopedia, https://www.mnopedia.org, accessed November 26, 2018.

2. "Revolt in the Northwest," *Fortune* (April 1936): 113–197.

3. Virginia Brainard Kunz, "A Period of National Tragedy—The Homeless and the Jobless in the 1930s," *Ramsey County History*, 26:1 (Spring 1991): 16–23.

4. Mary Lethert Wingerd, *Claiming the City: Politics, Faith, and the Power of Place in St. Paul* (Ithaca, N.Y.: Cornell University Press, 2001), 113, 252.

5. Ibid., 252.

6. "Banking Starts Rebuilding on a New Basis," *Commercial West*, March 11, 1933.

7. "Address by the Comptroller of the Currency," *Commercial West*, June 24, 1933, 30–32.

8. Ibid.

9. Michael Perino, *The Hellhound of Wall Street: How Ferdinand Pecora's Investigation of the Great Crash Forever Changed American Finance* (New York: Penguin Books, 2010), 3–6, 280–304.

10. Donald J. O'Grady, *History at Your Door: The Story of the St. Paul Pioneer Press and Dispatch* (St. Paul: Northwest Publications, 1983), 80–81.

11. "The Twin Cities: An Addendum," *Fortune* (July 1936): 86–142.

12. "The Great Northern," *Fortune* (December 1932): 71–108.

13. John F. Stover, *The Routledge Historical Atlas of the American Railroads* (New York: Routledge, 1999), 53–58.

14. Ralph W. Hidy, Muriel E. Hidy, Roy V. Scott, and Donald Hofsommer, *The Great Northern Railway* (Minneapolis: University of Minnesota Press, 1988), 199–200.

15. Herbert Spero, *Reconstruction Finance Corporation Loans to the Railroads, 1932–1937* (Boston: Bankers Publishing Company, 1939), 4–40, 164–167.

16. Hidy et al., 215, 246, 291.

17. James A. Stolpestad, "Building Through the Crash: St. Paul's New Directions in the 1930s," *Ramsey County History*, 50:3 (Fall 2015): 16–25.

18. Virginia Huck, *The 3M Story: Brand of the Tartan* (New York: Appleton-Century-Crofts, 1955); Virginia Huck, *The Many Worlds of Homer P. Clark* (St. Paul: West Publishing Company, 1980); James B. Bell, *From Arcade Steet to Main Street: A History of the Seeger Refrigeration Company, 1902–1984* (St. Paul: Ramsey County Historical Society, 2007); Ilan Moscovitz, "The Top 10 Depression Stocks," Motley Fool, https://www.fool.com, accessed June 12, 2009; and Kunz, 20.

19. Interview with Bonnie Mairs by the author, June 15, 2020.

20. Interview with Teedie Frankenbach by the author, June 12, 2020. Although she was named Louise at birth, she became known as Teedie soon afterward. "The story I was told is that Bobby [her brother, 19 months older] couldn't pronounce Louise and that's how Teedie came to be," she told the author in an email on January 17, 2021. "Sadly, it stuck!"

CHAPTER 3. THE BIRTH OF MAIRS & POWER

1. Irwin Collier, a retired professor who writes a wide-ranging and free-swinging blog about economists ("Economics in the Rear-View Mirror"), has suggested that Arthur Marget, who was Jewish, came to the University of Minnesota in 1927 after being a victim of discrimination. Marget, the top student in his class at Harvard, had been an assistant for Professor Allyn Young, an influential economist who had previously served as president of the American Economic Association. In a posting titled "Too Jewish for Chicago?" Collier suggested that Marget's effort to join the faculty at the University of Chicago failed in part because Professor Young sent a reference letter to the Chicago school that was "both glowing and explicit about his assistant's handicap"—that he was "one of the chosen people—i.e., a Jew." The letter said "the only thing that stands between Marget and success is his race. If you don't fill your place next year, you might do worse than to take him on for a year's trial." Collier cited the University of Chicago's archives as the source for the letter.

2. Email from Rich Arpi, archivist at the Ramsey County Historical Society, to the author, October 27, 2020.

3. Email from Ellen Holt-Werle, archivist at Macalester College, to the author, July 2, 2021.

4. Email from Teedie Frankenbach to the author, February 5, 2001.

5. Larry Millett, *Heart of St. Paul: History of the Pioneer and Endicott Buildings* (St. Paul: Minnesota Museum of Modern Art, 2016).

6. "Railroad and Bank Building," City of Saint Paul and Saint Paul Heritage Preservation Commission, 1988.

7. Email from Rob Mairs to the author with ledger records of trading by George Mairs Jr., 1927–1929, March 16, 2021.

8. George Mairs Jr., "A Study of the Investment Practices of the Larger Fire Insurance Companies with Special Reference to the Experience of the Continental Insurance Company and the Saint Paul Fire and Marine Insurance Company" (master's thesis, University of Minnesota, December 1930).

9. Interview with Rob Mairs by the author, March 19, 2021.

10. Letter from Margaret Long to George Mairs Jr., undated (probably early July 1932), Mairs & Power archives.

11. "Aims of New Investment Course Told by Mairs, Trustee-Teacher," *Mac Weekly*, February 23, 1934, p. 2.

12. Excerpt from *Stocks, Bonds, Bills, and Inflation (SBBI) Yearbook 2016* (Portland, Ore.: BV Resources, 2016).

13. Interview with Robert F. Garland by the author, February 1, 2021.
14. Interview with Dusty Mairs by the author, June 1, 2020.
15. "Wedding Notice," *Minneapolis Star Tribune*, December 6, 1925.
16. *St. Paul City Directories*, 1925–1927.
17. "Her Marriage Is Event of January in St. Paul," *Minneapolis Star Tribune*, January 12, 1926.
18. "Outlets," a collection of Louise Power's poetry published as a tribute to her by her six children in December 1982. She died in 1981.
19. Ritchie/Power wedding notice, *Minneapolis Star Tribune*, December 6, 1925.
20. Interview with Teedie Frankenbach by the author, March 2021.
21. Interview with Dusty Mairs by the author, April 2021.
22. Email from Amy Ensley, Wilson College, to the author, July 7, 2021.
23. *Minneapolis Star*, February 9, 1924, p. 13.
24. *Minneapolis Tribune*, November 17, 1925.
25. "Five Minnesota Mothers in a Ford," adapted from Louise Power's Journal by Anne Chapwell for the New Century Club, St. Paul, April 20, 2005, 1–31.
26. Senior page for George Mairs Jr., *1923 Yearbook*, Lafayette College, 1923.
27. Email from Rich Arpi.
28. Interviews with Dusty Mairs by the author and emails from Dusty Mairs to the author.
29. The invoice was not dated, but it was sent shortly after May 7, 1938, when George Jr. and Louise were married.
30. Email to the author from Teedie Frankenbach, January 4, 2021.
31. Interview with Ed Stringer by the author, July 14, 2020; email from Teedie Frankenbach to the author, January 16, 2021.
32. Joseph Kingman, "History of Encampment Forest Association," published in 1945 to commemorate the 25th anniversary of the Encampment Forest Association.
33. Interviews with Dusty Mairs by the author.
34. George III's description of his father's compensation is from brief summaries, preserved by his wife, of his career. He wrote them shortly before he died.
35. "Curious George," Gareth Hiebert's "Oliver Towne" column, *St. Paul Dispatch*, September 7, 1967.
36. From George III's summaries of his career.
37. The material about the Driscolls' portfolio came from discussions with Todd Driscoll and family records he preserved and provided for this project.
38. George Mairs Jr, Investment Counsel: Application for Investment Advisor's License, Minnesota Department of Commerce, July 13, 1943.
39. Email from Ronald J. DeSellier to the author, September 2020.

CHAPTER 4. THE PIVOT: SAYING GOODBYE TO FEAR

1. "What Is Investment Counsel?" an undated marketing brochure distributed by Mairs & Power, probably in 1954, copy in the Mairs & Power archives.
2. John Steele Gordon, *The Great Game: The Emergence of Wall Street as a World Power 1653–2000* (New York: Scribner, 1999), 249–251.
3. *The Pajama Game*, Wikipedia; lyrics for "Seven-and-a-Half Cents" are posted on several sites.
4. George C. Power Jr. was born in 1914; George A. Mairs Jr. in 1901; and George Mairs III in 1928.
5. Emails from Diane Power to the author provided much of the material for the profile of George C. Power Jr.
6. Interview with Charles "Todd" Driscoll, by the author, February 5, 2021.
7. Email from Peggie Klema to the author, February 19, 2021.
8. U.S. Army discharge papers for George C. Power Jr., July 31, 1946, in the Power family archives; email from Peter Robb to the author, February 17, 2021.
9. Interview with Peter Robb by the author, February 16, 2021.

10. Edwin J. Perkins, *Wall Street to Main Street: Charles Merrill and Middle-Class Investors* (Cambridge: Cambridge University Press, 1999).

11. Interview with Don Mains by the author, May 13, 2020.

12. Matthew P. Fink, *The Rise of Mutual Funds: An Insider's View* (New York: Oxford University Press, 2011); Hugh Bullock, *The Story of Investment Companies* (New York: Columbia University Press, 1959).

13. Ibid., 58.

14. Kenneth Lipartito and Carol Heher Peters, *Investing for Middle America: John Elliott Tappan and the Origins of American Express Financial Advisors* (New York: Palgrave: 2001).

15. Interview with Ed Stringer by the author, July 14, 2020.

16. Joe Nocera, *A Piece of the Action: How the Middle Class Joined the Money Class* (New York: Simon & Schuster, 1994).

17. An unsigned memo, apparently based on instructions from George Mairs Jr. to a secretary, explaining the reasons for incorporating, 1961, in the Mairs & Power archives.

CHAPTER 5. A GARDEN BLOOMS IN THE BACKYARD

1. John Cochrane, "Eugene Fama, Efficient Markets, and the Nobel Prize," *Chicago Booth Review*. This piece is adapted from a longer post on Cochrane's blog, "The Grumpy Economist."

2. In a brief written summary of his career shortly before he died, George III explained his view that the efficient markets theory doesn't apply to Mairs & Power's style of investing in Minnesota companies. Original in the Mairs & Power archives.

3. The U.S. Bureau of Labor Statistics is the source for the Consumer Price Index data.

4. Matthew P. Fink, *The Rise of Mutual Funds: An Insider's View* (New York: Oxford University Press, 2012), 110, 147.

5. Investment Company Institute, *Investment Company 2021 Fact Book* (Washington, D.C.: Investment Company Institute, 2021), 147; interviews by the author with Jon Theobald.

6. Minutes of June 22, 1970, meeting of the Mairs & Power Board of Directors. Mairs & Power archives.

7. www.medtronic.com.

8. Dusty Mairs provided 37 of George Mairs III's annual appointment books for this project. Mairs family archives.

9. Neal St. Anthony, "David Lilly Shaped the Modern-Day Toro," *Minneapolis Star Tribune*, February 18, 2014; Piper Jaffray & Hopwood report on Toro, January 8, 1963, Piper Jaffray & Hopwood Papers, Minnesota Historical Society, St. Paul, Minn.; www.toro.com.

10. "Ecolab Inc," MNOPEDIA: Minnesota's encyclopedia, https://www.mnopedia.org, accessed October 19, 2017; Piper Jaffray & Hopwood report on Economics Laboratory, June 29, 1965, Piper Jaffray & Hopwood Papers, Minnesota Historical Society, St. Paul, Minn.; Ecolab.com site.

11. John Brooks, *The Go-Go Years: The Drama and Crashing Finale of Wall Street's Bullish 60s* (New York: John Wiley & Sons, 1973).

12. Joe Nocera, *A Piece of the Action: How the Middle Class Joined the Money Class* (New York: Simon & Schuster, 1994), 34–52.

13. Brooks, 267–271.

14. "What Is the Nifty 50?" https://www.investopedia.com, accessed March 24, 2020.

15. Fink, 61.

16. Edwin J. Perkins, *Wall Street to Main Street: Charles Merrill and Middle-Class Investors* (Cambridge: Cambridge University Press, 1999)

17. Ibid., 222–223, 259.

CHAPTER 6. THE STRUGGLES OF THE '70S

1. The term "stagflation" refers to periods when the inflation rate is high, economic growth is slowing, and unemployment remains persistently high. The word is widely believed to have been popularized by Ian Macleod, a British politician in the Conservative Party, when

he used it in a speech to Parliament in 1965. "We now have the worst of both worlds—not just inflation on the one side or stagnation on the other, but both of them together," he declared. We have a sort of 'stagflation' situation."

2. Emails from Ronald J. DeSellier to the author. DeSellier, who was at Mairs & Power from 1973 until 1992, provided much of the descriptive material that appears in Chapters 6 and 7.

3. Minutes of June 16, 1975, meeting of the Mairs & Power Board of Directors.

4. John Rea and Richard Marcis, "Mutual Fund Shareholder Activity During U.S. Stock Market Cycles, 1944–1995," *Perspective*, 2:2 (March 1996): 10.

5. Matthew P. Fink, *The Rise of Mutual Funds: An Insider's View* (New York: Oxford University Press, 2011), 79.

6. National Bureau of Economic Research, https://www.nber.org. The NBER tracks the length and depth of U.S. recessions through its research in dating business cycles.

7. "Misery Index," Clay Halton, www.https://investopedia.com. This is a helpful discussion of the Misery Index. Until the 1970s, economists had generally believed that the inflation rate offset the unemployment rate and that therefore, the two rates could not rise at the same time. But in the 1970s, both often rose simultaneously. The index, an informal measure of the stagflation of this decade, was often cited by politicians of the party out of power to help regain power. Presidential candidate Jimmy Carter used it against President Gerald Ford in 1976, then presidential candidate Ronald Reagan returned the favor by using it against President Jimmy Carter in 1980. Later, the Misery Index was the name of a hardcore punk rock band, and more recently, of a television comedy show.

8. Fink, 80–81.

9. Ibid., 82.

10. "The Death of Equities: How Inflation is Destroying the Stock Market," *Business Week*, August 13, 1979.

CHAPTER 7. THE BULL ARRIVES; AN INDUSTRY THRIVES

1. Bennett Goodspeed drew attention from investors for his 1984 book, *The Tao Jones Averages: A Guide to Whole-Brained Thinking* (New York: Penguin Books, 1984). In his book, Goodspeed decried left-brain and right-brain thinking and the use of mathematical models, instead calling for a broad, humble, flexible, and adaptable approach to investing. Many of Goodspeed's recommendations reflected the investing style embraced by Mairs & Power: don't be too sure; stay diversified; stick to what you know; don't churn your account; mistakes are OK; avoid the pied piper.

2. John Steele Gordon, *The Great Game: The Emergence of Wall Street as a World Power 1653–2000*. (New York: Scribner, 1999) 287–290.

3. John H. Allan, "Merrill Lynch Buys White Weld, Old-Line Firm, for $50 Million," *New York Times*, April 15, 1978, p. 29.

4. Dave Beal, "Tradition: Winter Saturday Lunches Warm Up St. Paul Business," *St. Paul Pioneer Press*, January 25, 1983.

5. Malcolm McDonald, interview by the author, August 18, 2020. The Minnesota Club encountered serious financial difficulties in the late 1990s. In an email to the author, Jon Theobald said he had the unlucky timing of being president of the club in 1998–1999; thus, he had the responsibility of leading club members through painful discussions to sell its building and eventually to close the club. Much of the complex process of winding down the club's operations fell to Theobald, who called multiple board and membership meetings to work through the crisis. He negotiated the sale of the club's building to retired West Publishing executive John Nasseff, who in turn put $7 million into the property and then sold it to Minnesota Sports and Entertainment, which also owns the Minnesota Wild professional hockey team. Theobald said longtime club member George Mairs III, impressed by how he had

handled the situation, approached him in 2001 to move to Mairs & Power. That was how Theobald came to join the firm.

6. Email from Ronald J. DeSellier to the author.

7. Stock prices are from https://finance.yahoo.com.

8. Emails from DeSellier to the author; minutes of Mairs & Power Board of Directors meeting, June 30, 1992.

9. Joe Nocera, *A Piece of the Action: How the Middle Class Joined the Moneyed Class* (New York: Simon & Schuster, 1994), 276–284.

10. Ibid, 240–249, 385, 405.

11. Kristen Grind, Tom McGinty, and Sarah Krouse, "The Morningstar Mirage: Investors Everywhere Think a 5-Star Rating from Morningstar Means a Mutual Fund Will Become a Top Performer—It Doesn't," *Wall Street Journal*, October 25, 2017; Morningstar CEO Kunal Kapoor, Letter to the WSJ Editors, *Wall Street Journal*, November 2, 2017.

12. Matthew P. Fink. *The Rise of Mutual Funds: An Insider's View* (New York: Oxford University Press: 2011), 147.

13. Ibid., 148

CHAPTER 8. FROM ANONYMITY TO CELEBRITY

1. John Steele Gordon, *The Great Game: The Emergence of Wall Street as a World Power, 1653–2000* (New York: Scribner, 1999) 285-286.

2. Emails from Ron DeSellier to the author; interview by the author with Jon Theobald; interview by the author with Dusty Mairs.

3. The story about George III's first car comes from a booklet of memories of George III collected from friends and family by Dusty Mairs shortly after her husband died; the detail about his first paycheck is from the brief summaries of his career that he wrote after he retired.

4. Interview with Mark Henneman by the author, October 14, 2020.

5. Interview with Chip Emery by the author, June 29, 2020.

6. Interview with Jim Johnson by the author, July 8, 2020.

7. Interview with George Ficocello by the author, March 7, 2021.

8. Interviews with Dusty Mairs by the author. She provided significant material for this Chapter.

9. Interview with Don Mains by the the author, May 13, 2020.

10. Dusty Mairs, George Mairs III, recollections of his career.

11. Interview with Tom Kingston by the author, March 9, 2021.

12. Interview with Dr. Edward Cheng by the author, March 17, 2021.

13. Booklet of memories of George III (see note 3 above).

14. Interviews with Peter Robb by the author, February 16, 2021, and May 13, 2021.

15. Jason Zweig, "Zen Stock Picking," *Forbes*, December 19, 1994. The author's story about Mairs & Power, mentioned in the preface, appeared in the *St. Paul Pioneer Press* on January 16, 1995.

16. Shelley Neumeier, "Finding Steady Stocks in a Turbulent Market," *Fortune*, October 17, 1994.

17. Interview with Peter Robb by the author; interview with Michelle (Maltby) Lindenfelser by the author.

18. Fleming Meeks with Nanette Byrnes and Emily Harrison, "Best Mutual Funds for 1997," *Smart Money*, February 1997. 100–101.

19. Interview with Bob Struyk by the author, July 1, 2020.

20. In a discussion with the author, Donald M. Hall, who wrote *Generation of Wealth* (Minneapolis: Nodin Press, 2014) said he didn't know of any Twin Cities med-tech companies that emerged from the Medtronic cluster with a stock that performed as well as St. Jude stock did.

21. Valspar, https://www.company-histories.com; "Obituary Angus Wurtele, Valspar CEO, *PaintSquare*, September 20, 2017; "Sherwin-Williams Closes Deal for Valspar, *Minneapolis Star Tribune*, June 2, 2017, 2D; Rohan Preston and Pat Pfeifer, "C. Angus Wurtele:

For Former Valspar CEO, the Arts Brought Pure Joy," *Minneapolis Star Tribune*, September 5, 2017, 1B; Joe Carlson, "Abbott to Finish St. Jude Purchase," *Minneapolis Star Tribune*, January 4, 2017, 1D.

22. Dave Beal, "Manny Tries Again: Manny Villafana Starts Up Companies the Way the Rest of Us Change Jobs," *St. Paul Pioneer Press*, August 13, 1990, 1F; Piper Jaffray & Hopwood report on St. Jude Medical, July 1983; Ian Bezek, "Hormel Foods: Why It's My Largest Position and I Just Bought More," *Seeking Alpha*, February 1, 2021.

23. Ben Zimmer, "Why Gertrude Stein's 'No There There' Is Everywhere," *Wall Street Journal*, February 2, 2018; "Swimming Naked When the Tide Goes Out," *Time*, February 2, 2009.

24. Many stories about Mairs & Power and its principals, most prominently George Mairs III, are in the scrapbook compiled by Dusty Mairs.

25. Jessica Pressler, "The Encyclopedia of 9/11: The Firm that Lost the Most," *New York*, Aug. 26, 2011; "The Macroeconomic Impacts of the 9/11 Attack," U.S. Department of Homeland Security, August 2009.

26. "Strong Capital Management and Founder Richard Strong Agree to Pay $140 Million to Settle Fraud Charges Concerning Undisclosed Mutual Fund Trading," https://www.sec.gov/news/2004-69.htm, accessed May 21, 2021.

27. James Atkinson, "The Mutual Fund Industry Scandal and What Is Being Done About It," University of Notre Dame, April 4, 2004; Matthew P. Fink, *The Rise of Mutual Funds: An Insider's View* (New York: Oxford University Press, 2001), 232–245.

CHAPTER 9. UP, DOWN, AND UP AGAIN

1. Matthew P. Fink, *The Rise of Mutual Funds: An Insider's View* (New York: Oxford University Press, 2011) 232–245.

2. The description of the Mutual Fund Board is based on interviews with Jim Alt, Norb Conzemius, Mary Schmid Daugherty, Chuck Dietz, Ed Stringer, and Jon Theobald, all of whom, except Theobald, have been independent trustees on the Board.

3. Interviews with Jon Theobald and Peter Robb by the author.

4. Email from Andy Adams to the author, August 13, 2021.

5. Countless retrospectives have been written about the financial crisis of 2008–2009, with many differing viewpoints. One that may not get enough attention is the observation that a wide swath of the investment community engaged in "group-think" in the years before the crisis. Critics argue that during the run-up to the crisis, many if not most of Wall Street's principal players willfully blinded themselves to the questionable practices that wound up causing so much of the trouble.

6. Bethany McLean and Joe Nocera, *All the Devils Are Here: The Hidden History of the Financial Crisis* (New York: Portfolio, 2010); Steve Schaefer, "The Great Recession's Biggest Bankruptcies: Where Are They Now?" *Forbes*, August 10, 2011.

7. "Business Cycle Dating," National Bureau of Economic Research, www.nber.org, 2021.

8. Email from Jon Theobald to the author.

9. Joe Nocera, *A Piece of the Action.* (New York: Simon & Schuster, 1994) 327.

10. Neal St. Anthony, "George Mairs III Gave Money a Good Name," *Minneapolis Star Tribune*, June 4, 2010.

11. David Falkof, Morningstar.com: video interview with Mark Henneman and Bill Frels after they were named as Morningstar's Domestic Equity Fund Managers of the Year for 2012, January 5, 2013.

CHAPTER 10. TYING THE STRANDS TOGETHER

1. Much of the material from this Chapter came from discussions with and emails from Jon Theobald, who was CEO during 2012–2017 and has been retired since then.

2. New fee scale sent by Mairs & Power to all advisory clients in March 2014.

3. Email from Jon Theobald to the author.

4. Kevin Galvin, "The Necessities of Life— Available Early on the Frontier," *Ramsey County History*, 11:2 (Fall 1974): 12–13.

5. G. Richard Slade, "Crises and Panics and Mergers and Failures: St. Paul's Struggling Banks and How They Survived Their First 75 Years," *Ramsey County History*, (Winter 2002): 4-12. This is a richly detailed account of banking in St. Paul from the birth of the State of Minnesota up through the formation of the state's two large bank holding companies.

6. Email from Ron DeSellier to the author.

7. Interviews with Roger Katzenmaier by the author, July 7, 2020; with Peter Robb by the author, February 16, 2021.

8. Steve Brook, "Speculation Costs First Bank $310 Million," *St. Paul Pioneer Press*, January 1, 1989; Dave Beal, "First Bank Fumbles Toward a Takeover," *St. Paul Pioneer Press*, October 1, 1989.

9. G. Richard Slade, *Banking in the Great Northern Territory* (Afton: Afton Historical Society Press, 2005), 208.

10. Dave Beal, "Engineering Added Value, Innovative Technology Gave MTS a Good Name with Its Customers; Now the Company Is Making a Name for Itself in the Investment Community and Bringing Up the Price of Its Stock," *St. Paul Pioneer Press*, February 16, 1998.

11. Evan Ramstad, "$1.7B MTS Sale Takes a New Twist; Buyer Finds a Second Deal for a Major Part of the Eden Prairie Industrial Sensor Business," *Minneapolis Star Tribune*, January 23, 2021.

12. Interview with Norb Conzemius by the author, June 23, 2021.

CHAPTER 11. AMID UNCERTAINTY, PREPARING MAIRS & POWER FOR A NEW CENTURY

1. Interview with Andrea Stimmel by the author August 20, 2021.

2. Email from Mark Henneman, March 4, 2021. When the Covid-19 pandemic suddenly led to stay-at-home orders from various levels of government in mid-March 2020, investment firms and many other employers subsequently required their employees who could work from home to do so. All these sudden changes made the securities markets extremely unsettled. See Justin Baer with Heather Gillers and Gunjan Banerji, "The Day the Coronavirus Nearly Broke the Markets— Few Realize How Close to Collapse the Financial System Came on March 16," *Wall Street Journal*, May 21, 2020.

3. Callum Keown, "This Is the Greatest Threat to Big Tech's S&P Dominance, Goldman Says," *MarketWatch*, May 11, 2021.

4. Tony Thomas, Morningstar analyst, September 11, 2019. This was part of a Morningstar post titled "10 Superb Defensive Stock Funds," https://www.morningstar.com/articles/945364/10-superb-defensive-stock-funds. Thomas's comments about the Growth Fund's performance in 2021 are from an email from him to the author on August 24, 2021.

5. "Mairs & Power Launches Minnesota Municipal Bond ETF," March 12, 2021, press release from Mairs & Power.

6. Investment Company Institute, *2021 Mutual Fund Fact Book* (Washington, D.C.: Investment Company Institute, 2021), 220–222.

7. Email from Mark Henneman to the author, August 31, 2021.

8. Interviews with Andrea Stimmel by the author, August 20, 2021, and with Melissa Gilbertson by the author, August 26, 2021.

9. "New Research for Practitioners on How to Close the Gender Gap," CFA Institute Research Foundation, 2016.

10. "The Credit Suisse Gender 3000: Women in Senior Management," Credit Suisse Research Institute, September 23, 2014.

11. "Insights on Diversity and Inclusion," a series of reports posted by the McKinsey Global Institute, https://www.mckinsey.com, June 2021.

12. Mairs & Power Inc., Inclusion & Diversity Committee Initiatives; Committee Charter; Inclusion & Diversity Policy—Employee

Handbook, 2021, and an interview with Andrea Stimmel by the author.

13. Interview with Melissa Gilbertson by the author, August 26, 2021.

14. Interview with Mary Schmid Daugherty by the author, September 28, 2020.

15. Interviews with Mark Henneman by the author, October 14, 2020, and August 27, 2021; Mairs & Power Award for Investment Study, https://gustavus.edu.

16. Jeff Sommer, "Who Runs Mutual Funds? Very Few Women," *New York Times*, May 4, 2018.

17. Interview with Mark Salter, executive director of CFA Society of Minnesota, by the author, August 18, 2021; CFA Institute surveys of the membership of the Minnesota affiliate.

18. Interviews with Susanna Gibbons, Carlson School of Management, August 31, 2021, and Carol Schleif, August 29, 2021, by the author. Schleif, an investment professional in the Twin Cities since 1983, is the deputy chief investment officer for the BMO Family Office in Minneapolis.

19. Catalyst, a global nonprofit that has been seeking to help build workplaces that work for women since 1962, aggregated several studies about the status of women in the financial services industry in a post on June 29, 2020. Among the findings: While women accounted for 54 percent of employment in the U.S. financial sector in 2019, they were represented on the executive committees of only 26 percent of financial firms; in 2017, women in the financial sector in North America were much less likely to receive promotions and sponsors than men; in 2019, median weekly earnings for women lagged far behind pay for men working in similar occupations for investment professionals. https://www.catalyst.org/research/women-in-financial-services/

20. CFA Institute Research Foundation, 2016.

21. Interview with Mary Schmid Daugherty by the author.

22. "The Wolf of Wall Street," *Wikipedia*, August 21, 2021.

23. Interview with Melissa Gilbertson by the author, August 26, 2021; Jack Bogle's comment is from Evan Osnos, "Life After White Collar Crime," *The New Yorker*, August 30, 2021, p. 20.

24. Patrick Kennedy, "Miromatrix Is Latest Company to File for an IPO," *Minneapolis Star Tribune*, June 20, 2021.

25. Email from Andy Adams to the author, June 9, 2021.

26. "Mairs & Power Wins Best Mutual Fund Website Award," mairsandpower.com/about-us/company-news/item/78-best-mutual.

CHAPTER 12. THE BENEFITS OF PROXIMITY

1. Interview with Russell Kinnel by the author, February 25, 2021.

2. Presentation by Mark Henneman to the First Tuesday Luncheon, Carlson School of Management at the University of Minnesota, November 5, 2019.

3. Donald M. Hall, *Generation of Wealth* (Minneapolis: Nodin Press, 2014). Hall's book focuses on the rise of Control Data Corporation inspired innovation at other startups in the Twin Cities area. It also describes the local Twin Cities over-the-counter stock market of the late 1950s and the '60s.

4. Interview with Andy Adams by the author, December 11, 2020.

5. The rise of the other local funds reflected the strength and large number of Minnesota stocks from which investors could choose. The life span of these funds, however, was much shorter than that of the Growth Fund, which began concentrating on Minnesota stocks in the mid-1960s and eventually took much larger positions in them than the other funds. The Growth Fund continues this focus today.

6. Interview with Chuck Dietz by the author, June 8, 2020.

7. Patrick Kennedy, "The Star Tribune 100 Is Now the Star Tribune 50—Here's Why," *Minneapolis Star Tribune*, May 20, 2017.

8. Jason Thomas, "Where Have All the Public Companies Gone?" *Wall Street Journal*,

November 17, 2017. For more on this topic, see the testimony of Jay Ritter, finance professor at the University of Florida, before the Senate Committee on Banking, Housing, and Urban Affairs, March 6, 2012, and Bloomberg Editorial Board, "Where Have All the Public Companies Gone? Some Businesses Are Staying Private. Others Are Getting Bigger. That's Not Necessarily a Problem," April 9, 2018, https://www.bloomberg.com/opinion/articles/2018-04-09/where-have-all-the-u-s-public-companies-gone.

9. Interview with Mark Henneman by the author, October 14, 2020.

10. Michael Porter, *Competitive Strategy: Techniques for Analyzing Industries and Competitors* (New York: Simon & Schuster, 1980).

EPILOGUE

1. Interview with Andrea Stimmel by the author, August 20, 2021; interview with Mark Henneman by the author, August 27, 2021.

2. Persons of color accounted for 2 percent of Minnesota's population in 1973 vs. 21 percent in 2020, according to the Compass research unit at the Wilder Foundation in St. Paul.

3. The data on per capita income was aggregated by Louis D. Johnston, an economist at Saint John's University, Collegeville, Minn. He discussed the data in a presentation about Minnesota's economy on October 3, 2018, to faculty members, students, and supporters of Saint John's and the College of Saint Benedict and in an interview with the author on April 5, 2021. His lecture is posted at https://youtu.be/mwJFAolKqHO and Louis D. Johnston, "Exchange, Industry, and Adaptation: Economics in Minnesota," https://www.mnopedia.org/exchange-industry-and-adaptation-economics-minnesota, gives an overview of his historical analysis.

4. Interview with John Bergstrom by the author, September 3, 2021.

5. Interview with Fred Speece by the author, February 23, 2021.

6. This conclusion is the opinion of the author, who tries to keep up.

Index

G

Galbraith, John Kenneth, 77
Garland, Robert F., 45
Garretson, Don, 134
Gebhart, Michael, 25
Gehling, Marissa E., 224
Genentech, 204
General Electric Company, 75
General Mills Corporation, 4, 105
General Motors Corporation, 155
Giannini, A. P., 74, 77
Gibbons, Susanna, 190, 191
Gilbertson, Melissa M., 150, 168, 187, 188, 189,
 191, 224
Glass-Seagall Act (1933), 27
globalization, 123
"Go-Go Years"
 epitomized by fund managers' aggressive
  practices, 92
 hot mutual funds during that time, 89–90
 term coined by John Brooks for the late 1960s,
  88–89
Goldman Sachs, 100
Google (Alphabet) Corporation, 182, 183, 204
Gordon, John Steele, 63–64, 71, 123
Graco Corporation, 4, 205, 206, 207
Graham, Benjamin, 1–2, 71
Grand Rapids, Minn., 165, 166, 167
Great Depression, 23–29, 44, 46, 64, 216
Great Northern Railway, 19, 20, 23, 29–30, 39,
 40, 44, 45, 53, 56, 57
 competition from other commercial carriers,
  30–31
 financial problems in the 1930s, 31–33
Great Recession of 2007-2009, 154–157
Great Society programs, 83
Growth Fund, 1, 4, 5, 40–41, 49, 66, 78, 104,
 128, 161, 199
 adds ADC Telecom stock, 182
 attracts more retail investors, 79
 as a barometer of Minnesota's business
  activity, 81
 becomes less Minnesota-centric, 205
 Bill Frels named its co-manager, 144
 blowout returns for 1995, 139
 bullish market between 2013 and 2018, 163

buys shares of Dayton Hudson, 201
buys shares of Deluxe, 201
buys shares of H. B. Fuller, 201
buys shares of Jamf Holdings, 192
buys shares of Medtronic, 201
buys shares of Rosemount Engineering, 201
buys shares of Tonka, 201
classified as a large blend fund, 184
discovered by the financial press, 136–139
does well in 2016, 175
doubles its assets between 1988 and 1994,
 123–124
expands in 1997, 139–140
expands search for stocks beyond six nearby
 states, 205
flagship fund at Mairs & Power, 2–3
focuses on Minnesota public companies in the
 1960s, 82
fund assets by year, 194
gains Proto Labs from the Small Cap Fund, 208
George III advocates starting it, 131
George III steps down as its manager, 150
the impact of the COVID-19 pandemic on the
 fund, 179–180
impact of the Great Recession on it, 156–157
impact of the sluggish economy on, 95
inching into Minnesota stocks, 77
it illustrates the benefits of regional investing,
 197–208
its commitment to stocks in the state and
 region, 207–208, 215
its origins at Mairs & Power, 73–76
its performance helped by globalization, 123
its performance in the 1970s, 105
its performance shifts from 2019 headwinds to
 2020 tailwinds, 181–182, 184
its ranking in the mid-1990s, 136
its returns slip during the dot-com bubble,
 143–144
its soaring assets, 130
its strong performance in 2005, 154
its strong results from 1966 to 1972, 82–83
its success has paralleled the improved
 economy of Minnesota, 212–215
its takeoff in the 1960s due to Minnesota
 stocks, 84–88

ABOUT THE AUTHOR

Dave Beal worked for daily newspapers in six states, mostly as a business editor and columnist for the *St. Paul Pioneer Press* and earlier for the *Milwaukee Journal*. He is a past president of SABEW, the nation's leading organization for business and financial journalists. Dave holds graduate and undergraduate degrees in journalism from Syracuse University and the University of Illinois at Champaign-Urbana, respectively. In 2002, he and Fred Zimmerman, a business professor at the University of St. Thomas, published *Manufacturing Works: The Vital Link between Production and Prosperity* (Dearborn Financial Pub.). Dave and his wife, Caroline, live in the Twin Cities and have six children and 14 grandchildren.